BIBLIOGRAPHY OF OFFICIAL STATISTICAL YEARBOOKS AND BULLETINS

GOVERNMENT DOCUMENTS BIBLIOGRAPHIES

Series Editor   Steven D. Zink

The other titles in this series are:

An Annotated Guide to Current National Bibliographies
by Barbara L. Bell

Checklist of Government Directories, Lists and Rosters
by Richard I. Korman

Guide to Statistical Materials Produced by Governments and Associations in the United States
by Juri and Jean Slemmons Stratford

Guide to Presidential Advisory Commissions, 1973–1981
by Steven D. Zink

GOVERNMENT DOCUMENTS
BIBLIOGRAPHIES

Bibliography of Official Statistical Yearbooks and Bulletins

Gloria Westfall

CHADWYCK-HEALEY INC
ALEXANDRIA, VA

© 1986 Gloria Westfall
All rights reserved. No part of this work
may be reproduced, stored in a retrieval system,
or transmitted in any form or by any means,
electronic, mechanical, photocopying or otherwise
without the prior permission of the
copyright owner.

First published 1986 by:
Chadwyck-Healey Inc.
1021 Prince Street
Alexandria, VA 22314

Distributed outside the USA by:
Chadwyck-Healey Ltd
Cambridge Place
Cambridge CB2 1NR
England

Reprinted 1988

ISBN: 0 85964 124 4

Library of Congress Cataloging in Publication Data

Westfall, Gloria
  Bibliography of official statistical yearbooks and bulletins.
  (Government documents bibliographies)
  1. Statistics—Periodicals—Bibliography.
I. Title. II. Series.
Z7551.W47 1986 HA155. 016.31 86-17191

British Library Cataloguing in Publication Data

Westfall, Gloria
  Bibliography of official statistical
  yearbooks and bulletins.—(Government
  documents bibliographies)
  1. Statistics—History—19th century—
  Bibliography 2. Statistics—History—
  20th century—Bibliography
  I. Title II. Series
  016.0014′22 Z7551

Printed by Unwin Brothers Ltd.
Old Woking, Surrey.

To Alfred, Jennifer and Kristin

CONTENTS

Africa

Algeria	1-3
Angola	4-5
Benin	6-7
Botswana	8-9
Burkina Faso	10-11
Burundi	12-13
Cameroon	14-17
Cape Verde	18-20
Central African Republic	21-23
Chad	24-26
Congo	27-28
Djibouti	29-30
Egypt	31-32
Equatorial Guinea	33-34
Ethiopia	35
Gabon	36-38
Gambia	39-40
Ghana	41-44
Guinea	45
Guinea-Bissau	46-47
Ivory Coast	48-49
Kenya	50-51
Lesotho	52-53
Liberia	54-56
Libya	57-58
Madagascar	59
Malawi	60
Mali	61-62
Mauritania	63-64
Mauritius	65

Morocco	66-67
Mozambique	68-70
Niger	71-72
Nigeria	73-74
Reunion	75-77
Rwanda	78-79
Sao Tome and Principe	80
Senegal	81-83
Seychelles	84
Sierra Leone	85-86
Somalia	87-88
South Africa	89-91
Sudan	92
Swaziland	93-94
Tanzania	95-97
Zanzibar	96
Togo	98-99
Tunisia	100-102
Uganda	103-104
Zaire	105-106
Zambia	107-109
Zimbabwe	110-111

Americas

Antigua and Barbuda	112
Argentina	113-114
Bahamas	115-116
Barbados	117-119
Belize	120
Bermuda	121
Bolivia	122-124
Brazil	125-126
British Virgin Islands	127
Canada	128-129
Cayman Islands	130
Chile	131-134
Colombia	135-137
Costa Rica	138
Cuba	139-141

Dominica	142
Dominican Republic	143
Ecuador	144-145
El Salvador	146-147
French Guiana	148-149
Grenada	150
Guadeloupe	151-153
Guatemala	154-155
Guyana	156-157
Haiti	158-159
Honduras	160
Jamaica	161-163
Martinique	164-165
Mexico	166-168
Montserrat	169
Netherlands Antilles	170-171
Nicaragua	172-173
Panama	174
Paraguay	175-176
Peru	177-179
Puerto Rico	180
St. Christopher and Nevis	181
St. Lucia	182
St. Vincent and the Grenadines	183
Surinam	184-185
Trinidad and Tobago	186
United States of America	187
Uruguay	188
Venezuela	189-190

Asia

Afghanistan	191-192
Bahrain	193
Bangladesh	194-195
Bhutan	196
Brunei	197
Burma	198-200
China	201
China (Republic)	202-204

Cyprus	205-206
Hong Kong	207-209
India	210-212
Indonesia	213-215
Iran	216
Iraq	217-218
Israel	219-220
Japan	221-223
Jordan	224
Kampuchea	225-226
Korea (South)	227-229
Kuwait	230-231
Laos	232-233
Lebanon	234-235
Macau	236-237
Malaysia	238
Peninsular Malaysia	239-240
Sabah	241-242
Sarawak	243-244
Maldives	245
Mongolia	246-247
Nepal	248
Oman	249
Pakistan	250-252
Philippines	253-256
Qatar	257
Saudi Arabia	258
Singapore	259-260
Sri Lanka	261-263
Syria	264
Thailand	265-267
Turkey	268-270
United Arab Emirates	271
Abu Dhabi	272
Vietnam	273
Yemen	274
Yemen (People's Democratic Republic)	275

Europe

Albania	276-277
Austria	278-279
Belgium	280-282
Bulgaria	283-284
Czechoslovakia	285-287
Denmark	288-289
Finland	290-291
France	292-293
Germany (East)	294-295
Germany (West)	296-298
Gibraltar	299
Greece	300-302
Hungary	303-305
Iceland	306
Ireland	307-308
Italy	309-311
Liechtenstein	312
Luxembourg	313-314
Malta	315-316
Netherlands	317-319
Norway	320-321
Poland	322-324
Portugal	325-326
Romania	327-328
San Marino	329-330
Soviet Union	331-333
Spain	334-336
Sweden	337-338
Switzerland	339-340
United Kingdom	341-342
Northern Ireland	343-344
Scotland	345
Wales	346
Yugoslavia	347-349

Oceania

Australia	350-352

Fiji	353-354
French Polynesia	355-356
Guam	357
Kiribati	358
New Caledonia	359
New Zealand	360-362
Niue	363-364
Pacific Islands (Trust Territory)	365-366
Papua New Guinea	367-368
Solomon Islands	369-370
Tonga	371
Tuvalu	372
Vanuatu	373
Western Samoa	374

PREFACE

Some 80 new countries have come into being since the Library of Congress published *Statistical yearbooks: an annotated bibliography of the general statistical yearbooks of major political subdivisions of the world*, and its companion volume for statistical bulletins in the early 1950s. At the same time, developments in political, economic and social policy and practice have changed the kinds of questions data users ask, while technological advances in communication and automation have made it possible to collect and manipulate data on a scale unheard of in the early 1950s. As a result, a host of new yearbooks and bulletins have appeared in the last 30 years and significant changes have occurred in the content and format of many of those established earlier.

In spite of these developments, no bibliography devoted exclusively to official statistical yearbooks and bulletins has been published in recent years. There have, of course, been bibliographies which have included national statistical office compendia and bulletins in addition to other statistical sources. The most useful of these are the latest editions of Joan Harvey's well-known volumes of sources for social, economic and market research published by CBD Research Ltd., *Statistics--Africa* (1978), *Statistics--America*, (1980), *Statistics--Asia & Australasia*, (1983) and *Statistics--Europe* (1981). While Harvey's works represent a tour de force in their breadth of coverage, they do not attempt to include detailed analyses of subject content, but simply list chapter or section headings. They record current titles only, omitting title and agency name variations and continuation notes.

Another excellent source of information on official yearbooks and bulletins is the bibliography entitled 'Governmental and intergovernmental serial publications containing vital or migration statistics,' published at irregular intervals in *Population index*, most recently in v. 46, no. 4, winter, 1980. It is, however, limited to yearbooks and bulletins which contain data on vital statistics and migration, and it omits any information on the history of the publications cited.

In view of this situation, it seemed that a new bibliography analyzing the contents of recent editions of official yearbooks and bulletins and furnishing complete bibliographical descriptions of each title, would be welcomed by users of statistical data.

In an attempt to expand the usefulness of the bibliography, I have added several new features. For those who rely on yearbooks and bulletins primarily as guides to more detailed information, I have indicated whether or not the sources supplying the data published in the yearbooks and bulletins are identified and, if so, where this information may be found. For those whose research concerns the past rather than the present, I have included all citations to official historical statistics that I have been able to find. This information appears in two places: the title/agency variations and continuation notes at the beginning of the entry and in a paragraph headed *Historical statistics*, following the description of contents. Finally, as a service to those interested in filling in gaps in their collections, I have listed the titles and dates of editions available in microform or reprint and the publishers from which they may be secured.

SCOPE

I have defined general official statistical yearbooks as recurring publications of national statistical offices published annually or semi-annually or less frequently which contain statistical tables in more than one of the following categories: 1. physical environment; 2. demography; 3. economic affairs; 4. political affairs; and 5. social and cultural affairs. Classified as bulletins are publications with the same content and provenance published more often than annually, usually on a monthly or quarterly basis. Readers will note that in some cases the issues of bulletins described contain only economic information; these are included because data in other categories is known to have appeared in some issues or supplements. Both yearbooks and bulletins may contain narrative sections in addition to tables of numerical data.

When no publication of the types above is published, a substitute source of recent statistical data has been included, even if not published by the national statistical office of the country. I have found a yearbook or bulletin or a substitute source of general statistical information for every independent nation except Andorra, Monaco, Nauru, North Korea, and the Vatican City.

The bibliography includes all sovereign nations and those dependent territories for which a current yearbook or bulletin exists. Cross references are supplied for dependent territories included in another country's yearbook or bulletin.

Entries are limited to publications wholly or partially in the Roman or Cyrillic alphabet. At the present time, over half of the statistical offices in the world make their publications available in English.

I have not attempted to include yearbooks or bulletins below the national level except in cases where the areas they represent are not fully reported in a current publication of the national government of which they are part. Exceptions have been made for Abu Dhabi, Northern Ireland, Scotland, Wales.

Arrangement

Arrangement of entries is first by the five major regions of the world- Africa, Americas, Asia, Europe and Oceania-and then by country. The first title for each country is that of the most current general statistical yearbook or, if none exists, a substitute for it. Abridged editions of the first title and/or additional annual statistical compendia are listed next, followed by titles which have ceased. Statistical bulletins appear last.

Content of Entries

1. The first element in each entry is its serial number.
2. The title appears next, preceded by the symbol * in cases where it has ceased publication. Translations of non-English titles are provided in brackets.

3. The date of the first number issued in the series followed by a dash is recorded next, in cases where it has been possible to determine it. Dates of the last number issued are also given for series known to have ceased. A slash rather than a dash between dates ordinarily indicates the inclusive dates covered by a single number in a series. Dates of the data contained in the publications and the length of time elapsing between these dates and publication of the works described are points addressed in the descriptions of contents.

4. The imprint includes the name of the city of publication, in English, and the agency responsible for editing the publication, in the language used in the publication.

5. The frequency of the publication is indicated if not stated in the title, with one exception: yearbooks are assumed to be annual unless otherwise specified.

6. The languages appearing in the publication are reported next unless it is entirely in English.

7. The notes section includes the following: changes in series numbering or publishing patterns; variations in titles and in agency and country names; and continuations.

8. The description of contents includes an analysis of the subjects, dates and territorial areas covered in a recent edition or issue followed by notes indicating the inclusion of explanatory notes, sources, indexes, bibliographies and/or other features. A more detailed explanation of this section is given below. Ceased titles are analyzed only if no replacement for them has been found.

9. Sources for historical statistics not mentioned in the continuation notes are listed here. It should be noted that materials for sovereign nations for the period before they achieved independence are not listed unless currently available in microform. Colonial materials are covered in depth in the two Library of Congress publications mentioned earlier.

10. The availability of current issues is the next item in the entry. I have, of course, described the latest edition of each annual series that I was able to locate at the time I concluded the preparation of this bibliography in July, 1985. In cases where I was unable to find a copy of the latest edition to examine, I have recorded the date of the latest edition in the availability statement. A list of entry numbers for titles I did not personally examine is given at the end of the preface.

Since the dates of the most recent issues of monthly or quarterly bulletins are constantly changing, I have not attempted to secure the latest issue for my description, but have simply included the date of the issue described at the head of the annotation.

I have also listed the name and address of the distributor and the price of the current edition, if supplied by the office responsible for the publication. In cases where the price has not been supplied, but the publication is known not to be free, the word 'priced' is used.

11. The final statement gives the names of publishers of microform or reprint editions and the dates published by them. Congressional Information Services, Inc., is filming a new group of yearbooks, which extends coverage through 1984, or, in some cases, 1985. In addition, they are filming yearbooks for 1980-1984 for a number of countries not previously filmed. Further ordering information can be obtained from *Microforms in print* or *Guide to reprints*.

Analyses of contents

Since the format and content of both yearbooks and bulletins frequently change, I have noted the date of the edition or issue described and the number of pages of text and tables it contains at the beginning of the analysis of contents. The date of publication is also provided in cases where it is possible to determine it in order to give an indication of the differences which often exist between the date of the edition or issue and the publication date.

Subject Coverage

I have compiled a basic list of subject terms, a frankly subjective list based on my observations of the types of information users most frequently look for, and, more importantly, find, in yearbooks and bulletins, and have searched for these terms in all the materials included in the bibliography. I have tried to be as specific as possible. For example, instead of simply searching *vital statistics,* I have searched each of the following separate terms: *abortions, births, fertility, causes of death, deaths, divorces, illegitimate births, infant mortality, life expectancy,* and *marriages.* At the same time, I have tried to keep the list of terms within reasonable length.

Terms in the list are included in the descriptions if they are found in tables even if they do not appear in the table heading. A few terms unique to given publications have been added when it was felt that the importance of the subject warranted their inclusion.

There have, of course, sometimes been difficulties in defining terms. Consumption, for example, has generally been recorded wherever found, whether it refers to consumption of energy, food or a variety of consumer goods. Production, on the other hand, is not recorded as a separate term, it being understood that most of the publications offering data on industry or manufacturing report production figures.

It has also sometimes been difficult to decide in which categories to put a given term. Traffic accidents, for example, sometimes appear in yearbooks and bulletins in the section on vital statistics, sometimes with transportation, sometimes with health, and sometimes with justice. I have chosen to record them under justice, no matter where they appear in the yearbook or bulletin.

In order to make it possible for the reader to find out quickly whether a certain type of information has been included in a publication or not, I have grouped terms in 5 main categories:

1. PHYSICAL ENVIRONMENT;
2. DEMOGRAPHY;
3. ECONOMIC AFFAIRS;
4. POLITICAL AFFAIRS;
5. SOCIAL AND CULTURAL AFFAIRS.

Within these categories terms are grouped into sub-categories in alpabetical arrangement. A sample of the full list of terms searched is shown at the end of the preface.

The reader needs to be aware that the order of terms in my description is not that in the publication itself. Indexes and lists of tables in the original works must be utilized to find the specific tables and/or pages on which the data wanted will be found.

Chronological and territorial coverage

The time periods and areas covered by the edition or issue are described next. Since the dates covered vary enormously from one table to the next within most yearbooks and bulletins, emphasis is on the most recent period recorded and the range of dates included. Area breakdowns recorded include the following: 1. sub-national levels, such as states, provinces, and/or municipalities; 2. external territories; and 3. foreign countries. Readers should be aware that, in most cases, geographical area breakdowns are often restricted to a few tables, such as census results.

Methodology, sources, bibliographies and indexes

The inclusion of explanatory material and information on sources is mentioned next. Unfortunately, most publications include only the name of the agency responsible for furnishing the data; only a few report the titles of sources. Perhaps if users were to make their wishes on this subject known to statistical offices, more would include titles, as well as authors, of published sources.

Finally, the presence of such features as detailed tables of contents, notices of changes in format or content from previous editions, bibliographies and/or lists of publications of statistical offices, and subject indexes are indicated.

Acknowledgments

I am immensely grateful to the 85 national statistical offices who responded with comments and corrections to the drafts of the entries prepared for this bibliography I sent to them, and who, in many cases, also furnished later copies of publications. The bibliographies by Joan Harvey and the staff of *Population index* mentioned earlier were invaluable in providing a base on which to build this bibliography.

My deepest thanks go to the librarians of the Princeton University Libraries, the Statistical Reference Collection of the United Nations Dag Hammarskjold Library, and the International Monetary Fund/ World Bank Joint Library for permitting me to use their collections.

I also want to thank Indiana University for supporting this endeavor, particularly for the grant of a sabbatical leave which enabled me to complete it. I am grateful to my colleagues in the library, who offered aid in many ways. I particularly want to thank Sylvia Burbach and Carl Horne who translated East European publications for me. Finally, I want to thank my family for their support and encouragement throughout the preparation of the bibliography.

List of Terms Searched

PHYSICAL ENVIRONMENT

Climatology: precipitation, sunshine, temperature; *Environmental quality; Geography*: area and use of land, maps*.

DEMOGRAPHY

Population: arrivals and departures, census results from [years], distribution by age and sex, distribution by geographic/administrative area, ethnic groups, external migration, households and families, internal migration, population estimates and projections; *Vital statistics*: abortions, births, including illegitimate births, causes of death, deaths, divorces, fertility, infant mortality, life expectancy, marriages.

ECONOMIC AFFAIRS

Agriculture and food: farming, fishing, forestry; *Commerce and business*: companies, domestic commerce, exports, imports, tourism; *Finance*: banking and credit, money supply, securities; *Income and expenditure*: consumption, personal income, prices; *Industry*: communication, construction, energy, manufacturing, mining, transportation, water; *National accounts*: balance of payments, gross domestic product, gross national product, national income; *Public finance:* government expenditures, government revenue, planning and economic development.

POLITICAL AFFAIRS

Defense; Elections; Foreign aid.

SOCIAL AND CULTURAL AFFAIRS

Cultural and scientific activities: books and journals, cinema and performing arts, libraries, museums and galleries, newspapers, radio, television, science and research; *Education*: degrees conferred, educational attainment, enrollments, examination results, literacy, teaching staff; *Health*: disease, family planning, hospitals, medical personnel, public health; *Housing; Justice*: correctional institutions, courts, crimes, police, traffic accidents; *Labor*: employment and unemployment, foreign workers, labor force, labor-management relations, occupations, salaries and wages; *Religion; Social assistance; Social security; Sports and recreation.*

*Maps are included because of their value in interpreting statistical data even though they themselves usually do not contain statistics.

Titles not examined

I was unable to obtain copies of the following titles to examine: 2, 23, 25, 45, 104, 141, 190, 200, 226, 242, 244, 260, 275, 287, 301, 308, 359, 363, 370. Descriptions of contents which accompany some of these titles, have been furnished by the Statistical Office responsible for the publication.

Abbreviations and Acronyms Not Explained in the Text

CH: Chadwyck-Healey, Inc.
CIS: Congressional Information Service, Inc.
CNRS: Centre National de la Recherche Scientifique.
IDC: Inter Documentation Co. (American Distributor, Clearwater Publishing Co., Inc.)

AFRICA

ALGERIA

1. ***Annuaire statistique de l'Algérie*** [Statistical yearbook of Algeria]. 1926- Algiers: Direction des Statistiques et de la Comptabilité Nationale. French.

   1939/47 and 1963/64 numbered Nouvelle série.

   Agency name varies: 1926-57 by Service Centrale de Statistique; 1958-60 by Service de la Statistique Générale; 1961-74 by Sous-Direction des Statistiques. Continues *Statistique générale de l'Algérie*, 1867/72-1925, published by the Service de Statistique Générale.

   1980 edition published 1981, 423 p., contains statistical data in the following areas:

   PHYSICAL ENVIRONMENT
   Climatology: precipitation, temperature; *Geography*: area and use of land, maps.

   DEMOGRAPHY
   Population: Algerians resident in France; census results from 1856-1977; distribution by age and sex, distribution by geographic/administrative area, households and families, nomadic population, population estimates; *Vital statistics*: births, causes of death, deaths, divorces, fertility, infant mortality, life expectancy, marriages.

   ECONOMIC AFFAIRS
   Agriculture and food: farming, fishing, forestry; *Commerce and business*: exports, imports, tourism; *Finance*: banking and credit, money supply; *Income and expenditure*: consumption, prices; *Industry*: communication, energy, manufacturing, mining, transportation; *National accounts*: balance of payments, gross domestic product, national income; *Public finance*: government expenditures, government revenue.

   SOCIAL AND CULTURAL AFFAIRS
   Cultural and scientific activities: books and journals, cinema, libraries, museums and galleries, newspapers, radio, television; *Education*: degrees conferred, enrollments, examination results, language of instruction, literacy, teaching staff; *Health*: disease, hospitals, medical personnel, public health; *Housing*; *Justice*: correctional institutions, courts; *Labor*: employment, labor force, occupations, salaries and wages; *Social security*.

   Latest data are for 1979, with time series for varying periods. Vital statistics are provided to 1901. In addition to the national level, data are included for wilayaat (departments) and selected foreign countries.

   Notes accompanying the tables indicate the names of the agencies furnishing the data. Explanatory notes provided at the beginnings of chapters include descriptions of the geography, climate, administrative organization, educational and judicial systems of the country.

A list of official statistical publications is provided at the end of the volume.Latest edition published: 1981. Available from the Office National des Statistiques, 8-10 rue des Moussebiline, BP 55, Algiers. Price DA50.

The following years are available in microform: CH: 1926-64 and *Statistique générale de l'Algérie,* 1867-1925. CIS: 1970,1972,1974,1976. IDC: 1939/47-1961; 1963/64; 1966/67.

2. **Statistiques: revue de l'Office National des statistiques** [Statistics: review of the National Office of Statistics]. 1980- Algiers: Office National des Statistiques. Quarterly. French and Arabic.

   Replaces *Bulletin trimestriel de statistiques* [Quarterly bulletin of statistics] (see entry 3).

   Available from the Office National des Statistiques, 8-10 rue des Moussebiline, BP 55, Algiers. Price DA5.

3. ***Bulletin trimestriel de statistiques** [Quarterly bulletin of statistics]. 1964-80. Algiers: Direction des Statistiques et de la Comptabilité Nationale. French.

   Title varies: 1970-72 as *Bulletin de statistiques générales.* Agency varies: 1964-74 by Sous-Direction des Affaires, Economiques [et Financières]. Continues *Bulletin de statistiques générales,* published by the Service de Statistiques Générales, 1949-63.

   Nos. 1 and 2, Jan. and June, 1980, 57 p., contain data on the following subjects:

   PHYSICAL ENVIRONMENT
   Climatology: precipitation, temperature.

   DEMOGRAPHY
   Population: arrivals and departures; *Vital statistics*: births, causes of death, deaths, divorces, infant mortality, marriages.

   ECONOMIC AFFAIRS
   Agriculture and food: farming, fishing; *Commerce and business*: domestic commerce, exports, imports; *Income and expenditure*: prices; *Industry*: communication, energy, transportation.

   SOCIAL AND CULTURAL AFFAIRS
   Health: disease.

   Most data are monthly or quarterly for 1980 or 1979.

ANGOLA

4. ***Anuário estatístico/ Annuaire statistique** [Statistical yearbook]. 1933-74. Luanda: Direcção dos Serviços de Estatística, 1935-75. Portuguese and French.

Agency name varies: 1933-65 by Direcção dos Serviços de Economia e Estatística Geral; 1968-72 by Direcção Provincial dos Serviços de Estadística and Instituto Nacional de Estadística.

1973 edition published 1975, 393 p., contains statistical data in the following areas:

PHYSICAL ENVIRONMENT
Climatology: precipitation, sunshine, temperature; *Geography*: area of land.

DEMOGRAPHY
Population: arrivals and departures, census results from 1940 and 1970, distribution by geographic/administrative area, population estimates; *Vital statistics*: births, causes of death, deaths, divorces, infant mortality, marriages.

ECONOMIC AFFAIRS
Agriculture and food: farming, fishing, forestry; *Commerce and business*: domestic commerce, exports, imports, tourism; *Finance*: banking and credit, money supply; *Income and expenditure*: consumption, prices; *Industry*: communication, construction, energy, manufacturing, mining, transportation; *National accounts*: National income; *Public finance*: government expenditures, government revenue, planning and economic development.

SOCIAL AND CULTURAL AFFAIRS
Cultural and scientific activities: books and journals, cinema and performing arts, libraries, museums and galleries, newspapers, radio; *Education*: enrollments, teaching staff; *Health*: disease, hospitals, medical personnel, public health; *Justice*: correctional institutions, courts, police, traffic accidents; *Labor*: labor-management relations; *Religion*; *Sports*.

Most data are for 1973 and the preceding 4 years. In addition to the national level, data are included for districts and cities.

Notes indicating the agencies furnishing the data are found at the end of most tables. There is a detailed list of tables in the back of the volume.

Available in microform: CH: 1933-73. CIS: 1970-72.

5. *****Boletim mensal de estatística** [Monthly bulletin of statistics]. 1945-73? Luanda: Direcção dos Serviços de Estatística. Monthly. Portuguese.

For variations in agency name, see previous entry. Continues: *Boletim trimestral de estatística*, 1933-34, 1942-43.

V. 30, no. 12, Dec., 1974, 145 p., contains statistical data in the following areas:

PHYSICAL ENVIRONMENT
Climatology: precipitation, sunshine, temperature; *Geography*: area of land.

DEMOGRAPHY
Population: census results from 1970; distribution by age and sex, distribution by geographic/administrative area; *Vital statistics*: births, causes of death, deaths.

ECONOMIC AFFAIRS
Agriculture and food: farming, fishing, forestry; *Commerce and business*: companies, domestic commerce, exports, imports, tourism; *Finance*: banking and credit; *Income and expenditure*: consumption, prices; *Industry*: communication, construction, energy, manufacturing, mining, transportation; *National accounts*: balance of payments; *Public finance*: government expenditures, government revenue.

SOCIAL AND CULTURAL AFFAIRS
Cultural and scientific activities: books and journals, cinema and performing arts, libraries, museums and galleries,*Education*: enrollments, teaching staff; *Health*: disease, public health; *Justice*: courts; *Labor*: labor force; *Sports*.

Most data are monthly for Dec.,1974 and annual for 1 year. In addition to the national level, data are included for districts and cities.

Notes accompanying a few of the tables indicate the names of the agencies furnishing the data.

BENIN

6. ***Annuaire statistique*** [Statistical yearbook]. 1965- Cotonou: Institut National de la Statistique et de l'Analyse Economique. French.

Editions before 1975 published under the earlier name of the country, Dahomey. Agency name varies: Earlier, Direction de la Statistique.

No. 6, 1980, 280 p., contains statistical data in the following areas:

PHYSICAL ENVIRONMENT
Climatology: precipitation, temperature; *Geography*: area of land.

DEMOGRAPHY
Population: preliminary census results from 1979, distribution by age and sex, distribution by geographic/administrative area, population estimates; *Vital statistics*: births, deaths.

ECONOMIC AFFAIRS
Agriculture and food: farming, fishing, forestry; *Commerce and business*: domestic commerce, exports, imports; *Finance*: banking and credit, money supply; *Income and expenditure*: consumption, prices; *Industry*: communication, energy, mining, transportation; *National accounts*: balance of payments, gross domestic product, national income; *Public finance*: government expenditures, government revenue.

POLITICAL AFFAIRS
Foreign aid.

SOCIAL AND CULTURAL AFFAIRS
Education: enrollments, examination results, teaching staff; *Health*: disease, public health; *Justice*: crimes, police; *Labor*: labor force.

Most data are for 1978 or 1977 and the preceding 2 to 7 years. In addition to the national level, data are included for provinces and principal cities.

Notes accompanying the tables indicate the names of the agencies furnishing the data. Explanatory notes are provided at the beginnings of chapters.

Available from Institut National de la Statistique et de l'Analyse Economique, BP 323, Cotonou.

Available in microform: CH: 1965, 1967, 1969, 1973, 1975.

7. ***Bulletin de statistique*** [Bulletin of statistics]. 1966- Cotonou: Institut National de la Statistique et de l'Analyse Economique. Frequency varies. French.

No. 41, [July-Dec.] 1977, 23 p., contains statistical data in the following areas:

PHYSICAL ENVIRONMENT
Climatology: precipitation, temperature.

DEMOGRAPHY
Vital statistics: births, deaths.

ECONOMIC AFFAIRS
Agriculture and food: farming, fishing; *Income and expenditure*: prices; *Industry*: construction, energy, manufacturing, transportation.

SOCIAL AND CULTURAL AFFAIRS
Justice: crimes, traffic accidents.

Most data are monthly for the dates of the issue and annual for the preceding 2 years. In addition to the national level, data are included for provinces and cities. Notes accompanying the tables show the agencies furnishing the data.

Available from Institut National de la Statistique et de l'Analyse Economique, BP 323, Cotonou.

BOTSWANA

8. ***Statistical abstract.*** 1966- Gaborone: Central Statistics Office.

1979 edition published 1980, 94 p., contains statistical data in the following areas:

PHYSICAL ENVIRONMENT
Climatology: precipitation, temperature; *Geography*: area of land.

DEMOGRAPHY
Population: projections; *Vital statistics*: causes of death (hospital in-patients only).

ECONOMIC AFFAIRS
Agriculture and food: farming; *Commerce and business*: exports, imports, tourism; *Finance*: banking and credit, securities; *Income and expenditure*: cost of living, prices; *Industry*: communication, energy, mining, transportation; *National accounts*: balance of payments, gross domestic product; *Public finance*: government expenditures, government revenue.

SOCIAL AND CULTURAL AFFAIRS
Education: enrollments, teaching staff; *Health*: disease, hospitals, medical personnel; *Justice*: correctional institutions, crimes; *Labor*: employment, foreign workers, salaries and wages.

Most data are for 1979 or 1978. Time series may be provided for as many as 11 years. In addition to the national level, data are included for districts.

Commentaries are provided at the beginnings of sections. Notes accompanying the tables indicate the names of the agencies furnishing the data. There is a list of publications of the Central Statistics Office from 1969 to 1979.

Latest edition published: 1983. Available from Central Statistics Office, Private Bag 0024, Gaborone. Also for sale by the Government Printer, PO Box 87, Gaborone. Price: P2.

9. ***Statistical bulletin.*** 1976- Gaborone: Central Statistics Office. Quarterly.

V. 8, no. 1, Mar.,1983, 47 p., contains statistical data in the following areas:

PHYSICAL ENVIRONMENT
Climatology: precipitation.

DEMOGRAPHY
Population: arrivals and departures, census results from 1971 and 1981.

ECONOMIC AFFAIRS
Agriculture and food: farming; *Commerce and business*: exports, imports; *Finance*: banking and credit; *Income and expenditure*: cost of living, prices; *Industry*: construction, energy, mining, transportation; *National accounts*: balance of payments, gross domestic product; *Public finance*: government expenditures, government revenue.

SOCIAL AND CULTURAL AFFAIRS
Education: enrollments.*Labor*: employment, recruitment for South African mines.

Most data are monthly or quarterly for 2 to 4 years. Latest data are for the quarter preceding the date of the issue.

Notes accompanying some of the tables indicate the names of the agencies furnishing the data and a list of official statistical materials is given.

Available from Central Statistics Office, Private Bag 0024 , Gaborone. Also for sale by the Government Printer, PO Box 87, Gaborone. Price: P2.

BURKINA FASO

No yearbook or bulletin published since Burkina Faso became the official name of this country on August 4, 1984 has been found. Titles published under the country's earlier name, Upper Volta, include:

10. ***Bulletin annuaire d'information statistique et économique*** [Annual bulletin of statistical

and economic information]. 1958/59- Ougadougou: Institut National de la Statistique et de la Démographie. French.

Published as a supplement to *Bulletin mensuel d'information statistique et économique* [Monthly bulletin of statistical and economic information] (see entry 11), sometimes separately and sometimes in the last monthly issue for the year.

Title varies: Earlier, *Bulletin annuaire statistique et économique*; *Bulletin mensuel d'information économique et statistique*; *Supplément au bulletin mensuel de statistique*; *Bulletin annuaire de statistique*. Agency name varies: 1958/59-60 by Bureau des Etudes Economiques et de la Statistique; 1961 by Service de la Statistique; later by Direction [Division] de la Statistique et des Etudes Economiques; Direction des Comptes Economiques et de la Conjoncture and Direction de la Statistique et de la Mécanographie.

No. 19, n. s. 1978, 59 p., contains statistical data in the following areas:

PHYSICAL ENVIRONMENT
Climatology: precipitation, temperature.

ECONOMIC AFFAIRS
Commerce and business: exports, imports; *Finance*: banking and credit, money supply; *Income and expenditure*: prices; *Industry*: energy, manufacturing, transportation, water; *Public finance*: government revenue.

SOCIAL AND CULTURAL AFFAIRS
Health: disease, public health.

Most data are monthly for 1978 and annual for the current and 2 preceding years. Commentaries are provided in Part II. There is a list of tables at the beginning of the volume.

Available from the agency, BP 374, Ouagadougou. Priced.

11. ***Bulletin mensuel d'information statistique et économique.*** [Monthly bulletin of statistical and economic information]. 1960- Ougadougou: Institut National de la Statistique et de la Démographie. French.

Title varies: Earlier: *Bulletin [de] statistique*. For agency variations, see entry 10.

V.20, n.s., 1979, 64 p., contains monthly data for the current year and annual figures for the preceding 2 years on most of the same subjects as the preceding entry.

Available from the agency, BP 374, Ouagadougou. Priced.

BURUNDI

12. ***Annuaire statistique*** [Statistical yearbook]. 1962/65- Bujumbura: Service National des Etudes et Statistiques. 1966-. French.

Published as a supplement to its *Bulletin statistique* (see entry 13).

Agency varies: 1966-1976 published by Département des [de la] Statistique[s]; 1977 by Département des Etudes et Statistiques.

No. 47, 1982 edition, published June, 1983, 134 p. contains statistical data in the following areas:

PHYSICAL ENVIRONMENT
Geography: area of land.

DEMOGRAPHY
Population: census results from 1979, distribution by age and sex, distribution by geographic/administrative area, population estimates.

ECONOMIC AFFAIRS
Agriculture and food: farming, fishing, forestry; *Commerce and business*: exports, imports, tourism; *Finance*: banking and credit, money supply; *Income and expenditure*: consumption, prices; *Industry*: communications, energy, manufacturing, mining, transportation; *National accounts*: balance of payments, *Public finance*: government expenditures, government revenue.

SOCIAL AND CULTURAL AFFAIRS
Education: enrollments, literacy, teaching staff; *Health*: disease, hospitals, medical personnel, public health; *Labor*: employment, labor force, occupation, salaries and wages; *Religion*; *Social security*.

Most data are for 1982 and/or 1981 and varying numbers of earlier years. In addition to the national level, data are included for provinces and communes.

Introductory notes are provided at the beginnings of chapters. Notes accompanying the tables indicate the names of the agencies furnishing the data.

Available from the Service National des Etudes et Statistiques, B.P. 1156, Bujumbura. Price: FB1800, domestic; FB1120, foreign.

Available in microform: CH: 1969-75. IDC: 1962/65-71; 1973; 1975-79.

13. ***Bulletin statistique*** [Statistical bulletin]. 1966- Bujumbura: Service National des Etudes et Statistiques. Quarterly. French.

Title varies slightly: Some issues as *Bulletin statistique trimestriel*.
No. 80, 4th quarter of 1982, 106 p., contains statistical data in the following areas:

ECONOMIC AFFAIRS
Commerce and business: exports, imports; *Income and expenditure*: prices; *Industry*: energy, manufacturing, transportation; *National accounts*: balance of payments; *Public finance*: government revenue.

Most data are monthly and/or quarterly for the quarter of issue and the corresponding period of the previous year. In addition to the national level, data are included for some cities.

Notes accompanying the tables indicate the names of the agencies furnishing the data.

Available from the Service National des Etudes et Statistiques, B.P. 1156, Bujumbura. Price: FBu1800, domestic, per year; FB1120, foreign, per year.

CAMEROON

14. ***Note annuelle de statistique*** [Annual statistical note]. 1964- Yaoundé: Direction de la Statistique et de la Comptabilité Nationale. 2 issues per year. French.

    1981 edition, 160 p., contains statistical data in the following areas:

    DEMOGRAPHY
    Population: distribution by age and sex, population estimates; *Vital statistics*: births, deaths, fertility, life expectancy.

    ECONOMIC AFFAIRS
    Agriculture and food: farming; *Commerce and business*: companies, exports, imports; *Finance*: banking and credit, money supply; *Income and expenditure*: prices; *Industry*: communication, industrial production, transportation.

    Most data are for 1981 or 1980 and the preceding year. A narrative section precedes the statistical tables. Notes accompanying the tables indicate the names of the agencies furnishing the data. There is a detailed list of tables at the beginning of the volume, an alphabetical subject index, and a bibliography of official statistical materials.

    Latest edition published: 1982. Available from the Direction de la Statistique et de la Comptabilité Nationale, BP 660, Yaoundé. Price: CFA 4,000 per issue, domestic; 7,500 per annum, domestic; 12,000, foreign.

    Available in microform: CH: 1973-75. CIS: 1973/74. IDC: 1973/74-1979-80.

15. ***Le Cameroun en chiffres*** [Cameroon in figures]. Yaoundé: Direction de la Statistique et de la Comptabilité Nationale. Annual. French.

    1982 edition, 11 p., contains statistical data in the following areas:

    PHYSICAL ENVIRONMENT
    Geography: maps.

    DEMOGRAPHY
    Population: distribution by age, distribution by sex, distribution by geographic/ administrative area.

    ECONOMIC AFFAIRS
    Agriculture and food: farming; *Commerce and business*: enterprises, exports, imports, tourism; *Finance*: money supply; *Income and expenditure*: prices; *Industry*: communication, energy, transportation, water; *National accounts*: gross domestic product; *Public finance*: government expenditures, government revenue.

    SOCIAL AND CULTURAL AFFAIRS
    Education: enrollments, teaching staff; *Labor*: labor force.

    Most data are for 1981/82 and the preceding 2 years.

Available from the Direction de la Statistique et de la Comptabilité Nationale, BP 660, Yaoundé.

16. ***Bulletin mensuel de statistique*** [Monthly bulletin of statistics]. 1968- Yaoundé: Direction de la Statistique et de la Comptabilité Nationale. French.

V. 9, no. 11, Nov., 1982, 41 p., contains statistical data in the following areas:

ECONOMIC AFFAIRS
Agriculture and food: farming; *Commerce and business*: exports, imports; *Finance*: banking and credit, money supply; *Income and expenditure*: prices.

Most data are monthly for 1982 and annual for the preceding year. Notes accompanying the tables indicate the names of the agencies furnishing the data.

Available from the Direction de la Statistique et de la Comptabilité Nationale, BP 660, Yaoundé. Price: CFA 500 per issue; 5,000 domestic, and 8,000, foreign, per year.

17. *****Note trimestrielle de statistique*** [Quarterly statistical note]. 1964-73. Yaoundé: Direction de la Statistique et de la Comptabilité Nationale. French.

Title varies: Earlier, *Note trimestrielle sur la situation économique du Cameroun.*

CAPE VERDE

No currently published yearbook has been found for Cape Verde. The following title offers a variety of current statistics:

18. ***Primeiro plano nacional de desenvolvimento, 1982/85.*** [Praia]: Secretaria de Estado da Cooperação e Planeamento, 1983. Portuguese.

V. 1, 144 p. and annexes, contains statistical data in the following areas:

DEMOGRAPHY
Population: census results from 1960-1980, distribution by age and sex, population projections; *Vital statistics*: births, deaths.

ECONOMIC AFFAIRS
National accounts: balance of payments, gross domestic product; *Public finance*: government expenditures, government revenue, planning and economic development.

POLITICAL AFFAIRS
Foreign aid.

SOCIAL AND CULTURAL AFFAIRS
Education: literacy; *Labor*: employment and unemployment, labor force.

Most data are for 1980, with planning expenditures for 1982/85.

Available from the Secretaria de Estado da Cooperação e Planeamento, Rua Guerra, Mendes 39, Praia.

19. ***Anuário estatístico** [Statistical yearbook]. 1933-1951/52. Praia: Secção de Estatística, 1934-1952. Portuguese.

    Available in microform: CH: 1933-51/52.

20. **Boletim trimestral de estatística** [Quarterly bulletin of statistics]. 1949- Praia: Serviço Nacional de Estatística. Quarterly. Portuguese and French.

    V. 3, no. 3, 1982, 29 p., contains statistical data in the following areas:

    DEMOGRAPHY
    Population: arrivals and departures, external migration; *Vital statistics*: births, deaths.

    ECONOMIC AFFAIRS
    Commerce and business: exports, imports; *Income and expenditure*: consumption, prices; *Industry*: communication, energy, manufacturing, mining, transportation; *Public finance*: government revenue.

    POLITICAL AFFAIRS
    Foreign aid.

    Most data are quarterly or monthly for 1981 or 1980 and the same period for the preceding year. In addition to the national level, data are included for islands.

    Available from Serviço Nacional de Estatística, rue du 12 septembre, Praia.

CENTRAL AFRICAN REPUBLIC

21. **Annuaire statistique** [Statistical yearbook]. 1962- Bangui: Direction de la Statistique Générale et des Etudes Economiques. Irregular (three editions have been published: 1962, 1970 and 1978). French.

    Agency varies: 1962 issued by Direction de la Statistique et de la Conjoncture.

    1978 edition, 276 p., contains statistical data in the following areas:

    PHYSICAL ENVIRONMENT
    Climatology: precipitation, sunshine, temperature; *Geography*: maps.

    DEMOGRAPHY
    Population: census results from 1975, distribution by age and sex, distribution by geographic/administrative area, households and families, population estimates, rate of urbanization.

    ECONOMIC AFFAIRS
    Agriculture and food: farming, forestry; *Commerce and business*: enterprises, exports, imports, services, tourism; *Finance*: banking and credit; *Income and expenditure*: consumption, prices; *Industry*: construction, energy, manufacturing, mining, transportation; *National accounts*: gross domestic product; *Public finance*: government expenditures, government revenue.

SOCIAL AND CULTURAL AFFAIRS
Education: enrollments, examination results, teaching staff; *Health*: disease, hospitals, medical personnel, public health; *Housing*; *Labor*: occupations, salaries and wages; *Social assistance*; *Social security*.

Most data are for 1978 and the preceding 7 years. In addition to the national level, data are included for prefectures, sub-prefectures and cities.

Commentaries are provided at the beginnings of chapters. Notes accompanying the tables indicate the names of agencies furnishing the data.

Available from Direction de la Statistique Générale et des Etudes Economiques, BP 732, Bangui. Price: CFA4,000, domestic; 8,000, Europe by air mail; 10,000, America, Asia, Oceania by air mail.

Available in microform: CH: 1962.

22. **Bulletin trimestriel de statistique** [Quarterly bulletin of statistics]. 1960- Bangui: Direction de la Statistique Générale et des Etudes Economiques. Quarterly. French.

Agency varies: Earlier by the Service de la Statistique Générale and by the Direction de la Statistique et de la Conjoncture. Continues the same title published by the Bureau de la Statistique Générale of Ubangi-Shari, 1952-1958.

No. 157-159, 1st qtr., 1982, série spéciale, published July, 1983, 51 p., contains statistical data in the following areas:

PHYSICAL ENVIRONMENT
Climatology: precipitation, sunshine, temperature.

DEMOGRAPHY
Vital statistics: births, deaths, divorces, marriages.

ECONOMIC AFFAIRS
Agriculture and food: farming; *Commerce and business*: exports, imports; *Finance*: banking and credit, money supply; *Income and expenditure*: prices; *Industry*: communication, energy, manufacturing, mining, transportation; *Public finance*: government expenditures, government revenue.

Most data are annual figures for 1981 and/or 1980. In addition to the national level, data are included for the city of Bangui. Notes accompanying the tables indicate the names of the agencies furnishing the data.

Available from the address in entry 21. Priced.

23. **Bulletin d'informations statistiques** [Bulletin of statistical information]. 1960- Bangui: Direction de la Statistique Générale et des Etudes Economiques. Monthly. French.

Title varies: Some issues titled *Bulletin mensuel de statistique* [Monthly bulletin of statistics]. For agency variations, see preceding entry. Continues same title published by Bureau de la Statistique Générale of Ubangi-Shari, 1952-1958.

CHAD

24. ***Annuaire statistique du Tchad*** [Statistical yearbook of Chad]. 1966- N'Djamena: Sous-Direction de la Statistique. Annual. French.

Not published in 1971 and 1973. 1974 numbered Nouvelle série. Publication temporarily suspended with 1975?

Agency name varies: 1966-68 by Service de la Statistique Générale; 1969-72: Direction de la Statistique et des Etudes Economiques.

V. 2, n.s., 1975, 223 p., contains statistical data in the following areas:

PHYSICAL ENVIRONMENT
Climatology: precipitation, temperature; *Geography*: area of land.

DEMOGRAPHY
Population: distribution by age and sex, distribution by geographic/administrative area.

ECONOMIC AFFAIRS
Agriculture and food: farming; *Commerce and business*: domestic commerce, establishments, exports, imports, tourism; *Finance*: banking and credit, money supply; *Income and expenditure*: consumption, prices; *Industry*: energy, manufacturing, transportation, water; *National accounts*: gross domestic product; *Public finance*: government expenditures, government revenue.

POLITICAL AFFAIRS
Foreign aid.

SOCIAL AND CULTURAL AFFAIRS
Cultural and scientific activities: newspapers, radio; *Education*: enrollments; *Health*: disease, hospitals, medical personnel, public health; *Sports and recreation*.

Most data are for 1975 and varying numbers of preceding years, usually 5. In addition to the national level, data are included for prefectures, county seats, and centers over 5,000.

Commentaries are provided at the beginnings of chapters. Notes accompanying the tables indicate the names of the agencies furnishing the data.

Will be available from the agency, BP 453, N'Djamena, when publication is resumed. Priced.

Available in microform: CH: 1969-70, 1972, 1974, 1975. CIS: 1974. IDC: 1966-71, 1974.

25. ***Tchad - Relance économique en chiffres, année 1983*** [Chad - Economic progress in figures for the year 1983]. N'Djamena: Direction de la Statistique, des Etudes Economiques et Démographiques, 1984. 125 p. French.

This title temporarily replaces both the yearbook, entry 24, and the bulletin, entry 26.

Available from the address in entry 24 for CFA 5,000.

26. ***Bulletin de statistique*** [Bulletin of statistics]. 1951- N'Djamena: Direction de la Statistique, des Etudes Economiques et Démographiques. Frequency varies. French.

   Title varies: Some issues as *Bulletin mensuel de statistique.* Agency name varies: 1951-60 by Bureau de la Statistique; 1961-62 by Service de la Statistique; 1963-68: Service de la Statistique Générale; 1969-72: Direction de la Statistique et des Etudes Economiques; 1973-77?: Sous-Direction de la Statistique.

   No. 226, 3rd qtr., 1977, contains statistical data in the following areas:

   PHYSICAL ENVIRONMENT
   Climatology: precipitation, temperature.

   DEMOGRAPHY
   Vital statistics: births, deaths, marriages.

   ECONOMIC AFFAIRS
   Commerce and business: domestic commerce, exports, imports; *Finance*: banking and credit; *Income and expenditure*: consumption, prices; *Industry*: communication, energy, manufacturing, transportation; *Public finance*: government expenditures, government revenue.

   Most data are monthly for the latest year and annual for the preceding 3 years. The latest data are for the quarter on the cover of the issue. Notes accompanying the tables indicate the names of the agencies furnishing the data.

   Available from the address given in entry 24.

COMOROS

Receipt of a *Statistical bulletin,* dated March, 1983, was recorded by the U.N. Economic Commission for Africa Library.

CONGO

27. ***Annuaire statistique*** [Statistical yearbook]. 1958/63- Brazzaville: Centre National de la Statistique et des Etudes Economiques. Irregular; eds. published 1966, 1969, and 1974. French.

   Agency name varies slightly.

   1974 edition, 330 p., contains statistical data in the following areas:

   PHYSICAL ENVIRONMENT
   Climatology: precipitation, temperature; *Geography*: area of land, maps.

   DEMOGRAPHY
   Population: distribution by geographic/administrative area, population estimates; *Vital statistics*: causes of death, infant mortality.

ECONOMIC AFFAIRS
Agriculture and food: farming, fishing, forestry; *Commerce and business*: exports, imports; *Finance*: banking and credit; *Income and expenditure*: consumption, prices; *Industry*: manufacturing, mining, transportation; *Public finance*: government expenditures, government revenue.

SOCIAL AND CULTURAL AFFAIRS
Education: enrollments, teaching staff; *Health*: disease, hospitals, medical personnel, public health.

Most data are for 1973 and the preceding 7 years. In addition to the national level, data are included for regions and municipalities.

Commentaries are provided at the beginnings of chapters. Sources of data are discussed at the end of the volume.

Available from the agency at BP 2031, Brazzaville.

Available in microform: CH: 1958/63, 1969. IDC: 1969, 1974.

28. ***Bulletin mensuel [rapide] de statistique*** [[Rapid] monthly bulletin of statistics]. 1958- Brazzaville: Centre National de la Statistique et des Etudes Economiques. Monthly. French.

No. 154, Jan., 1980, 25 p., contains statistical data in the following areas:

PHYSICAL ENVIRONMENT
Climatology: precipitation, temperature.

DEMOGRAPHY
Vital statistics: births, deaths, divorces, infant mortality, marriages.

ECONOMIC AFFAIRS
Agriculture and food: farming, fishing, forestry; *Finance*: banking and credit, money supply; *Industry*: energy, manufacturing, mining, transportation; *Public finance*: government expenditures, government revenue.

SOCIAL AND CULTURAL AFFAIRS
Health: disease, public health.

Most data are monthly for the date on the cover and the preceding 3 months and annual for the preceding 2 years. A list of the publications of the agency is provided in each issue.

Available from the address given in entry 27. Priced?

DAHOMEY

See BENIN

DJIBOUTI

29. ***Annuaire statistique de Djibouti*** [Statistical yearbook]. 1975/78- Djibouti: Direction Nationale de la Statistique. French.

    1981 edition, 133 p., contains statistical data in the following areas:

    PHYSICAL ENVIRONMENT
    Climatology: precipitation, temperature; *Geography*: maps.

    DEMOGRAPHY
    Population: Refugees; *Vital statistics*: births, deaths.

    ECONOMIC AFFAIRS
    Agriculture and food: farming, fishing; *Commerce and business*: enterprises, exports, imports: *Finance*: banking and credit; *Income and expenditure*: consumption, prices; *Industry*: communication, construction, energy, mining, transportation; *National accounts*: balance of payments, gross domestic product; *Public finance*: government expenditures, government revenue.

    POLITICAL AFFAIRS
    Elections.

    SOCIAL AND CULTURAL AFFAIRS
    Cultural and scientific activities: circulation of official gazettes, radio, television; *Education*: enrollments, examination results, teaching staff; *Labor*: employment, salaries and wages; *Social security*; *Sports and recreation*.

    Most data are for 1981 or 1980 and the preceding 1 or 2 years. Explanatory notes accompany some sections. Notes accompanying the tables indicate the names of the agencies furnishing the data.

    Latest edition published: 1982. Available from the agency, BP 1846, Djibouti.

30. ***Bulletin trimestriel de statistique*** [Quarterly bulletin of statistics]. 1970- Djibouti: Direction Nationale de la Statistique. Quarterly. French.

    Title varies slightly: some issues as *Bulletin de statistique et de documentation.*

    No. 34, 2nd qtr., 1982, 50 p., contains statistical data in the following areas:

    PHYSICAL ENVIRONMENT
    Climatology: precipitation, temperature.

    DEMOGRAPHY
    Vital statistics: births, deaths.

    ECONOMIC AFFAIRS
    Commerce and business: domestic commerce; *Finance*: banking and credit, money supply; *Income and expenditure*: consumption, prices; *Industry*: communication, construction, energy, mining, transportation; *Public finance*: government expenditures, government revenue.

SOCIAL AND CULTURAL AFFAIRS
Justice: traffic accidents; *Labor*: employment, salaries and wages.

Most data are monthly, semi-annual or annual for 1982 or 1981 and the preceding 2 years. Notes accompanying the tables indicate the names of the agencies furnishing the data.

Available from the address given in entry 29.

EGYPT

31. ***Statistical yearbook.*** 1952/61- Cairo: Central Agency for Public Mobilisation and Statistics. Annual.

   Title varies: 1952/61-1952/72 as *Statistical handbook*. Country name 1958-71: United Arab Republic.

   1952/82 edition published 1983, 317 p., contains statistical data in the following areas:

   ## PHYSICAL ENVIRONMENT
   Climatology: precipitation, temperature; *Geography*: map.

   ## DEMOGRAPHY
   Population: census results from 1882-1976, distribution by age and sex, distribution by geographic/administrative area, households, population estimates; *Vital statistics*: births, deaths, divorces, marriages.

   ## ECONOMIC AFFAIRS
   Agriculture and food: farming, land ownership; *Commerce and business*: cooperatives, exports, imports, tourism; *Income and expenditure*: consumption, prices; *Industry*: communication, construction, energy, manufacturing, mining, transportation; *National accounts*: gross domestic product, national income.

   ## SOCIAL AND CULTURAL AFFAIRS
   Cultural and scientific activities: cinema and performing arts, libraries, museums and galleries, radio, television; *Education*: degrees conferred, educational attainment, enrollments, examination results, graduates of higher education institutions, teaching staff; *Health*: hospitals, public health; *Housing*; *Labor*: employment, occupations; *Social security*.

   Most data are for 1982 and the preceding 5 years, plus 1952. In addition to the national level, data are included for governorates and towns. There are comparative statistics for selected foreign countries. Commentaries are provided at the beginnings of most chapters.

   Historical statistics. Statistics for earlier periods are found in the *Annuaire statistique*, 1873-1962, published by the Statistical Department of the Ministry of Finance and Economy, 1909, Direction de la Statistique, 1910-12; and the Département de la Statistique Générale, 1913-42/43. Other sources for the 19th century are the *Statistique de l'Egypte....1863-72*, and the *Tableaux statistiques/ Statistical returns*, 1881-97, both published by the Statistical Department.

Available from the agency, PO Box 2086, Cairo.

Available in microform: CH: 1952/64-1952/71. CIS: 1952/70-1952/74; 1952/76-1952/78. IDC: 1952/68, 1952/71-1952/74. The following years of the *Annuaire statistique* are also offered: CH: 1901-59; IDC: 1909-62. CH provides 1881-97 of *Tableaux statistiques/ Statistical returns*.

32. **Statistical abstract.** 1965- Cairo: Central Agency for Public Mobilisation and Statistics. Irregular.

This is an English version of an abridged edition of the annual statistical abstract published in Arabic. It offers less detailed coverage of the same subjects as entry 31.

Available in microform: CH: 1951-71; IDC: 1967-72.

No general bulletin of statistics has been found for Egypt.

EQUATORIAL GUINEA

33. *Reseña estadística de la República de Guinea Ecuatorial* [Statistical review of the Republic of Equatorial Guinea]. Malabo: Dirección General [Tecnica] de Estadística. Spanish.

1981, 117 p., contains statistical data in the following areas:

PHYSICAL ENVIRONMENT
Climatology: precipitation, temperature; *Geography*: area of land, maps.

DEMOGRAPHY
Population: census results from 1932-1960; *Vital statistics*: births, deaths, fertility, infant mortality, life expectancy.

ECONOMIC AFFAIRS
Agriculture and food: farming, fishing, forestry; *Commerce and business*: exports, imports; *Income and expenditure*: consumption, prices; *Industry*: energy; *Public finance*: government expenditures and government revenue at national and municipal levels.

SOCIAL AND CULTURAL AFFAIRS
Education: enrollments, teaching staff; *Health*: hospitals, public health; *Religion*.

Data are for the latest year available, with time series to 1948 provided in some cases. In addition to the national level, data are included for provinces and districts. Notes accompanying some of the tables indicate the names of the agencies furnishing the data.

Available from the Dirección General de Estadística, Malabo.

34. *Boletín estadístico* [Statistical bulletin]. 1981- Malabo: Dirección General de Estadística. Irregular. Spanish.

3rd ed., 1983, published June, 1983, 106 p., contains statistical data in the following areas:

PHYSICAL ENVIRONMENT
Climatology: precipitation, temperature; *Geography*: area of land.

DEMOGRAPHY
Population: distribution by geographic/administrative area, population estimates.

ECONOMIC AFFAIRS
Agriculture and food: farming; *Commerce and business*: exports, imports; *Income and expenditure*: consumption; *Industry*: energy, transportation; *National accounts*: balance of payments; *Public finance*: government expenditures, government revenue.

SOCIAL AND CULTURAL AFFAIRS
Education: enrollments, teaching staff.

Most data are for 1982 and the preceding 1 or 2 years. In addition to the national level, data are included for provinces and districts.

Notes accompanying the tables indicate the names of the agencies furnishing the data.

Available from the address given in entry 33.

ETHIOPIA

35. ***Statistical abstract.*** 1963- Addis Ababa: Central Statistical Office. English and Amharic.

1980 edition published 1982, 304 p., contains statistical data in the following areas:

PHYSICAL ENVIRONMENT
Climatology: precipitation, temperature; *Geography*: area of land; map.

DEMOGRAPHY
Population: arrivals and departures, distribution by age and sex, distribution by geographic/administrative area, households and families, population estimates and projections.

ECONOMIC AFFAIRS
Agriculture and food: farming; *Commerce and business*: exports, imports; *Finance*: banking and credit, money supply; *Income and expenditure*: consumption, prices; *Industry*: communication, construction, energy, manufacturing, mining, transportation; *National accounts*: balance of payments, gross domestic product; *Public finance*: government expenditures, government revenue.

SOCIAL AND CULTURAL AFFAIRS
Education: degrees conferred, enrollments, teaching staff; *Health*: disease, hospitals, medical personnel; *Justice*: correctional institutions, courts; *Labor*: employment in manufacturing.

Most data are for 1980 or 1979 and the preceding 2 to 4 years. In addition to the national level, data are included for awraja [sub-regions] and towns.

Explanatory notes at the beginning of sections sometimes include the names of the agencies furnishing the data. There is a detailed list of tables at the beginning of the volume.

Available from the Central Statistical Office, PO Box 1143, Addis Ababa.

Available in microform: CH: 1963-76. CIS: 1970-72, 1975. IDC: 1963-71, 1980.

No general statistical bulletin has been found for Ethiopia.

GABON

36. ***Situation économique, financière et sociale de la République Gabonaise*** [Economic, financial and social situation of the Republic of Gabon]. 1959- Libreville: Direction Générale de la Statistique et des Etudes Economiques. French.

    Agency varies: 1961 by Service de la Statistique et des Etudes Economiques; 1962-69 by Service National de la Statistique [et des Etudes Economiques]. Issued as supplements to *Bulletin mensuel de statistique*.
    1981 edition, 141 p., contains statistical data in the following areas:

    ECONOMIC AFFAIRS
    Agriculture and food: farming, fishing, forestry; *Commerce and business*: exports, imports, tourism; *Finance*: banking and credit, money supply; *Income and expenditure*: prices; *Industry*: construction, energy, manufacturing, mining, transportation, water; *Public finance*: government expenditures, government revenue.

    POLITICAL AFFAIRS
    Foreign aid.

    SOCIAL AND CULTURAL AFFAIRS
    Education: enrollments, examination results, teaching staff; *Health*: hospitals, medical personnel, public health; *Social assistance*; *Social security*.

    Most data are for 1981 and the preceding year. Time series for 5 years are frequently included. In addition to the national level, data are included for regions.

    Commentaries are provided at the beginnings of chapters. Notes accompanying some of the tables indicate the names of the agencies furnishing the data.

    Available from the agency, BP 179, Libreville.

    Available in microform: CH: 1961-71.

37. ***Annuaire statistique*** [Statistical yearbook]. 1964- Libreville: Direction [Générale] de la Statistique et des Etudes Economiques. Irregular; editions for 1964, 1968, 1970/75 published. French.

    Agency name varies: 1964 by Service National de la Statistique; 1968 by Service National de la Statistique et des Etudes Economiques.

    1970-75 edition, 180 p., contains statistical data in the following areas:

PHYSICAL ENVIRONMENT
Climatology: precipitation, temperature; *Geography*: map.

DEMOGRAPHY
Population: distribution by age and sex, distribution by geographic/administrative area.

ECONOMIC AFFAIRS
Agriculture and food: farming, fishing, forestry; *Commerce and business*: exports, imports, tourism; *Finance*: banking and credit, money supply; *Income and expenditure*: consumption, prices; *Industry*: energy, manufacturing, mining, transportation; *National accounts*: gross domestic product; *Public finance*: government expenditures, government revenue.

SOCIAL AND CULTURAL AFFAIRS
Education: enrollments, examination results, teaching staff; *Health*: hospitals, public health; *Labor*: employment, salaries and wages; *Social assistance*; *Social security*.

Most data are for 1969-1975. The 1964 edition includes statistics for the period 1957 to 1964. In addition to the national level, data are included for regions/provinces and municipalities. Commentaries including discussions of sources are provided at the beginnings of some chapters.

Available from the agency, BP 179, Libreville.

38. ***Bulletin mensuel de statistique*** [Monthly bulletin of statistics]. 1959- Libreville: Direction [Générale] de la Statistique et des Etudes Economiques. French.

For agency name changes, see entry 37.

[Jan.-June], 1983, 31 p., contains statistical data in the following areas:

ECONOMIC AFFAIRS
Agriculture and food: farming, forestry; *Commerce and business*: exports, imports; *Finance*: banking and credit; *Industry*: energy, mining, transportation, water.

Most data are for the first 6 months of 1983 and the corresponding period of the preceding year, plus annual figures for the preceding year. Notes accompanying the tables indicate the names of the agencies furnishing the data.

Available from the address in entry 37. Priced?

GAMBIA

39. ***The Gambia trade directory.*** Banjul: Ministry of Finance and Trade, 1983. 91 p.

This directory of exporters, importers, and trade organizations includes statistics in the following areas:

DEMOGRAPHY
Population: census results from 1973, ethnic groups, population estimates; *Vital statistics*: life expectancy.

ECONOMIC AFFAIRS
Agriculture and food: farming, fishing; *Commerce and business*: exports, imports, tourism; *Income and expenditure*: cost of living, prices; *Industry*: mining, transportation; *National accounts*: balance of payments, gross domestic product; *Public finance*: government expenditures, government revenue.

SOCIAL AND CULTURAL AFFAIRS
Education: enrollments, teaching staff; *Labor*: employment, labor force; *Religion*.

Most data are for 1981/82 and the preceding year. Notes accompanying some of the tables indicate the names of the agencies furnishing the data.

Available from the Ministry, The Quadrangle, Banjul.

40. **Statistical summary.* 1964-1967/68. Bathurst: Statistics Office.

This brief compilation of climatological, demographic, economic, political and social statistics was published by the Government Printer in the Sessional papers of the House of Representatives as follows: 1964 as no. 7 of 1965; 1965 as no. 6 of 1966; 1966/67 as no. 9 of 1967; and 1967/68 as no. 5 of 1969.

Available in microform: CH: 1964-1967/68.

No general statistical bulletin of statistics for the Gambia has been found.

GHANA

41. *Economic survey.* 1955- Accra: Central Bureau of Statistics. Annual, except for the following years which were published together: 1972/74; 1975/76; 1977-79; 1977-80.

1977-80 edition, published 1981, 320 p., contains statistical data in the following areas:

DEMOGRAPHY
Population: arrivals and departures.

ECONOMIC AFFAIRS
Agriculture and food: farming, fishing, forestry; *Commerce and business*: exports, imports, tourism; *Finance*: banking and credit, money supply; *Income and expenditure*: consumption, prices; *Industry*: communication, construction, energy, manufacturing, mining, transportation; *National accounts*: balance of payments, gross domestic and gross national product, national income; *Public finance*: government expenditures, government revenue, planning and economic development.

POLITICAL AFFAIRS
Foreign aid.

SOCIAL AND CULTURAL AFFAIRS
Education: enrollments; *Labor*: employment and unemployment, labor-management relations, salaries and wages.

Most data are annual figures for 1977-1980. Notes indicating sources accompany a few of the tables.

Latest edition published: 1981. Available from the agency at PO Box 1098, Accra. Price: $20.00.

42. **Statistical yearbook.** 1961- Accra: Central Bureau of Statistics.

Publication temporarily suspended with 1969/1970 edition.

1967/68, 240 p., contains statistical data in the following areas:

PHYSICAL ENVIRONMENT
Climatology: precipitation, temperature; *Geography*: area of land, maps.

DEMOGRAPHY
Population: arrivals and departures, census results from 1960, distribution by sex, distribution by geographic/administrative area, ethnic groups.

ECONOMIC AFFAIRS
Agriculture and food: farming, fishing, forestry; *Commerce and business*: domestic commerce, establishments, exports, imports; *Finance*: banking and credit, money supply; *Income and expenditure*: consumption, prices; *Industry*: communication, energy, manufacturing, mining, transportation, water; *National accounts*: balance of payments, gross domestic product, national income; *Public finance*: government expenditures, government revenue.

POLITICAL AFFAIRS
Elections.

SOCIAL AND CULTURAL AFFAIRS
Cultural and scientific activities: libraries, newspapers, performing arts; *Education*: enrollments, literacy, teaching staff; *Health*: disease, hospitals, medical personnel, public health; *Justice*: correctional institutions, courts, crimes, traffic accidents; *Labor*: employment and unemployment, labor force, occupations, salaries and wages; *Religion*.

Most data are for 1968 and 1967, plus varying numbers of earlier years. In addition to the national level, data are included for regions and municipalities.

Commentaries are provided at the beginnings of some chapters. Notes accompanying the tables indicate the names of the agencies furnishing the data. There is an alphabetical subject index and a list of publications of the Central Bureau of Statistics.

Available in microform: *Statistical yearbook*: CH: 1961-70. CIS: 1969/70. IDC: 1961-67/68.

43. **Statistical handbook.** 1967- Accra: Central Bureau of Statistics.

Publication temporarily suspended with 1970.

A less detailed version of entry 42, with coverage of most of the same topics.

44. **Quarterly digest of statistics.** 1952- Accra: Central Bureau of Statistics.

V.1, no. 3, Dec., 1981, 70 p., contains statistical data in the following areas:

ECONOMIC AFFAIRS
Agriculture and food: farming; *Commerce and business*: exports, imports; *Finance*: banking and credit, money supply; *Income and expenditure*: consumption, prices; *Industry*: energy, manufacturing, mining, transportation; *National accounts*: balance of payments; *Public finance*: government expenditures, government revenue, planning and economic development.

SOCIAL AND CULTURAL AFFAIRS
Education: enrollments, teaching staff; *Labor*: employment , salaries and wages.

Most data are monthly for 1981 and the preceding 2 years, with annual figures for the preceding 9 years. Sources of data are not given.

Available from the address given in entry 41. Price: $10.00 per issue.

GUINEA

No statistical abstract has been found for Guinea.

45. ***Bulletin spécial de statistique*** [Special bulletin of statistics]. 1962- Conakry: Service de la Statistique Générale. Quarterly. French.

GUINEA-BISSAU

46. ***Anuário estatístico*** [Statistical yearbook]. 1974- Bissau: Direcção Geral de Estadístico. Portuguese.

1977 edition, 152 p., contains statistical data in the following areas:

PHYSICAL ENVIRONMENT
Climatology: precipitation, temperature; *Geography*: area of land, maps.

DEMOGRAPHY
Population: census results from 1950, 1960, 1970.

ECONOMIC AFFAIRS
Agriculture and food: farming, fishing, forestry; *Commerce and business*: exports, imports; *Finance*: banking and credit; *Industry*: communication, manufacturing, transportation; *Public finance*: government expenditures, government revenue.

SOCIAL AND CULTURAL AFFAIRS
Education: enrollments, teaching staff; *Health*: hospitals, medical personnel.

Most data are for 1977 and the preceding 2 years. Time series may be provided for as many as 15 years. Notes of explanation accompany most chapters.

Available from the agency, CP 6, Bissau. Priced.

Available in microform: CH: 1947-58 of the *Anuário estadístico*.

47. ***Boletim trimestral de estadística*** [Quarterly bulletin of statistics]. 1974- Bissau: Direcção Geral de Estatística. Portuguese.

1st qtr.,1982, 31 p., contains statistical data in the following areas:

PHYSICAL ENVIRONMENT
Climatology: precipitation, sunshine, temperature.

DEMOGRAPHY
Population: arrivals and departures, distribution by geographic/administrative area; *Vital statistics*: births in hospitals and clinics.

ECONOMIC AFFAIRS
Agriculture and food: farming, fishing; *Commerce and business*: exports, imports, tourism; *Income and expenditure*: prices; *Industry*: communication, manufacturing, transportation; *Public finance*: government expenditures, government revenue.

SOCIAL AND CULTURAL AFFAIRS
Health: disease, hospitals, public health; *Justice*: traffic accidents.

Most data are for the first quarter of 1982, with some annual figures for 1981 and 1982. Some data are included for regions.

Available from the address given in entry 47. Priced.

IVORY COAST

48. ***La Côte d'Ivoire en chiffres; Annuaire statistique*** [The Ivory Coast in figures; Statistical yearbook]. 1975- Abidjan: Direction de la Statistique. Irregular. French.

1980/81 edition, 324 p., contains statistical data in the following areas:

PHYSICAL ENVIRONMENT
Climatology: precipitation, temperature; *Geography*: area and use of land, maps.

DEMOGRAPHY
Population: census results from 1975, distribution by age and sex, distribution by geographic/administrative area, population projections.

ECONOMIC AFFAIRS
Agriculture and food: farming, fishing, forestry; *Commerce and business*: companies, exports, imports, tourism; *Finance*: banking and credit; *Income and expenditure*: consumption, prices; *Industry*: communication, construction, energy, manufacturing, mining, transportation; *National accounts*: balance of payments, gross domestic product; *Public finance*: government expenditures, government revenue.

POLITICAL AFFAIRS
Foreign aid.

SOCIAL AND CULTURAL AFFAIRS
Education: enrollments, examination results, teaching staff; *Health*: hospitals, medical personnel, public health.

Most data are for 1979 and/or 1978 and varying numbers of earlier years. In addition to the national level, data are included for regions and departments. Explanatory notes appear at the beginning of many sections. Notes accompanying most of the tables indicate the names of agencies furnishing the data. Also included are a government directory, the investment code and a list of agencies offering aid to foreign investors.

Available from the agency at BP V 55, Abidjan. Priced.

Available in microform: CH: 1975. IDC: 1975.

49. *Bulletin mensuel de statistique* [Monthly bulletin of statistics]. 1948- Abidjan: Direction de la Statistique. French.

V. 34, nos. 8-9, Sept., 1981, 130 p., contains statistical data in the following areas:

PHYSICAL ENVIRONMENT
Climatology: precipitation, sunshine, temperature.

ECONOMIC AFFAIRS
Commerce and business: exports, imports; *Finance*: banking and credit, money supply; *Income and expenditure*: consumption, prices; *Industry*: communication, energy, transportation.

SOCIAL AND CULTURAL AFFAIRS
Labor: salaries and wages.

Most data are monthly or quarterly for 4 years. Latest data are for 3 to 6 months earlier than the date of the issue. Notes accompanying the tables indicate the names of the agencies furnishing the data.

Available from the address given in entry 48. Priced.

KENYA

50. *Statistical abstract.* 1961- Nairobi: Central Bureau of Statistics.

Agency varies: 1961-64 by the Economics and Statistics Division; 1965-71 by the Statistics Division (attached to the Ministry of Economic Planning and Development, 1965-69; the Ministry of Finance and Economic Planning, 1970; and the Ministry of Finance and Planning, 1971). Continues the *Statistical abstract [of the Colony and Protectorate of Kenya]*, issued by the East Africa High Commission, East African Statistical Dept. (Kenya Unit), 1955-60.

1984, 276 p., contains statistical data in the following areas:

PHYSICAL ENVIRONMENT
Climatology: precipitation, sunshine, temperature; *Geography*: area and use of land.

DEMOGRAPHY
Population: arrivals and departures, census results from 1911-1979, distribution by age and sex, distribution by geographic/administrative area, race and tribe, external migration; *Vital statistics*: births, deaths.

ECONOMIC AFFAIRS
Agriculture and food: farming, fishing, forestry; *Commerce and business*: establishments, exports, imports, tourism.*Finance*: banking and credit, money supply, securities; *Income and expenditure*: consumption, prices; *Industry*: communication, construction, energy, manufacturing, mining, transportation; *National accounts*: balance of payments, gross domestic product, gross national product; *Public finance*: government expenditures and government revenue for central government and local authorities, planning and economic development.

POLITICAL AFFAIRS
Membership of the National Assembly.

SOCIAL AND CULTURAL AFFAIRS
Cultural and scientific activities: radio, television; *Education*: educational attainment, enrollments, examination results, teaching staff; *Health*: disease, family planning, hospitals, medical personnel, public health; *Housing*; *Justice*: correctional institutions, courts, crimes, traffic accidents; *Labor*: employment, labor-management relations, salaries and wages; *Social security*.

Most data are for 1983 and varying numbers of earlier years. In addition to the national level, data are included for provinces, districts and major towns.

Commentaries are provided at the beginnings of chapters. Notes accompanying the tables indicate the names of the agencies furnishing the data.

Available from the Government Printer, Printing and Stationery Dept., PO Box 30128, Nairobi. Price: sh100.

Available in microform: CH: 1961-76. CIS: 1970-72, 1974, 1976-80. IDC: 1961-69, 1972-73, 1975-80. The *Statistical abstract* of the East African Statistical Dept., 1955-60, is available from both CH and IDC.

51. **Kenya statistical digest.** 1963- Nairobi: Central Bureau of Statistics. Quarterly.

For agency variations, see previous entry.

V. 21, no. 4, 1982, 35 p., contains statistical data in the following areas:

PHYSICAL ENVIRONMENT
Climatology: precipitation.

DEMOGRAPHY
Population: arrivals and departures; population estimates.

ECONOMIC AFFAIRS
Agriculture and food: farming; *Commerce and business*: companies, exports, imports, tourism; *Finance*: banking and credit; *Income and expenditure*: consumption, prices; *Industry*: construction, manufacturing, transportation; *National accounts*: gross domestic product; *Public finance*: government revenue.

SOCIAL AND CULTURAL AFFAIRS
Health: family planning; *Labor*: employment, salaries and wages.

Most data are monthly or quarterly for the current year to date on cover, with quarterly figures for 2 preceding years and annual figures for 5 years. Notes accompanying the tables indicate the names of the agencies furnishing the data.

Available from the address given in entry 50. Price: sh15 per issue; sh60 per year.

LESOTHO

52. ***Annual statistical bulletin.*** 1963/64- Maseru: Bureau of Statistics.

1982 edition published August, 1983, 200 p., contains statistical data in the following areas:

PHYSICAL ENVIRONMENT
Climatology: precipitation, sunshine, temperature; *Geography*: area of land.

DEMOGRAPHY
Population: census results from 1976, distribution by age and sex, distribution by geographic/administrative area, households and families, population projections; *Vital statistics*: births, causes of death of migrant laborers, deaths in hospitals, fertility, infant mortality, life expectancy.

ECONOMIC AFFAIRS
Agriculture and food: farming, forestry; *Commerce and business*: exports, imports, tourism; *Finance*: banking and credit; *Income and expenditure*: consumption, prices; *Industry*: communication, mining, transportation; *National accounts*: gross domestic product, gross national product; *Public finance*: government expenditures, government revenue.

SOCIAL AND CULTURAL AFFAIRS
Education: enrollments, examination results, teaching staff; *Health*: hospitals, medical personnel, public health; *Justice*: correctional institutions, crimes; *Labor*: migrant mine labor.

Most data are for 1981 and/or 1980. There are a few time series for as many as 10 years. In addition to the national level, data are included for districts.

Commentaries, which include discussions of sources, are provided at the beginnings of sections. Some tables are accompanied by notes indicating the names of the agencies furnishing the data. A price list of publications available from the Bureau of Statistics is provided.

Latest edition published: 1983, 216p. Available from the agency at PO Box 455, Maseru. Priced.

Available in microform: CH: 1963-73. CIS: 1971, 1973, 1976, 1977.

53. *Quarterly statistical bulletin.* 1976- Maseru: Bureau of Statistics.

V.2, no. l, July, 1977, 50 p., contains statistical data in the following areas:

PHYSICAL ENVIRONMENT
Climatology: precipitation, sunshine, temperature.

ECONOMIC AFFAIRS
Commerce and business: exports, imports.*Industry*: transportation; *Public finance*: government expenditures, government revenue.

SOCIAL AND CULTURAL AFFAIRS
Health: disease, public health; *Justice*: correctional institutions,*Labor*: employment, foreign workers.

Most data are monthly for the current and preceding year. Latest data are for 3 months before the date of the issue. There are some time series for 5 years. In addition to the national level, data are included for districts. Notes accompanying the tables indicate the names of the agencies furnishing the data.

Available from the address given in entry 52. Priced.

LIBERIA

54. *Economic survey of Liberia.* 1967- Monrovia: Bureau of Statistics.

Statistical tables are contained in Part II, entitled 'Statistical abstract'. 1980 edition published Oct, 1980, 166 p., contains statistical data in the following areas:

DEMOGRAPHY
Population: distribution by age and sex, distribution by geographic/administrative area, population estimates; *Vital statistics*: births, deaths, infant mortality, life expectancy.

ECONOMIC AFFAIRS
Agriculture and food: farming; *Commerce and business*: exports, imports; *Finance*: banking and credit, money supply; *Income and expenditure*: consumption, prices; *Industry*: communication, energy, transportation, water; *National accounts*: balance of payments, gross domestic product; *Public finance*: government expenditures, government revenue, planning and economic development.

POLITICAL AFFAIRS
Foreign aid.

SOCIAL AND CULTURAL AFFAIRS
Education: enrollments, graduates of higher education institutions by field, teaching staff; *Health*: disease, hospitals, medical personnel; *Housing*; *Labor*: labor force.

Most data are for 1980 and varying numbers of earlier years. There are some monthly figures. In addition to the national level, data are included for counties.

Commentaries and explanations are found in Part I. Notes accompanying some of the tables indicate the names of the agencies furnishing the data.

Available from the agency at PO Box 9016, Monrovia.

55. ***Quarterly statistical bulletin of Liberia.*** 1970- Monrovia: Bureau of Statistics.

No.13/14, 1st qtr., 1974, 92 p., contains statistical data in the following areas:

DEMOGRAPHY
Population: arrivals and departures.

ECONOMIC AFFAIRS
Agriculture and food: farming, fishing, forestry; *Commerce and business*: exports, imports, services; *Finance*: banking and credit; *Income and expenditure*: prices; *Industry*: construction, energy, manufacturing, mining, transportation; *National accounts*: gross domestic product and gross national product, national income; *Public finance*: government expenditures, government revenue.

SOCIAL AND CULTURAL AFFAIRS
Labor: employment, salaries and wages.

Quarterly issues usually have monthly and/or quarterly data for the quarter of the issue and the 2 preceding quarters, plus annual figures for 4 years. One issue a year is entitled 'annual summary' and has figures for the year of the issue and/or the preceding year, plus annual figures for varying periods of time.

Sources are discussed at the beginning of the issue and a few of the tables have notes indicating the names of the agencies furnishing the data.

Available from the address given in entry 54.

56. ***Statistical newsletter.*** 1981?- Monrovia: Bureau of Statistics.

In addition to statistical tables, dealing mostly with economic questions, each issue has an article devoted to a special topic. No. 4, 1982, 27 p., had a survey of adult education in Liberia in 1980, as well as statistical tables on accidents, banking and credit, exports, government expenditures and receipts, imports, money supply, and prices.

Available from the address in entry 54.

LIBYA

57. ***Statistical abstract of Libya.*** 1958/62- Tripoli: Census and Statistics [Statistical] Department. Arabic and English.

1978 edition published 1980, 256 p., contains statistical data in the following areas:

AFRICA : LIBYA

PHYSICAL ENVIRONMENT
Climatology: precipitation, temperature.

DEMOGRAPHY
Population: census results from 1954, 1964, 1973, distribution by age and sex, distribution by geographic/administrative area, external migration, households and families, internal migration, population estimates and projections; *Vital statistics*: births, deaths, divorces, fertility, marriages.

ECONOMIC AFFAIRS
Agriculture and food: farming; *Commerce and business*: exports, imports, tourism; *Finance*: banking and credit, money supply; *Income and expenditure*: cost of living, prices; *Industry*: communication, construction, energy, manufacturing, mining, transportation; *National accounts*: balance of payments, gross domestic product, national income; *Public finance*: government expenditures, government revenue, planning and economic development.

SOCIAL AND CULTURAL AFFAIRS
Education: educational attainment, enrollments, teaching staff; *Health*: hospitals, medical personnel, public health; *Justice*: crimes, traffic accidents; *Labor*: employment, labor force, occupations, salaries and wages; *Religion*; *Social assistance*; *Social security*.

Most data are for 1978 or 1977. There are time series for 5 to 10 year periods. In addition to the national level, data are included for provinces. Sources are discussed at the beginnings of sections and some tables have notes indicating the names of the agencies furnishing the data.

Latest edition published: 1980? Available from the agency at 40 Sharia Damascus, Tripoli.

Available in microform: CH: 1958/62-74. CIS: 1970, 1972, 1974, 1976-78. IDC: 1958/62-74.

58. ***Quarterly bulletin of statistics.*** 1950- Tripoli: Census and Statistics Department. English and Arabic.

4th qtr., 1976, 9 p., contains statistical data in the following areas:

DEMOGRAPHY
Population: arrivals and departures; *Vital statistics*: births, deaths, divorces, marriages.

ECONOMIC AFFAIRS
Commerce and business: exports, imports; *Finance*: banking and credit, money supply; *Income and expenditure*: cost of living, prices; *Industry*: construction, energy, manufacturing, transportation.

Most data are monthly for the quarter on the cover and the preceding two quarters.

Available from the address in entry 57.

MADAGASCAR

No current general statistical yearbook has been found for Madagascar. Only economic statistics are included in the semi-annual *Situation économique au 1er janvier* [Economic situation on January 1st], 1968- , published by the Institut National de la Statistique et de la Recherche Economique.

Historical statistics. Statistics for the period prior to 1951 are found in the *Annuaire statistique de Madagascar, 1938-51,* published by the Service de Statistique Générale in 1953, and available in microfiche from CH.

59. **Bulletin mensuel de statistique** [Monthly bulletin of statistics]. 1955- Antananarivo: Institut National de la Statistique et de la Recherche Economique. French.

Country name 1958-1975: Malagasy Republic. Agency name varies: 1955-60 by Service de Statistique Générale. Continues *Bulletin de statistique générale de Madagascar et dépendances,* published by the Service de Statistique Générale, 1949-54.

No. 300/301, Sept./Oct., 1980, 29 p., contains statistical data in the following areas:

PHYSICAL ENVIRONMENT
Climatology: precipitation, temperature.

ECONOMIC AFFAIRS
Commerce and business: exports, imports; *Finance*: banking and credit; *Income and expenditure*: consumption, prices; *Industry*: construction, energy, manufacturing, mining, transportation; *Public finance*: government expenditures, government revenue.

SOCIAL AND CULTURAL AFFAIRS
Labor: employment.

Most data are monthly for current year. Latest data are for the month before the date of the issue. Notes accompanying the tables indicate the names of the agencies furnishing the data.

Available from Imprimerie Nationale, BP 38, CCP 9901, Antananarivo. Priced.

MALAWI

60. **Malawi statistical yearbook.** 1972- Zomba: National Statistical Office.

Continues *Compendium of statistics*, published by the Ministry of Development and Planning, 1965, and the Department of Census and Statistics, 1966, 1970.

1982 edition published May, 1984, 173 p., contains statistical data in the following areas:

PHYSICAL ENVIRONMENT
Climatology: precipitation, temperature; *Geography*: area of land.

DEMOGRAPHY

Population: arrivals and departures, census results from 1901-1977, distribution by age and sex, distribution by geographic/administrative area, race; *Vital statistics*: births in hospitals and clinics, deaths, infant and maternal mortality, vital statistics for Europeans and Asians.

ECONOMIC AFFAIRS

Agriculture and food: farming, fishing, forestry; *Commerce and business*: companies, domestic commerce, exports, imports, tourism; *Finance*: banking and credit: *Income and expenditure*: prices; *Industry*: communication, construction, energy, manufacturing, mining, transportation, water; *National accounts*: balance of payments, gross domestic product; *Public finance*: government expenditures, government revenue, planning and economic development.

SOCIAL AND CULTURAL AFFAIRS

Education: educational attainment of Africans, enrollments, examination results, graduates of the University of Malawi, teaching staff; *Health*: disease, hospitals, medical personnel, public health; *Housing*; *Justice*: traffic accidents; *Labor*: employment, Malawians working abroad, salaries and wages.

Most data are for 1981 and varying numbers of earlier years. In addition to the national level, data are included for regions and districts. Notes accompanying the tables indicate the names of the agencies.

Available from the agency, PO Box 333, Zomba. Price K8.50.

Available in microform: CH: 1972-74. CIS: 1972, 1974. *Compendium of statistics*, CH: 1965-66, 1970. CIS: 1970.

No general statistical bulletin has been found for Malawi. The *Monthly statistical bulletin* published by the National Statistical Office since 1971 is devoted to economic statistics.

MALI

61. ***Annuaire statistique du Mali*** [Statistical yearbook of Mali]. 1960- Bamako: Direction Nationale de la Statistique et de l'Informatique.

Title varies slightly: *Annuaire statistique de la République Mali* used for some years.

1981 edition, published Aug., 1983, 242 p., contains statistical data in the following areas:

PHYSICAL ENVIRONMENT

Climatology: precipitation, temperature; *Geography*: maps.

DEMOGRAPHY

Population: census results from 1976, distribution by age and sex, distribution by geographic/administrative area, population estimates; *Vital statistics*: births, causes of death, deaths, infant mortality, marriages.

ECONOMIC AFFAIRS
Agriculture and food: farming, fishing, forestry; *Commerce and business*: exports, imports; *Finance*: banking and credit, money supply; *Income and expenditure*: consumption, prices; *Industry*: communication, energy, transportation; *Public finance*: government expenditures, government revenue.

SOCIAL AND CULTURAL AFFAIRS
Education: enrollments, examination results, percent of school age population in school, teaching staff; *Health*: disease, hospitals, medical personnel, public health.

Most data are for 1981 and varying numbers of earlier years. In addition to the national level, data are included for regions.

Notes accompanying the tables indicate the names of the agencies furnishing the data. An introduction provides a chronology of important events during 1981 and a description of the geography and history of Mali.

Historical statistics. *Mali a handbook of historical statistics*, by Pascal and Eleanor Imperato, Boston: G.K. Hall, 1982, 339 p., contains data for the period between 1935 and 1975.

Latest edition published: 1982, 296 p. Available from the agency in Koulouba, Bamako. Price: $100.

62. ***Bulletin mensuel de statistique*** [Monthly bulletin of statistics]. 1959- Bamako: Direction Nationale de la Statistique et de l'Informatique.

No. 2, Feb., 1983, 45 p., contains statistical data in the following areas:

PHYSICAL ENVIRONMENT
Climatology: precipitation, temperature.

DEMOGRAPHY
Vital statistics: causes of death, deaths, infant mortality.

ECONOMIC AFFAIRS
Agriculture and food: farming; *Commerce and business*: exports; *Finance*: banking and credit; *Income and expenditure*: prices; *Industry*: energy, transportation; *Public finance*: government expenditures, government revenue.

Most data are for the month of the issue and the preceding month, plus the same period for the preceding year. In addition to the national level, data are included for regions. Notes accompanying the tables indicate the names of the agencies furnishing the data.

Available from the address in entry 61. Price: $100 per year.

MAURITANIA

63. ***Annuaire statistique*** [Statistical yearbook]. 1968- Nouakchott: Direction de la Statistique et des Etudes Economiques. French.

1975/1976 edition, 166 p., contains statistical data in the following areas:

PHYSICAL ENVIRONMENT
Climatology: precipitation, temperature; *Geography*: area of land.

DEMOGRAPHY
Population: distribution by geographic/administrative area.

ECONOMIC AFFAIRS
Agriculture and food: farming, fishing, forestry; *Commerce and business*: domestic commerce, exports, imports, tourism; *Finance*: banking and credit; *Income and expenditure*: prices; *Industry*: communication, mining, transportation; *Public finance*: government expenditures, government revenue, planning and economic development.

SOCIAL AND CULTURAL AFFAIRS
Education: enrollments, examination results, teaching staff; *Health*: disease, hospitals, public health; *Social security*.

Most data are for 1975 and 1976. In addition to the national level, data are included for regions and departments. Notes accompanying the tables indicate the names of the agencies furnishing the data.

Available from the agency, BP 240, Nouakchott. Priced?

64. ***Bulletin mensuel statistique*** [Monthly statistical bulletin]. 1960- Nouakchott: Direction de la Statistique et des Etudes Economiques. Irregular. French.

Title varies: Earlier years as *Bulletin statistique et économique*.

No. 3, May-June, 1978, 36 p., contains statistical data in the following areas:

PHYSICAL ENVIRONMENT
Climatology: precipitation, temperature.

ECONOMIC AFFAIRS
Commerce and business: exports, imports; *Finance*: banking and credit; *Industry*: energy, manufacturing, transportation; *Public finance*: government revenue.

SOCIAL AND CULTURAL AFFAIRS
Health: disease.

Most data are for the months of the issue and the same period for the preceding year. Notes accompanying the tables indicate the names of the agencies furnishing the data.

Available from the address given in entry 63. Priced.

MAURITIUS

65. ***Bi-annual digest of statistics.*** 1966- Rose Hill: Central Statistical Office. Semi-annual.

Continues two earlier titles by the same agency, the *Quarterly digest of statistics,* 1961-66, and the *Year book of statistics,* 1946-1959.

V. 18, no. 12 Dec., 1983 edition published May, 1984, 144 p., contains statistical data in the following areas:

PHYSICAL ENVIRONMENT
Climatology: precipitation, temperature; *Geography*: area and use of land.

DEMOGRAPHY
Population: arrivals and departures, census results from 1846-1972, distribution by age and sex, distribution by geographic/administrative area, long-term emigrants, population estimates and projections; *Vital statistics*: births, causes of death, deaths, fertility, infant mortality, life expectancy, marriages.

ECONOMIC AFFAIRS
Agriculture and food: farming, fishing; *Commerce and business*: exports, imports, tourism; *Finance*: banking and credit, money supply; *Income and expenditure*: prices; *Industry*: communication, construction, energy, manufacturing, transportation; *National accounts*: balance of payments, gross national product; *Public finance*: government expenditures, government revenue.

SOCIAL AND CULTURAL AFFAIRS
Cultural and scientific activities: radio, television; *Education*: degrees conferred, enrollments, teaching staff; *Health*: disease, hospitals, medical personnel, public health; *Labor*: employment, salaries and wages; *Social assistance*; *Social security*.

Most data are for 1983 and the preceding 4 years. In addition to data for the whole country and the Island of Mauritius, there are some data for the Island of Rodrigues and other islands. Notes accompanying some tables indicate the names of the agencies furnishing the data.

Available from the Government Printing Office, Elizabeth II Ave., Port-Louis. Price: R50 per issue.

Available in microform: CH: 1966-76; 1961-66 of *Quarterly digest of statistics*; 1946-59 of *Year book of statistics*. CIS: 1981.

MOROCCO

66. ***Annuaire statistique du Maroc*** [Statistical yearbook of Morocco]. 1925- Rabat: Direction de la Statistique. Annual (irregular). French and Arabic.

Title varies: 1925-54 as *Annuaire statistique de la zone française du Maroc*. Agency varies: 1925-38 by Direction Générale de l'Agriculture, du Commerce et de la Colonisation and Service du Commerce et de l'Industrie; 1939- by Service [Central] des Statistiques, then by Division des Statistiques.

1982 edition, 372 p., contains statistical data in the following areas:

PHYSICAL ENVIRONMENT
Climatology: precipitation, sunshine, temperature; *Geography*: area of land, maps.

DEMOGRAPHY
Population: arrivals and departures, census results from 1960, 1971, distribution by age and sex, distribution by geographic/administrative area, households and families, population estimates; *Vital statistics*: causes of death.

ECONOMIC AFFAIRS
Agriculture and food: farming, fishing, forestry; *Commerce and business*: enterprises, establishments, exports, handicrafts, imports, tourism; *Finance*: banking and credit, money supply; *Income and expenditure*: consumption, prices; *Industry*: communication, construction, energy, manufacturing, mining, transportation; *National accounts*: balance of payments, gross domestic product, national income; *Public finance*: government expenditures, government revenue.

SOCIAL AND CULTURAL AFFAIRS
Cultural and scientific activities: cinema; *Education*: educational attainment (of urban labor force only), enrollments, examination results, teaching staff; *Health*: disease, family planning, hospitals, medical personnel, public health; *Justice*: courts, traffic accidents; *Labor*: employment and unemployment, labor force, occupations, salaries and wages; *Sports and recreation*.

Most data are for 1981 and varying numbers of earlier years. In addition to the national level, data are included for regions, provinces, and cities.

Explanatory notes are provided at the beginnings of chapters. Notes accompanying the tables indicate the names of the agencies furnishing the data. There is a detailed list of tables at the end of the volume.

Available from the agency, BP 178, Rabat. Price: DH110.

Available in microform: CH: 1925-1929, 1932-76. CIS: 1971, 1973, 1976. IDC: 1947-71, 1973-76.

67. ***Bulletin mensuel de statistique*** [Monthly bulletin of statistics]. 1957- Rabat: Direction de la Statistique. Temporarily quarterly. French and Arabic.

For agency name changes, see entry 66. Continues: *La conjoncture économique marocaine*, 1947-56, published by the Service Central des Statistiques.

Dec., 1982, 94 p., contains statistical data in the following areas:

PHYSICAL ENVIRONMENT
Climatology: precipitation, sunshine, temperature.

DEMOGRAPHY
Population: arrivals and departures.

ECONOMIC AFFAIRS
Agriculture and food: fishing; *Commerce and business*: exports, handicrafts, imports, tourism; *Finance*: banking and credit, money supply; *Income and expenditure*: prices; *Industry*: communication, construction, energy, manufacturing, mining, transportation; *Public finance*: government expenditures, government revenue.

SOCIAL AND CULTURAL AFFAIRS
Cultural and scientific activities: television; *Labor*: salaries and wages.

Most data are monthly and/or quarterly for the dates of the issue and cumulative for the current year to those dates. Corresponding figures for the same periods of the preceding year are also provided. Notes accompanying the tables indicate the names of the agencies furnishing the data.

Available from the address in entry 66. Price: DH242.00 per year.

MOZAMBIQUE

68. **Moçambique: informação estatística** [Mozambique; statistical information]. 1980- Maputo: Commissão Nacional do Plano, 1982. Portuguese.

1980/81 edition published June, 1982, 74 p., contains statistical data in the following areas:

PHYSICAL ENVIRONMENT
Climatology: precipitation, temperature; *Geography*: area of land, maps.

DEMOGRAPHY
Population: distribution by geographic/administrative area.

ECONOMIC AFFAIRS
Agriculture and food: farming; *Commerce and business*: domestic commerce, exports, imports; *Industry*: communication, manufacturing, transportation; *Public finance*: government expenditures, government revenue.

SOCIAL AND CULTURAL AFFAIRS
Cultural and scientific activities: books and journals, cinema and performing arts, newspapers, radio; *Education*: enrollments, literacy, teaching staff; *Health*: hospitals, medical personnel, public health.

Most data are for 1980 and 1981. In addition to the national level, data are included for provinces. The introduction to the volume describes the political and administrative organization of the country.

Available from the Centro de Documentação Económica, Commissão Nacional do Plano, CP 2051, Maputo. Price: $U.S.5.00, airmail postage included.

Recent statistics are also available in the **Economic report,** published by the Commission in both English and Portuguese. The latest edition, published in Jan., 1984, $15, was not available for examination.

69. *****Anuário estatístico/ Annuaire statistique** [Statistical yearbook]. 1926/28-73. Lourenço Marques: Direcção dos Serviços de Estatística. Portuguese and French.

Title varies slightly. The name of the agency appears on its publications in the following forms in addition to the one listed above: Direcção Provincial dos Serviços de [Economia e de] Estatística Geral; Instituto Nacional de Estadística; Repartiçao

[Central or Técnica] de Estatística [Geral]; Direcção dos Serviços de Economia e de Estatística Geral.

1973 edition published 1976, 422 p., contains statistical data in the following areas:

PHYSICAL ENVIRONMENT
Climatology: precipitation, sunshine, temperature; *Geography*: area and use of land, maps.

DEMOGRAPHY
Population: arrivals and departures, census results from 1928-70, distribution by age and sex, distribution by geographic/administrative area, ethnic groups, households and families; *Vital statistics*: births, illegitimate births, causes of death, deaths, divorces, infant mortality, marriages.

ECONOMIC AFFAIRS
Agriculture and food: farming, fishing, forestry; *Commerce and business*: exports, imports, tourism; *Finance*: banking and credit; *Income and expenditure*: prices; *Industry*: communication, construction, energy, manufacturing, mining, transportation; *National accounts*: balance of payments.

SOCIAL AND CULTURAL AFFAIRS
Cultural and scientific activities: books and journals, cinema and performing arts, libraries, museums and galleries, newspapers, radio; *Education*: enrollments, teaching staff; *Health*: disease, hospitals, public health; *Justice*: correctional institutions, courts, crimes, police, traffic infractions; *Labor*: manpower, salaries and wages; *Religion*; *Social assistance*; *Social security*; *Sports and recreation*.

Most data are for 1973. There are time series for varying periods. In addition to the national level, data are included for districts.

Notes accompanying some of the tables indicate the names of the agencies furnishing the data. There is a detailed list of tables at the beginning of the volume.

Some years available from the agency in entry 68.

Available in microform: CH: 1926/28-73; 1970,1971,1973. IDC: 1947-66, 1968-73.

70. ***Boletim mensal de estatística/ Bulletin mensuel de statistique** [Monthly bulletin of statistics]. 1929-75. Lourenço Marques: Direcção dos Serviços de Estatística. Portuguese and French.

Title varies slightly. For agency name variations, see entry 69.

V. 14, no. 12, Dec., 1973, 119 p., contains statistical data in the following areas:

PHYSICAL ENVIRONMENT
Geography: area of land.

DEMOGRAPHY
Population: arrivals and departures; *Vital statistics*: births, causes of death, deaths, infant mortality, marriages.

ECONOMIC AFFAIRS
Agriculture and food: farming, fishing, forestry; *Commerce and business*: domestic commerce, societies, tourism; *Finance*: banking and credit; *Income and expenditure*: consumption; *Industry*: communication, construction, energy, manufacturing, mining, transportation; *Public finance*: government expenditures, government revenue.

SOCIAL AND CULTURAL AFFAIRS
Cultural and scientific activities: cinema and performing arts, museums, radio; *Health*: disease; *Housing*; *Justice*: courts; *Labor*: unemployment, labor force, salaries and wages; *Social assistance*; *Social security*.

Most data are for 1973 and the preceding 2 years. In addition to the national level, data are included for districts and cities.

Some issues available from the agency in entry 68.

NIGER

71. ***Annuaire statistique*** [Statistical yearbook]. 1962- Niamey: Direction de la Statistique et des Comptes Nationaux. Irregular; eds. published 1962, 1967, 1978/79. French.

Agency name varies: Earlier by Service de la Statistique [et de la Mécanographie].

1978/79 edition, 210 p. contains data in the following areas:

PHYSICAL ENVIRONMENT
Climatology: precipitation, temperature; *Geography*: maps.

DEMOGRAPHY
Population: census results from 1977, distribution by age, distribution by sex, distribution by geographic/administrative area, population estimates; *Vital statistics*: fertility, infant and maternal mortality.

ECONOMIC AFFAIRS
Agriculture and food: farming; *Commerce and business*: exports, imports, tourism; *Finance*: banking and credit, money supply; *Income and expenditure*: consumption, prices; *Industry*: communication, energy, manufacturing, mining, transportation, water; *National accounts*: balance of payments, gross domestic product; *Public finance*: government expenditures, government revenue, planning and economic development (5th Plan, 1979-83).

SOCIAL AND CULTURAL AFFAIRS
Cultural and scientific activities: languages spoken, newspapers; *Education*: educational attainment, enrollments, examination results, literacy, percent of school age population in school, teaching staff; *Health*: disease, hospitals, medical personnel, public health; *Labor*: employment, salaries and wages.

Most data are for 1979 or 1978 and varying numbers of earlier years, usually 4. In addition to the national level, some data are provided for departments and arrondissements (districts).

Notes accompanying the tables indicate the names of the agencies furnishing the data.

There is a detailed list of tables at the beginning of each chapter. The first two chapters contain descriptions of the geography and the political-administrative organization of the country.

Available from the Direction de la Statistique et des Comptes Nationaux of the Ministère du Plan, Niamey.

72. ***Bulletin de statistique*** [Bulletin of statistics]. 1959- Niamey: Direction de la Statistique et des Comptes Nationaux. Quarterly. French.

For agency name variations, see entry 71.

No. 88, 4th qtr., 1980, 37 p., contains statistical data in the following areas:

PHYSICAL ENVIRONMENT
Climatology: precipitation, temperature.

ECONOMIC AFFAIRS
Agriculture and food: farming.*Finance*: banking and credit; *Income and expenditure*: prices; *Industry*: energy, manufacturing, transportation.

Most data are monthly or quarterly for the quarter of the issue and the preceding 1 to 3 years. In addition to the national level, data are included for departments. Notes accompanying some of the tables indicate the names of the agencies furnishing the data.

Available from the Direction de la Statistique et des Comptes Nationaux of the Ministère du Plan, Niamey.

NIGERIA

73. ***Annual abstract of statistics.*** 1960- Lagos: Federal Office of Statistics.

1981 edition published 1981, 169 p., contains statistical data in the following areas:

PHYSICAL ENVIRONMENT
Climatology: precipitation, sunshine, temperature; *Environmental quality*: radiation in Nigeria; *Geography*: area of land, maps.

DEMOGRAPHY
Population: arrivals and departures, distribution by age and sex, distribution by geographic/administrative area, external migration, population estimates and projections; *Vital statistics*: causes of death.

ECONOMIC AFFAIRS
Agriculture and food: farming, fishing; *Commerce and business*: domestic commerce, exports, imports; *Finance*: banking and credit, money supply, securities; *Income and expenditure*: consumption, prices; *Industry*: communication, construction, energy, manufacturing, mining, transportation; *National accounts*: balance of payments, gross domestic product, national income; *Public finance*: government expenditures, government revenue.

AFRICA : NIGERIA

POLITICAL AFFAIRS
Elections.

SOCIAL AND CULTURAL AFFAIRS
Education: degrees conferred, enrollments, teaching staff; *Health*: disease, hospitals, medical personnel, public health; *Justice*: correctional institutions, crimes; *Labor*: employment, productivity in mining, salaries and wages.

Most data are for 1975-79. In addition to the national level, data are included for states. Notes accompanying the tables indicate the names of the agencies furnishing the data. Later data are available in *Economic and social statistics bulletin* published in 1984 and 1985.

Available from the agency at PM Bag 12528, Lagos. Price: ₦ 5.00.

Available in microform: CH: 1960-61, 1963-73. CIS: 1970-73. IDC: 1960, 1963-64, 1966-70, 1972-73, 1975.

74. ***Digest of statistics.*** 1952- Lagos: Federal Office of Statistics. Quarterly.

V. 27, Dec., 1979, 63 p., contains statistical data in the following areas:

DEMOGRAPHY
Population: arrivals and departures, census results from 1963, population estimates and projections.

ECONOMIC AFFAIRS
Agriculture and food: farming; *Commerce and business*: exports, imports; *Finance*: banking and credit, money supply; *Income and expenditure*: consumption, prices; *Industry*: energy, manufacturing, mining, transportation; *National accounts*: balance of payments, gross domestic product; *Public finance*: government expenditures, government revenue.

SOCIAL AND CULTURAL AFFAIRS
Justice: correctional institutions, crimes; *Labor*: employment, productivity, salaries and wages.

Most data are monthly or quarterly for two years, with annual figures for varying periods of time. Latest data are for the month preceding the date of issue. In addition to the national level, data are included for states. Notes accompanying the tables indicate the names of the agencies furnishing the data.

Available from the address given in entry 73. Price: ₦ 2.00 per issue.

REUNION

75. ***Panorama de l'économie de la Réunion*** [Panorama of the economy of Reunion]. 1981- Sainte-Clothilde: Institut National de la Statistique et des Etudes Economiques (France), Service Régional de la Réunion. French.

Published as an annual supplement to *L'économie de la Réunion: revue d'information économique et sociale,* described in entry 77.

Replaces: *Mémento statistique* and *Statistiques et indicateurs économiques*, published by Institut National de la Statistique et des Etudes Economiques (France), Service Départemental de la Réunion.

1984 edition, published March, 1984, 130 p., contains statistical data in the following areas:

PHYSICAL ENVIRONMENT
Climatology: precipitation, sunshine, temperature; *Geography*: area of land, maps.

DEMOGRAPHY
Population: census results from 1646-1982, distribution by age and sex, distribution by geographic/administrative area, external migration, households and families; *Vital statistics*: abortions, births, including illegitimate births, causes of death, deaths, divorces, fertility, infant mortality, marriages.

ECONOMIC AFFAIRS
Agriculture and food: farming, fishing; *Commerce and business*: domestic commerce, exports, imports, tourism; *Finance*: banking and credit, money supply; *Income and expenditure*: consumption, personal income, prices; *Industry*: communication, construction, energy, manufacturing, transportation; *National accounts*: gross domestic product; *Public finance*: government expenditures and government revenue for the department and local authorities (aggregate only).

SOCIAL AND CULTURAL AFFAIRS
Cultural and scientific activities: television; *Education*: diplomas conferred, enrollments, examination results, literacy, teaching staff; *Health*: disease, hospitals, medical personnel, public health; *Housing*; *Justice*: traffic accidents; *Labor*: employment and unemployment, labor force, salaries and wages; *Social assistance*; *Social security*; *Sports and recreation*.

Most data are for 1983 and the 4 preceding years. In addition to the national level, data are included for arrondissements (districts) and municipalities.

Commentaries are provided at the beginnings of chapters. Notes accompanying the tables indicate the names of the agencies furnishing the data. There is a detailed list of tables at the beginning of the volume and an alphabetical subject index at the end.

Available from the Observatoire Economique de la Réunion, Institut National de la Statistique et des Etudes Economiques (France), 4 rue de l'Ecole, Sainte-Clothilde, 97490. Price: F30.

76. **Annuaire statistique de la Réunion** [Statistical yearbook of Reunion]. 1952/55-1969/72, 1976- Sainte-Clothilde: Institut National de la Statistique et des Etudes Economiques (France), Service Départemental de la Réunion. Irregular. French.

Currently issued in multiple fascicles in the series, entitled *Documents*. Numbers issued so far are:

I. *Situation, relief, climat, organisation administrative, élections* [Geography, climate, administrative organization, elections]. (Document no. 16) 1976. 60 p.

IV. *Pêche, forêts, agriculture* [Fishing, forests, agriculture]. (Document no. 28) 1979. 132 p.

VI. *Transports, postes et télécommunications information* [Transportation post and telecommunications information]. (Document no. 36) 1981. 80 p.

VII. *Le Commerce extérieur de la Réunion, 1966 à 1978* [Foreign trade of Reunion, 1966-1978]. (Document no. 29) 1979. 153 p.

The series begun in 1976 covers the period from 1973 until the date of publication, with time series back to the 1950s in many cases. Sources are discussed at the beginnings of chapters.

Available from the address in entry 75. Price: F10 per volume.

Available in microform: CIS: 1969/72.

77. ***L'économie de la Réunion: revue d'information économique et sociale*** [The economy of Reunion: review of economic and social information]. 1982- Sainte-Clothilde: Institut National de la Statistique et des Etudes Economiques (France), Service Régional de la Réunion. Bimonthly. French.

A supplement entitled, *Panorama de l'économie de la Réunion*, [Panorama of the economy of Reunion], described in entry 75, is published annually.

Each issue contains articles on various topics, many of which include statistics. Most issues also include a section entitled 'Indicateurs économiques', which includes monthly or quarterly data for a maximum period of 12 months or 9 quarters. Latest data are for 2 to 4 months before the date of issue and cover such topics as births and deaths, construction, farming, fishing, labor market, manufacturing, salaries, tourism, and transport.

Historical statistics. Monthly statistics for earlier periods were found in an annual publication, *Economie de la Réunion: séries statistiques mensuelles* [The Economy of Reunion: monthly statistical series], 1977-79, and the monthly, *Bulletin de statistiques mensuelles* [Bulletin of monthly statistics], 1964-77, both published by the Institut National de la Statistique et des Etudes Economiques (France), Service Départemental de la Réunion.

Available from the address in entry 75. Price: F80 per year, domestic; F120 per year, abroad.

See also entries under*France*.

RWANDA

78. ***Bulletin de statistique: supplément annuel*** [Bulletin of statistics: annual supplément]. 1964- Kigali: Direction Générale de la Statistique. Annual. French.

No. 9, 1982, 151 p., contains statistical data in the following areas:

AFRICA : SAO TOME AND PRINCIPE

PHYSICAL ENVIRONMENT
Climatology: precipitation, temperature.

DEMOGRAPHY
Population: migration, population estimates; *Vital statistics*: births, deaths, marriages.

ECONOMIC AFFAIRS
Agriculture and food: farming; *Commerce and business*: exports, imports, tourism; *Finance*: banking and credit, money supply; *Income and expenditure*: consumption, prices; *Industry*: communication, construction, energy, mining, transportation, water; *National accounts*: balance of payments; *Public finance*: government expenditures, government revenue.

SOCIAL AND CULTURAL AFFAIRS
Education: enrollments, teaching staff; *Health*: disease, hospitals, medical personnel, public health; *Social security*.

Most data are for 1981, with time series for varying periods. In addition to the national level, data are included for prefectures. Notes accompanying some of the tables indicate the names of the agencies furnishing the data.

Latest edition published: No. 10-11, 1984, published January 1984, 144 p. Available from the agency, BP 46, Kigali. Included in annual subscription to *Bulletin de statistique*, described in entry 79.

79. ***Bulletin de statistique*** [Bulletin of statistics]. 1964- Kigali: Direction Générale de la Statistique. Quarterly. French.

   Emphasis is on economic statistics. Some issues include demographic and/or social data.

   Figures are monthly, quarterly or semi-annual for the current year and preceding years. The latest data are for about 2 months before the date of the issue.

   Available from the address in entry 78. Price: $U.S.8 per issue, foreign; $U.S.32.00 per year, foreign.

SAO TOME AND PRINCIPE

No general statistical yearbook is currently published for Sao Tome and Principe.

80. ***Boletim trimestral de estatística*** [Quarterly bulletin of statistics]. 1929- São Tomé?: Repartição Provincial dos Serviços de Estatística. Frequency varies: earlier, monthly. French and Portuguese.

   Topics covered vary from issue to issue. V. IV, no. 14, 2nd quarter, 1974, 41 p., contains statistical data in the following areas:

PHYSICAL ENVIRONMENT
Climatology: precipitation, sunshine, temperature.

DEMOGRAPHY
Population: arrivals and departures, census results from 1970, distribution by age and sex (of labor force only); *Vital statistics*: births, including illegitimate births, causes of death, deaths.

ECONOMIC AFFAIRS
Agriculture and food: farming, fishing, forestry; *Commerce and business*: exports, imports; *Finance*: banking and credit; *Income and expenditure*: consumption, prices; *Industry*: communication, energy, manufacturing, transportation; *Public finance*: government expenditures, government revenue.

SOCIAL AND CULTURAL AFFAIRS
Health: disease; *Labor*: labor force, salaries and wages.

Latest data are for the quarter preceding the date of the issue. There are quarterly and annual time series of varying lengths.

SENEGAL

81. ***Situation économique du Sénégal*** [Economic situation of Senegal]. 1962- Dakar: Direction de la Statistique. French.

1980 edition, 342 p., contains statistical data in the following areas:

DEMOGRAPHY
Population: census results from 1976, distribution by age and sex, distribution by geographic/administrative area, ethnic groups, internal migration; *Vital statistics*: fertility.

ECONOMIC AFFAIRS
Agriculture and food: farming, fishing; *Commerce and business*: exports, imports, tourism; *Finance*: banking and credit, money supply; *Income and expenditure*: consumption, prices; *Industry*: communication, construction, energy, manufacturing, mining, transportation, water; *National accounts*: gross domestic and gross national product, national income; *Public finance*: government expenditures, government revenue.

SOCIAL AND CULTURAL AFFAIRS
Education: educational attainment, enrollments, examination results, literacy, teaching staff; *Health*: disease, hospitals, medical personnel, family planning, public health; *Justice*: courts, crimes; *Labor*: employment and unemployment, labor force.

Most data are for 1980, with time series for varying periods. There are a few monthly series. In addition to the national level, data are included for regions.

Explanatory notes accompany some sections and agencies furnishing the data are indicated for some of the tables. There is a detailed listing of tables at the end of the volume.

Available from the agency at BP 116, Dakar. Priced.

Available in microform: CH: 1962-68, 1970-72, 1974-76.

82. *Le Sénégal en chiffres* [Senegal in figures]. 1976- Dakar: Société Africaine d'Edition for the Ministère des Finances et des Affaires Economiques. Irregular. French.

The 1982/1983 edition, 304 p., contains statistical data in the following areas:

PHYSICAL ENVIRONMENT
Climatology: precipitation, sunshine, temperature; *Geography*: area of land, maps.

DEMOGRAPHY
Population: census results from 1976, distribution by age and sex, distribution by geographic/administrative area, ethnic groups, external and internal migration; *Vital statistics*: births, deaths, fertility, infant mortality, life expectancy.

ECONOMIC AFFAIRS
Agriculture and food: farming, fishing; *Commerce and business*: domestic commerce, enterprises, exports, imports, tourism; *Finance*: banking and credit, money supply; *Income and expenditure*: consumption, prices; *Industry*: communication, construction, energy, manufacturing, mining, transportation, water; *National accounts*: balance of payments, gross domestic product, national income; *Public finance*: government expenditures, government revenue, planning and economic development.

POLITICAL AFFAIRS
Foreign aid.

SOCIAL AND CULTURAL AFFAIRS
Cultural and scientific activities: journals, newspapers; *Education*: enrollments, examination results, teaching staff; *Health*: disease, hospitals, medical personnel, public health; *Justice*: correctional institutions, courts, crimes; *Labor*: employment and unemployment, labor force, occupations, salaries and wages.

Most data are for 1980 or 1979 and varying numbers of earlier years. In addition to the national level, some data are provided for regions. Commentaries are provided at the beginnings of chapters. Notes accompanying the tables indicate the names of the agencies furnishing the data.

Available from the Société Africaine d'Edition, BP 1877, Dakar.

Available in microform: IDC: 1978.

83. *Bulletin statistique et économique [mensuel]* [Statistical and economic bulletin [monthly]]. 1959- Dakar: Direction de la Statistique. French.

Nos. 1-2, 1982, 72 p., contain only climatological data and economic statistics in the following areas: banking and credit, construction, energy, exports, farming, government expenditures and government revenue, imports, manufacturing, money supply, tourism, transportation.

Most data are monthly for the current and preceding year. The latest data are for the month of the issue. Annual figures are given for 2 to 5 years. In addition to the national level, data are given for regions.

Notes indicating the agencies furnishing the material are given at the beginning of some tables.

AFRICA : SENEGAL

Available from the address given in entry 81.

SEYCHELLES

84. ***Statistical abstract.*** 1977- Victoria: Statistics Division.
    1983 edition, 126 p., contains statistical data in the following areas:

    PHYSICAL ENVIRONMENT
    Climatology: precipitation, sunshine, temperature; *Geography*: area of land.

    DEMOGRAPHY
    Population: distribution by age and sex, external migration, population estimates and projections; *Vital statistics*: births, causes of death, deaths, fertility, infant mortality, life expectancy.

    ECONOMIC AFFAIRS
    Agriculture and food: farming, fishing; *Commerce and business*: exports, imports, tourism; *Finance*: banking and credit, money supply; *Income and expenditure*: prices; *Industry*: communication, energy, manufacturing, transportation; *National accounts*: balance of payments, gross domestic product; *Public finance*: government expenditures, government revenue.

    SOCIAL AND CULTURAL AFFAIRS
    Education: enrollments, examination results, teaching staff; *Health*: disease, hospitals, medical personnel, public health; *Justice*: crimes; *Labor*: employment and unemployment, salaries and wages.

    Most data are for 1983 and the preceding 4 years. Notes accompanying the tables indicate the names of the agencies furnishing the data. A list of publications available from the Statistics Division appears at the end of the abstract.

    Available from the agency at PO Box 206, Victoria. Price: R60.00

    The *Quarterly statistical bulletin* was discontinued in 1982 and replaced by a number of separate bulletins. Those covering retail trade and tourism are issued monthly, those covering external trade, employment and production, quarterly, and those offering employment and demographic data, semi-annually.

SIERRA LEONE

85. ***Annual digest of statistics.*** 1968- Freetown: Central Statistics Office.

    Cover title: *Annual statistical digest.*

    No. 12, 1982, 50 p., contains statistical data in the following areas:

    PHYSICAL ENVIRONMENT
    Climatology: precipitation, temperature; *Geography*: area of land.

DEMOGRAPHY
Population: census results from 1974, distribution of population by geographic/administrative area; *Vital statistics*: births, deaths, infant mortality, marriages.

ECONOMIC AFFAIRS
Agriculture and food: farming; *Commerce and business*: establishments, exports, imports; *Income and expenditure*: prices; *Industry*: communication, manufacturing, mining, transportation; *National accounts*: gross domestic product; *Public finance*: government expenditure, government revenue.

SOCIAL AND CULTURAL AFFAIRS
Education: enrollments, teaching staff; *Health*: hospitals, medical personnel, public health; *Justice*: traffic accidents; *Labor*: employment.

Most data are for 1982 and preceding periods of varying length. In addition to the national level, data are included for provinces and districts.

Explanatory notes are grouped at the end of the volume. Notes accompanying some of the tables indicate the names of the agencies furnishing the data. There is a detailed list of tables at the beginning of the volume.

Latest edition published: 1984, published June 1985, 61p. Available from the agency, Tower Hill, Freetown.

Available in microform: CH: 1968-71, 1976. CIS: 1970, 1975.

86. *Statistical bulletin.* 1963- Freetown: Central Statistics Office. Quarterly.

Title varies: 1963-66 as *Quarterly statistical bulletin.*

No issues after 1971 located. Dec., 1971 edition, 72 p., contains statistical data in the following areas:

PHYSICAL ENVIRONMENT
Climatology: precipitation, temperature.

DEMOGRAPHY
Population: population projections; *Vital statistics*: births, deaths.

ECONOMIC AFFAIRS
Agriculture and food: farming; *Commerce and business*: exports, imports; *Finance*: banking and credit, money supply; *Income and expenditure*: prices; *Industry*: energy, transportation; *Public finance*: government expenditures, government revenue.

SOCIAL AND CULTURAL AFFAIRS
Education: enrollments, teaching staff; *Health*: hospitals; *Labor*: employment and unemployment.

Most data are annual for 1971 and varying numbers of preceding years. A few figures are on a quarterly basis. In addition to the national level, data are included for provinces. Notes accompanying the tables indicate the names of the agencies furnishing the data.

Available from the address given in the previous entry.

SOMALIA

87. ***Statistical abstract/ Koobaha staatistikada.*** 1964- Mogadishu: Central Statistical Department. English and Somali; 1964-71 in Italian and French.

    Title varies: 1964-71 as *Compendio statistico/ Statistical abstract.* Agency varies: 1964-68 by Statistical Department of the Ministry of Planning and Coordination.

    1980 edition published Dec., 1982, 110 p., contains statistical data in the following areas:

    PHYSICAL ENVIRONMENT
    Climatology: precipitation, temperature; *Geography*: area of land.

    DEMOGRAPHY
    Population: distribution by regions.

    ECONOMIC AFFAIRS
    Agriculture and food: farming; *Commerce and business*: establishments, exports, imports; *Finance*: banking and credit, money supply; *Income and expenditure*: consumption, prices; *Industry*: communication, energy, manufacturing, transportation; *Public finance*: government expenditures, government revenue, economic development.

    SOCIAL AND CULTURAL AFFAIRS
    Education: enrollments, teaching staff; *Health*: disease, medical personnel, public health; *Justice*: crimes, traffic accidents; *Labor*: employment, salaries and wages.

    Most data are for 1980 and preceding periods of varying length, usually 2 to 5 years. In addition to the national level, data are included for regions, districts and towns.

    General and technical notes are provided at the beginning of the volume. Notes accompanying the tables indicate the names of the agencies furnishing the data. There is a detailed list of tables at the beginning of the volume.

    Available from the agency, PO Box 1742, Mogadishu. Priced.

    Available in microform: CH: 1964-73. CIS: 1970-72, 1974-75. IDC: 1964-73, 1975-78.

88. ***Monthly statistical bulletin/ Faafinta Istaatistikada bisha.*** 1966- Mogadishu: Central Statistical Dept. Somali and English.

    Topics covered vary in different issues. Data are for the 3 months corresponding to the date of the issue and the same period in the preceding 2 years.

    Available from the address in entry 87. Priced.

SOUTH AFRICA

89. ***South Africa; official yearbook of the Republic of South Africa.*** 1974- Pretoria: Department of Foreign Affairs and Information. Also published in Afrikaans.

    Continues: *Official yearbook of the Union [of South Africa] and of Basutoland, Bechuana-*

land Protectorate and Swaziland, 1910/16-60, published by the Bureau of [Census and] Statistics.

1984 edition, 1058 p., contains a statistical appendix, in addition to detailed narrative accounts of economic, political, social and cultural conditions in South Africa. Topics covered in tables, which represent only a fraction of the statistics in the main body of the work include:

PHYSICAL ENVIRONMENT
Climatology: precipitation, sunshine, temperature; *Environment*: provincial reserves; *Geography*: area and use of land, maps.

DEMOGRAPHY
Population: census results from 1904-1980, distribution by age and sex, distribution by geographic/administrative area, ethnic groups, external migration, home languages, internal migration, population estimates and projections; *Vital statistics*: births, causes of death, deaths, divorces, fertility, life expectancy, marriages.

ECONOMIC AFFAIRS
Agriculture and food: farming, forestry; *Commerce and business*: domestic commerce, establishments, exports, imports, tourism; *Finance*: banking and credit, money supply, securities; *Income and expenditure*: consumption, personal income, prices; *Industry*: communication, energy, manufacturing, mining, transportation; *National accounts*: balance of payments, gross domestic product, national income; *Public finance*: government expenditures, government revenue, planning and economic development.

POLITICAL AFFAIRS
Defense; *Elections*.

SOCIAL AND CULTURAL AFFAIRS
Cultural and scientific activities: libraries, museums and galleries, newspapers; *Education*: degrees awarded, enrollments, examination results, teaching staff; *Health*: disease, hospitals, medical personnel, public health; *Justice*: crimes, traffic accidents; *Labor*: employment and unemployment, labor force, labor-management relations, migrant workers, occupations, productivity, salaries and wages; *Religion*; *Social assistance*; *Social security*.

Data in Addendum I, entitled *Statistics in Brief,* cover agriculture, construction, education, electricity, finance, foreign trade, internal trade, labor, mining, manufacturing, migration, national accounts, population, prices, the purchasing power of the rand, and transportation.

Most data are for 1982. There are time series of varying lengths in the narrative section, while the statistical addendum includes comparative figures for 1960, 1970, and 1980 (plus 1981, in some cases). In addition to the national level, data are included for provinces and homelands.

Tables in the addendum have been prepared by the Central Statistical Services and the South African Reserve Bank. Some of the tables in the main body of the work include the names of the agencies furnishing the data. There is a bibliography at the end of each chapter as well as at the end of the volume, and an alphabetical subject index.

Distributed by the Department of Foreign Affairs and Information, Private Bag X152, Pretoria 0001. No price listed.

Available in microform: IDC: 1974-77, 1982.

90. **South African statistics/ Suid Afrikaanse statistieke.** 1964- Pretoria: Central Statistical Services. Biennial; annual 1964-66. English and Afrikaans.

Title varies: 1964-66 as *Statistical year book.* Agency varies: 1970-80 by Department of Statistics; 1964-68 by Bureau of [Census and] Statistics.

1982 edition, v. p., contains statistical data in the following areas:

PHYSICAL ENVIRONMENT
Climatology: precipitation, sunshine, temperature; *Geography*: maps.

DEMOGRAPHY
Population: census results from 1904-1980, distribution by age, distribution by sex, distribution by geographic/administrative area, ethnic groups, external migration, households and families, population estimates.*Vital statistics*: births, including legitimacy, causes of death, deaths, divorces, infant mortality, life expectancy, marriages.

ECONOMIC AFFAIRS
Agriculture and food: farming, fishing, forestry; *Commerce and business*: companies, domestic commerce, establishments, exports, imports, services, tourism; *Finance*: banking and credit, money supply, securities; *Income and expenditure*: consumption, personal income, prices; *Industry*: communication, construction, energy, manufacturing, mining, transportation; *National accounts*: balance of payments, gross domestic product, national income; *Public finance*: government expenditures and government revenue for the central and local governments (aggregate by province only).

SOCIAL AND CULTURAL AFFAIRS
Cultural and scientific activities: books and journals, cinema, home languages, newspapers, radio, television; *Education*: degrees conferred, educational attainment, enrollments, examination results, literacy, teaching staff; *Health*: disease, hospitals, medical personnel, public health; *Housing*; *Justice*: courts, traffic accidents; *Labor*: employment and unemployment, labor force, labor-management relations, occupations, salaries and wages; *Religion*; *Social security*.

Most data are for 1982 and/or 1981 and varying numbers of earlier years. Historical tables extending to 1915 or 1920, in some cases, are included in most chapters. In addition to the national level, data are included for provinces, homelands and statistical regions.

Commentaries, which include discussions of sources, are provided at the ends of chapters. There is a detailed list of tables and an alphabetical subject index.

Historical statistics. Statistics for earlier periods are found in *Union statistics for fifty years: jubilee issue, 1910-1960*, published by the Office of Census and Statistics.

Available from the Government Printer, Private Bag 85, Bosman St., Pretoria. Price: R6, domestic; R7, foreign.

Available in microform: CH: 1964-76, and *Union statistics for fifty years: jubilee issue, 1910-1960* published by the Office of Census and Statistics. CIS: 1970, 1972, 1974, 1980.

91. **Bulletin of statistics/ Bulletin van statistiek.** 1922- Pretoria: Central Statistical Services. Quarterly. English and Afrikaans.

    Title and frequency vary: 1922-61: *Monthly bulletin of Union statistics.* 1961-67: *Monthly bulletin of statistics.* Agency varies: 1969-83 by Department of Statistics; 1922-69 by Bureau of [Census and] Statistics.

    V. 17, no. 1, 1st qtr., 1983 edition, v. p., contains statistical data in the following areas:

    DEMOGRAPHY
    Population: external migration, population estimates; *Vital statistics*: births, deaths, divorces, infant mortality, marriages.

    ECONOMIC AFFAIRS
    Agriculture and food: farming; *Commerce and business*: companies, domestic commerce, exports, imports, tourism; *Finance*: banking and credit, money supply, securities; *Income and expenditure*: consumption, prices; *Industry*: construction, energy, manufacturing, mining, transportation; *National accounts*: gross domestic product; *Public finance*: government expenditures and government revenue for central government and provinces.

    SOCIAL AND CULTURAL AFFAIRS
    Justice: traffic accidents; *Labor*: employment and unemployment, labor force, labor-management relations, salaries and wages.

    Most data are monthly for 1982 and annual for the preceding year. Commentaries including discussions of sources are provided at the ends of sections. A list of official statistical publications is included at the end of the issue.

    Historical statistics. Statistics for 1919-1923 are found in *Quarterly abstract of Union statistics,* 1920-23, and the *Half-yearly abstract of Union statistics,* 1919-1920, published by the Office of Census and Statistics.

    Available from the address given in entry 90. Price: R4.20 per issue, domestic; R5, foreign. R16.80 per year, domestic; R20.00, foreign.

SUDAN

92. **Statistical yearbook.** 1970- Khartoum: Department of Statistics.

    1975/76 edition, published March, 1978, 187 p., contains statistical data in the following areas:

PHYSICAL ENVIRONMENT
Climatology: precipitation, temperature; *Geography*: area of land, maps.

DEMOGRAPHY
Population: distribution by age and sex, distribution by geographic/administrative area, population estimates.

ECONOMIC AFFAIRS
Agriculture and food: farming, forestry; *Commerce and business*: cooperatives, exports, imports; *Finance*: banking and credit, money supply; *Income and expenditure*: consumption, prices; *Industry*: communication, energy, transportation; *National accounts*: balance of payments, gross domestic product, national income; *Public finance*: government expenditures, government revenue, planning and economic development.

SOCIAL AND CULTURAL AFFAIRS
Education: enrollments, graduates of higher education institutions, literacy classes, teaching staff; *Health*: disease, hospitals, medical personnel, public health; *Justice*: traffic accidents.

Most data are for 1975/76 and the preceding 1 or 2 years. In addition to the national level, data are included for provinces.

Notes accompanying the tables give the names of the agencies furnishing the data. There is a detailed list of tables at the beginning of each chapter.

Available from the agency, PO Box 700, Khartoum.

Available in microform: CIS: 1970.

SWAZILAND

93. ***Annual statistical bulletin.*** 1966- Mbabane: Central Statistical Office.

    1969 not published.

    Agency varies: 1966-68 by Statistical Office; 1970 by Department of Statistics.

    1981 edition published 1983, 115 p., contains statistical data in the following areas:

    PHYSICAL ENVIRONMENT
    Climatology: precipitation, temperature; *Geography*: area of land.

    DEMOGRAPHY
    Population: census results from 1898-1976, distribution by age and sex, distribution by geographic/administrative area, ethnic groups, external migration; *Vital statistics*: births, causes of death in hospitals only, deaths, fertility.

    ECONOMIC AFFAIRS
    Agriculture and food: farming, forestry; *Commerce and business*: companies, exports, imports, tourism; *Finance*: banking and credit, money supply; *Income and expenditure*: consumption, cost of living, prices; *Industry*: communication, construction, energy, manufacturing, mining, transportation; *National accounts*: balance of payments, gross

domestic and gross national product, national income; *Public finance*: government expenditures, government revenue.

SOCIAL AND CULTURAL AFFAIRS
Education: enrollments, examination results, teaching staff; *Health*: disease, family planning, hospitals, public health; *Justice*: correctional institutions, courts; *Labor*: employment, occupations, salaries and wages.

Most data are for 1981 and/or 1980 and varying periods of earlier years. In addition to the national level, data are included for districts.

Commentaries are provided at the beginnings of some sections. Notes accompanying the tables indicate the names of the agencies furnishing the data.

Available from the agency, PO Box 456, Mbabane. Priced.

Available in microform: CH: 1966-68, 170-76. CIS: 1970-78. IDC: 1966-79.

94. ***Quarterly digest of statistics.*** 1967- Mbabane: Central Statistical Office.

See entry 93 for agency name variations.

No. 40, March, 1977, contains statistical data in the following areas:

ECONOMIC AFFAIRS
Agriculture and food: farming; *Commerce and business*: exports, imports, tourism; *Finance*: banking and credit, money supply; *Income and expenditure*: consumption, prices; *Industry*: mining, transportation; *National accounts*: gross domestic and gross national product.

SOCIAL AND CULTURAL AFFAIRS
Health: hospitals.

Most data are monthly or quarterly for 1976 and/or 1975 and annual for the 4 preceding years. In addition to the national level, data are included for districts. Notes accompanying the tables indicate the names of the agencies furnishing the data.

Available from the address given in entry 93. Priced.

TANZANIA

95. ***Statistical abstract.*** 1961- Dar es Salaam: Bureau of Statistics. Irregular.

Not published 1967-69, 1974-1978.

Agency varies: 1961 by Economic and Statistics Division; 1962 by Statistics Division; 1963-66 by Central Statistical Bureau. Continues same title, 1938-60, issued by East Africa High Commission, East African Statistical Department (Tanganyika Branch).

1979 edition, published 1981, 434 p., contains statistical data in the following areas:

PHYSICAL ENVIRONMENT
Climatology: precipitation, sunshine, temperature; *Geography*: area of land, national parks.

DEMOGRAPHY
Population: census results from 1978, distribution by age and sex, distribution by geographic/administrative area, households and families.

ECONOMIC AFFAIRS
Agriculture and food: farming, forestry; *Commerce and business*: exports, imports, tourism; *Finance*: banking and credit; *Income and expenditure*: prices; *Industry*: communication, energy, manufacturing, mining, transportation; *National accounts*: gross domestic product; *Public finance*: government expenditures, government revenue.

POLITICAL AFFAIRS
Elections.

SOCIAL AND CULTURAL AFFAIRS
Education: educational attainment, enrollments, literacy, teaching staff; *Health*: hospitals, medical personnel, public health; *Justice*: correctional institutions, courts, crimes, traffic accidents; *Labor*: employment, labor force, non-citizen employees, occupations, salaries and wages.

Most data are for 1973 through 1979. In addition to Zanzibar as a whole, data are included for regions and districts. A separate statistical yearbook is also available for Zanzibar and is described in the next entry.

Commentaries are provided at the beginnings of chapters. Notes accompanying the tables indicate the names of the agencies furnishing the data. A bibliography of official statistical materials published from 1948 through 1981 is provided. There is a detailed list of tables at the beginning of the volume.

Available from the Government Publication Agency, PO Box 1801, Dar es Salaam. Priced.

Available in microform: CH: 1961-66, 1970, and *Statistical abstract*, 1938-60, issued by the East Africa High Commission, East African Statistical Department (Tanganyika Unit); CIS: 1970. IDC: 1964-66, 1970, 1973.

ZANZIBAR

96. ***Statistical abstract of Zanzibar.*** 1981- Zanzibar Town: Department of Statistics (Zanzibar).

V.II, 1982, 77 p., contains statistical data in the following areas:

PHYSICAL ENVIRONMENT
Climatology: precipitation, sunshine, temperature; *Geography*: area of land.

AFRICA : TANZANIA (ZANZIBAR)

DEMOGRAPHY
Population: census results from 1967 and 1978, distribution by age and sex, distribution by geographic/administrative area, external migration.

ECONOMIC AFFAIRS
Agriculture and food: farming, fishing, forestry; *Commerce and business*: exports, imports, tourism; *Finance*: banking and credit; *Industry*: communication, energy, manufacturing, transportation; *National accounts*: gross domestic product; *Public finance*: government expenditures, government revenue.

SOCIAL AND CULTURAL AFFAIRS
Education: enrollments, examination results, teaching staff; *Health*: hospitals, medical personnel; *Justice*: crimes; *Labor*: employment, salaries and wages.

Most data are for 1981 and the preceding 4 years. In addition to Zanzibar as a whole, data are included for islands, regions and districts. Notes accompanying the tables indicate the names of the agencies furnishing the data.

Available from the Zanzibar Government Printer, PO Box 261, Zanzibar. Price: Sh30.00

97. *Taarifa ya takwimu ya robo mwaka/ Quarterly statistical bulletin.* 1964- Dar es Salaam: Bureau of Statistics. Frequency varies: monthly 1964-71. Swahili and English.

Swahili title varies slightly. For agency variations, see entry 95. Continues: *Tanganyika monthly statistical bulletin*, 1951-64, published by the East Africa High Commission, East African Statistical Department (Tanganyika Unit).

V. 31, no. 1, June, 1981, 67 p., contains statistical data in the following areas:

PHYSICAL ENVIRONMENT
Climatology: precipitation.

DEMOGRAPHY
Population: census results from 1967, 1978, population estimates.

ECONOMIC AFFAIRS
Agriculture and food: farming, forestry; *Commerce and business*: exports, imports; *Finance*: banking and credit; *Income and expenditure*: prices; *Industry*: communication, manufacturing, mining, transportation; *National accounts*: gross domestic product.

Most data are monthly for 1980 and the preceding year and annual for 4 years. Data are usually for mainland Tanzania only.

Notes accompanying the tables indicate the names of the agencies furnishing the data. There is a list of official statistical publications in stock at the end of the issue.

Available from the address in entry 95. Priced.

TOGO

98. ***Annuaire statistique du Togo*** [Statistical yearbook of Togo]. 1966- Lomé: Direction de la Statistique. French.

    1977/78 edition, published Nov., 1980, 209 p., contains statistical data in the following areas:

    PHYSICAL ENVIRONMENT
    Climatology: precipitation, temperature; *Geography*: area of land.

    DEMOGRAPHY
    Population: census results from 1961, 1970, distribution by age and sex, distribution by geographic/administrative area, ethnic groups, households, population estimates.

    ECONOMIC AFFAIRS
    Agriculture and food: farming, fishing, forestry; *Commerce and business*: exports, imports; *Finance*: banking and credit, money supply; *Income and expenditure*: consumption, prices; *Industry*: communication, construction, energy, manufacturing, mining, transportation, water; *National accounts*: gross domestic product, national income.*Public finance*: government expenditures, government revenue.

    SOCIAL AND CULTURAL AFFAIRS
    Cultural and scientific activities: radio; *Education*: educational attainment, enrollments, examination results, literacy, percent of school-age population in school, teaching staff; *Health*: hospitals, medical personnel, public health; *Labor*: labor force, salaries and wages. *Religion*.

    Most data are for 1978 and 1977 and varying numbers of earlier years. There are some monthly data. In addition to the national level, data are included for regions and circonscriptions [districts].

    Explanatory notes are provided at the beginnings of sections. Notes accompanying the tables indicate the names of the agencies furnishing the data. There is a detailed list of tables at the end of the volume.

    Latest edition: 1981-1982, published Dec., 1983, 210 p. Available from the agency, BP 118, Lomé. Price: CFA3000.

    Available in microform: CH: 1966-73. CIS: 1970-73. IDC: 1966-1975/76.

99. ***Bulletin mensuel de statistique*** [Monthly bulletin of statistics]. 1952- Lomé: Direction de la Statistique. French.

    No. 2, Feb., 1981 74 p., contains statistical data in the following areas:

    PHYSICAL ENVIRONMENT
    Climatology: precipitation, sunshine, temperature.

    DEMOGRAPHY
    Vital statistics (in Lomé only): births, divorces, deaths and marriages.

ECONOMIC AFFAIRS
Agriculture and food: farming; *Commerce and business*: exports, imports; *Finance*: banking and credit; *Income and expenditure*: prices; *Industry*: construction, energy, transportation.

Most data are for the month of issue and annual for the preceding year. In addition, cumulative figures are provided for the current and preceding year through the date of the issue. Notes accompanying the tables indicate the names of the agencies furnishing the data.

Available from the address in entry 98. Priced.

TUNISIA

100. **Annuaire statistique de la Tunisie** [Statistical yearbook of Tunisia]. 1940/46- Tunis: Institut National de la Statistique. French.

Agency varies: 1940/46-55 by Service Tunisien des Statistiques; 1956-66 by Service des Statistiques. Continues: *Statistique générale de la Tunisie*, published by the Direction Générale de l'Agriculture, du Commerce et de la Colonisation.

V. 27, 1982, 295 p., contains statistical data in the following areas:

PHYSICAL ENVIRONMENT
Climatology: precipitation, temperature.

DEMOGRAPHY
Population: distribution by age and sex, distribution by geographic/administrative area, population estimates; *Vital statistics*: births, deaths, divorces, fertility, infant mortality, marriages.

ECONOMIC AFFAIRS
Agriculture and food: farming, fishing; *Commerce and business*: domestic commerce, exports, imports, tourism; *Finance*: banking and credit, money supply; *Income and expenditure*: consumption, prices; *Industry*: communication, construction, energy, manufacturing, mining, transportation, water; *National accounts*: gross domestic product; *Public finance*: government expenditures, government revenue.

SOCIAL AND CULTURAL AFFAIRS
Cultural and scientific activities: cinema and performing arts, libraries; *Education*: enrollments, examination results, percent of school-age population in school, teaching staff; *Health*: hospitals, medical personnel, public health; *Justice*: courts, traffic accidents; *Labor*: employment, Tunisian workers abroad.

Most data are for 1982 and the preceding 4 or 5 years. In addition to the national level, data are included for governorates.

Notes accompanying the tables indicate the names of the agencies furnishing the data. There is a list of the publications of the Institut National de Statistique inside the back cover and a detailed list of tables at the beginning of each chapter.

Historical statistics. Statistics for earlier periods are found in *Statistique générale de la*

Tunisie de 1881 à 1892, published by the Direction des Renseignements et des Contrôles Civils in 1893. From 1881 to 1912, they also appear in an annual publication of the French government, *Rapport au Président de la République sur la situation de la Tunisie*, subtitled *Statistique générale de la Tunisie*, from 1904-12.

Available from the Institut, BP 65, 70 rue Ech-cham, Tunis. Price: D3,500.

Available in microform: CH: 1940-1971 and *Statistique générale de la Tunisie*, 1913-1939. IDC: 1940/46-1972/73.

101. **L'Economie de la Tunisie en chiffres** [The Tunisian economy in figures]. 1960- Tunis: Institut National de la Statistique. French and Arabic.

    Agency varies: 1960-66 by Service des Statistiques.

    V. 21, n.s., 1982, published June, 1983, 170 p., contains statistical data in the following areas:

    PHYSICAL ENVIRONMENT
    Climatology: precipitation, temperature.

    DEMOGRAPHY
    Population: arrivals and departures, distribution by age and sex, distribution by geographic/administrative area, external migration.*Vital statistics*: births, deaths, divorces.

    ECONOMIC AFFAIRS
    Agriculture and food: farming, fishing; *Commerce and business*: companies, domestic commerce, exports, imports, tourism; *Finance*: banking and credit, money supply; *Income and expenditure*: consumption, prices; *Industry*: communication, energy, manufacturing, mining, transportation, water; *National accounts*: balance of payments, gross domestic product; *Public finance*: government expenditures, government revenue.

    SOCIAL AND CULTURAL AFFAIRS
    Cultural and scientific activities: cinema and performing arts, libraries, museums and galleries; *Education*: degrees conferred, enrollments, examination results, teaching staff; *Health*: hospitals, medical personnel, public health; *Justice*: traffic accidents; *Labor*: employment, Tunisian workers abroad, salaries and wages.

    Most data are for 1982 and the preceding 2 years. In addition to the national level, data are included for governorates.

    Notes accompanying the tables indicate the names of the agencies furnishing the data. There is a detailed list of tables at the beginning of each chapter.

    Available from the address in entry 100.

    Available in microform: IDC: 1960/61, 1973.

102. **Bulletin mensuel de statistique** [Monthly bulletin of statistics]. 1954- Tunis: Institut National de la Statistique. French and Arabic. For agency variations, see entry 100.

Continues: *Supplément mensuel de statistiques,* 1949-54, published by the Service des Statistiques.

No. 350, April-May, 1984, 43 p., contains statistical data in the following areas:

PHYSICAL ENVIRONMENT
Climatology: precipitation, temperature.

DEMOGRAPHY
Population: distribution by geographic/administrative area; *Vital statistics*: births, deaths, marriages.

ECONOMIC AFFAIRS
Commerce and business: domestic commerce, exports, imports, tourism; *Finance*: banking and credit, money supply; *Income and expenditure*: consumption, prices; *Industry*: communication, construction, energy, manufacturing, mining, transportation.

SOCIAL AND CULTURAL AFFAIRS
Labor: employment.

Most data are monthly for 12 months. Latest data are for 1 to 3 months before the date of the issue. In addition to the national level, data are included for governorates.

Notes accompanying the tables indicate the names of the agencies furnishing the data. Publications of the Institute are listed inside the front cover.

Available from the address in preceding entry 101. Price: D7,500 per year.

UGANDA

103. *Statistical abstract.* 1960- Entebbe: Statistics Division.

Agency varies: 1961-1962 by Statistics Branch. Continues the same title published by the East Africa High Commission, East African Statistical Department (Uganda Unit), 1957-1960.

1974 edition, published 1979, 137 p., contains statistical data in the following areas:

PHYSICAL ENVIRONMENT
Climatology: precipitation, sunshine, temperature; *Geography*: area and use of land.

DEMOGRAPHY
Population: ethnic groups, external migration, population projections.

ECONOMIC AFFAIRS
Agriculture and food: farming, fishing, forestry; *Commerce and business*: companies, exports, imports; *Finance*: banking and credit, money supply; *Income and expenditure*: consumption, cost of living, personal income, prices; *Industry*: communication, construction, energy, manufacturing, mining, transportation; *National accounts*: balance of payments, gross domestic product; *Public finance*: government expenditures, government revenue.

SOCIAL AND CULTURAL AFFAIRS
Education: enrollments, teaching staff; *Health*: disease, hospitals, medical personnel, public health; *Labor*: employment, salaries and wages.

Most data are for 1974 and the preceding 3 years, with some time series for longer periods. In addition to the national level, data are included for regions and districts.

Explanatory notes are provided at the beginnings of most chapters. Notes accompanying the tables indicate the names of the agencies beginning of the volume. A list of official statistical publications is provided.

Distributed by the Government Printer, PO Box 33, Entebbe. Priced.

Available in microform: CH: 1961-71, 1973. CIS: 1970-71, 1973. IDC: 1961-70. Both CIS and IDC offer 1957-60 of *Statistical abstract*, of the East African High Commission, East African Statistical Department (Uganda Unit).

104. ***Quarterly economic and statistical bulletin.*** 1965- Entebbe: Statistics Division. Publication suspended?

UPPER VOLTA

See BURKINA FASO.

ZAIRE

105. ***Annuaire statistique du Zaïre*** [Statistical yearbook of Zaire]. 1971- Kinshasa Gombe: Institut National de la Statistique. French.

1971 numbered new series.

Replaces *Bulletin trimestriel des statistiques générales* [Quarterly bulletin of general statistics], 1962-?, published by the Institut National de la Statistique and earlier by the Direction de la Statistique et des Etudes Economiques. It continued the *Bulletin [mensuel] des statistiques [générales] du Congo belge et du Ruanda Urundi/ [Maandelijks] statistisch bulletijn van algemene statistieken van Belgisch-Congo en Ruanda-Urundi*, 1955-61 (French and Dutch), published by the Direction de la Statistique of the Belgian Congo.

1979 edition, published Feb., 1982, 495 p., contains statistical data in the following areas:

PHYSICAL ENVIRONMENT
Climatology: precipitation, sunshine, temperature.*Geography*: area of land, maps.

DEMOGRAPHY
Vital statistics: births, deaths, divorces, marriages.

ECONOMIC AFFAIRS

Commerce and business: exports, imports, tourism; *Finance*: banking and credit, money supply; *Income and expenditure*: prices; *Industry*: construction, energy, manufacturing, mining, transportation; *National accounts*: balance of payments, gross domestic product; *Public finance*: government expenditures, government revenue.

SOCIAL AND CULTURAL AFFAIRS

Justice: correctional institutions, traffic accidents.

Most data are quarterly and/or monthly and annual for 1979 and/or 1978.

Historical statistics. Statistics for earlier periods may be found in the first and second editions of the *Annuaire*, published in 1971 and 1979, which offer data for 1958-1969 and 1969-1978, respectively, and in two series published by the Gouverneur Général of the Belgian Congo: *Discours*, 1953-57, and *Bulletin annuel des statistiques du Congo belge*, 1957-59, (cover title, *Statistiques relatives à l'année*).

Available from the agency, BP 8500, Building Onatra, Kinshasa Gombe.

Available in microform: CH: *Statistiques relatives à l'année*, 1957, 1959.

106. **Conjoncture économique** [Economic forecast]. 1960- Kinshasa Gombe: Département de l'Economie Nationale et de l'Industrie. French.

Contains statistical tables intermixed with narrative. [No.] 20, 1980-1981, published Dec., 1981, 580 p., includes figures showing the distribution of population by geographic area and ethnic groups, in addition to the following types of economic data: balance of payments, banking and credit, communication, companies, construction, consumption, energy, exports and imports, farming, foreign aid received, government expenditures, government revenue, manufacturing, mining, and transportation.

Most data are for 1981 and/or 1980 and the preceding 1 to 4 years, plus the reference year, 1968. There are some long time series; copper production is reported for the period 1911 to 1981, for example. There are a few figures for regions. No sources for tables are given.

Notes accompanying most of the tables give the names of the agencies furnishing the data. Commentaries are provided at the beginning of sections.

The quarterly bulletin of statistics has been replaced by the *Annuaire statistique du Zaïre* [Statistical yearbook of Zaire]. For more information on the bulletin, see entry 105.

ZAMBIA

107. **Zambia in figures.** 1980- Lusaka: Central Statistical Office.

1980 edition, published Jan., 1980, [8] p., contains statistical data in the following areas:

DEMOGRAPHY
Population: census results from 1969, 1974, distribution by age, distribution by sex, population projections.

ECONOMIC AFFAIRS
Agriculture and food: farming; *Commerce and business*: exports, imports; *Finance*: banking and credit, money supply; *Income and expenditure*: prices; *Industry*: communication, construction, energy, mining, transportation; *National accounts*: gross domestic product; *Public finance*: government expenditures, government revenue.

SOCIAL AND CULTURAL AFFAIRS
Education: enrollments; *Labor*: employment, labor force.

Most data are for 1979 and 3 preceding years.

Latest edition published: 1983. Available from the agency, Box 31908, Lusaka. Price: K0.50.

108. ***Statistical yearbook***. 1967- Lusaka: Central Statistical Office.

Publication suspended with 1971 edition.

1971 edition, published 1973, 192 p., contains statistical data in the following areas:

PHYSICAL ENVIRONMENT
Climatology: precipitation, temperature; *Geography*: area of land.

DEMOGRAPHY
Population: census results from 1963 and 1969, distribution by age and sex, distribution by geographic/administrative area, ethnic groups; *Vital statistics*: births.

ECONOMIC AFFAIRS
Agriculture and food: farming, fishing; *Commerce and business*: companies, domestic commerce, exports, imports; *Finance*: banking and credit, money supply; *Income and expenditure*: consumption, prices; *Industry*: communication, construction, energy, manufacturing, mining, transportation; *National accounts*: balance of payments, gross domestic product; *Public finance*: government expenditures, government revenue, planning and economic development.

SOCIAL AND CULTURAL AFFAIRS
Education: degrees conferred, enrollments, examination results, literacy, teaching staff; *Health*: disease, hospitals, public health; *Housing*; *Justice*: correctional institutions, courts, crimes, traffic accidents; *Labor*: unemployment, labor force, labor-management relations, occupations, salaries and wages.

Most data are for 1971 or 1970 and the preceding 2 to 7 years. In addition to the national level, data are included for provinces, districts and the main towns. Sources are listed at the beginnings of some chapters. There is a list of official statistical materials available from the Central Statistical Office at the end of the volume.

Distributed by the Government Printer, PO Box 30136, Lusaka.

Available in microform: CH: 1968-71. CIS: 1970-71. IDC: 1968-71.

109. ***Monthly digest of statistics.*** 1965- Lusaka: Central Statistical Office.

V. 18, nos. 7-9, July-Sept., 1982, 68 p., contains statistical data in the following areas:

DEMOGRAPHY
Population: census results from 1969 and 1980, distribution by geographic/administrative area, external migration.

ECONOMIC AFFAIRS
Agriculture and food: farming, fishing; *Commerce and business*: exports, imports; *Finance*: banking and credit, money supply; *Income and expenditure*: prices; *Industry*: construction, energy, manufacturing, mining, transportation; *National accounts*: balance of payments, gross domestic product, national income; *Public finance*: government expenditures, government revenue.

SOCIAL AND CULTURAL AFFAIRS
Education: enrollments; *Labor*: employment, labor-management relations, salaries and wages.

Most data are monthly or quarterly for the current and preceding year, with annual time series for varied periods of time. Latest data are for the month or quarter preceding the month of the issue. In addition to the national level, data are included for provinces and districts. The latest publications of the Central Statistical Office are listed at the end of the issue.

Available from the address given in entry 107. Price: K2.00 per issue; K20.00, plus postage per year.

ZIMBABWE

110. ***Annual economic review of Zimbabwe.*** 1965- Harare: Ministry of Finance, Economic Planning and Development.

Title varies: Earlier: *Economic survey of Zimbabwe*; 1965-77: *Economic survey of Rhodesia*.

1981 edition, published Aug., 1981, 68 p., contains a map and statistical tables in the following areas:

DEMOGRAPHY
Population: ethnic groups, population estimates.

ECONOMIC AFFAIRS
Agriculture and food: farming; *Commerce and business*: exports, imports, tourism; *Finance*: banking and credit, money supply; *Income and expenditure*: prices; *Industry*: construction, energy, manufacturing, mining; *National accounts*: balance of payments, gross domestic product, national income; *Public finance*: government expenditures, government revenue.

Data are for 1980 and varying numbers of earlier years. There is a list of tables at the beginning. Tables are prepared by the Central Statistical Office.

Historical statistics. Statistics for earlier years may be found in *Official yearbook of the colony of Southern Rhodesia containing general information and statistics,* 1924-1952, and *Statistical yearbook of Southern Rhodesia: the official annual of the social and economic conditions of the colony,* 1938, 1947, both issued by the Department of Statistics of Southern Rhodesia and both available in microform from CH.

Available from the agency, Ground Floor, Milton Building, Private Bag 7752, Causeway, Samora Machel Avenue, Harare. Priced.

111. **Monthly digest of statistics.** 1964- Harare: Central Statistical Office.

Country name before 1980: Rhodesia. Continues in part the *Monthly digest of statistics of the Federation of Rhodesia and Nyasaland,* 1954-64, published by the Central African Statistical Office, and the **Economic and statistical bulletin of Southern Rhodesia,** 1933/34-53, issued by the Central African Statistical Office, 1949-54, and the Department of Statistics, 1936-49.

April, 1983 edition, 85 p., contains statistical data in the following areas:

DEMOGRAPHY
Population: external migration, population estimates.

ECONOMIC AFFAIRS
Agriculture and food: farming, fishing, forestry; *Commerce and business*: companies, domestic commerce, exports, imports; *Finance*: banking and credit, money supply, securities; *Income and expenditure*: prices; *Industry*: construction, energy, manufacturing, mining, transportation; *National accounts*: balance of payments, gross domestic product, national income; *Public finance*: government expenditures, government revenue.

SOCIAL AND CULTURAL AFFAIRS
Education: enrollments; *Housing*; *Justice*: traffic accidents; *Labor*: employment, salaries and wages.

Most data are monthly or quarterly for current year and preceding 2 years and annual for 5 years. Latest data are for 2 to 4 months before the date of the issue. There are time series of varying lengths. Notes at the end of the volume include a discussion of sources. A list of official statistical publications is given at the beginning of the issue.

Available from the agency, PO Box 8063, Causeway, Harare. Priced.

AMERICAS

ANTIGUA AND BARBUDA

112. ***Statistical yearbook.*** 1975- St. John's: Statistics Office.

1978 edition, 99 p., contains statistical data in the following areas:

PHYSICAL ENVIRONMENT
Climatology: precipitation, temperature; *Geography*: area of land.

DEMOGRAPHY
Population: arrivals and departures, distribution by age and sex, distribution by geographic/administrative area, households and families, population estimates.*Vital statistics*: births, including illegitimate births, deaths, divorces, marriages.

ECONOMIC AFFAIRS
Agriculture and food: farming, fishing; *Commerce and business*: domestic commerce, exports, imports, tourism; *Finance*: banking and credit; *Income and expenditure*: cost of living, prices; *Industry*: communication, construction, energy, manufacturing, transportation; *National accounts*: gross domestic product; *Public finance*: government expenditures, government revenue.

SOCIAL AND CULTURAL AFFAIRS
Education: enrollments, teaching staff; *Health*: disease, medical personnel, public health; *Housing*; *Justice*: correctional institutions, courts, crimes, traffic accidents; *Labor*: employment, labor force, labor-management relations, occupations, salaries and wages; *Social security*.

Most data are for 1977 and the preceding 5 years. In addition to the national level, data are included for parishes. Notes accompanying the tables indicate the names of the agencies furnishing the data.

Latest edition: 1982, published Aug., 1983, 118 p. Available from the agency, Redcliffe St., St. John's. Priced.

Available in microform: CH: 1975-76.

ARGENTINA

113. ***Anuario estadístico*** [Statistical yearbook]. 1944-50, 1973- Buenos Aires: Instituto Nacional de Estadística y Censos. Irregular. Spanish.

Not published 1951-56; 1974-77.

Title varies: 1948-57 as *Anuario estadístico de la República Argentina*. Agency varies: 1944-47 by Dirección General de Estadística y Censos; 1948-50, 1957 by Dirección Nacional [General] del Servicio Estadístico [Nacional]. Continues: *Anuario de la Dirección General de Estadística,* 1892-1914.

1981/82 edition, 706 p., contains statistical data in the following areas:

PHYSICAL ENVIRONMENT
Climatology: precipitation, sunshine, temperature; *Environment*: national parks and reserves; *Geography*: area and use of land.

DEMOGRAPHY
Population: census results from 1869-1980, distribution by age and sex, distribution by geographic/administrative area, external migration, internal migration, population estimates and projections; *Vital statistics*: births, including illegitimate births, causes of death, deaths, infant mortality, life expectancy, marriages.

ECONOMIC AFFAIRS
Agriculture and food: farming, fishing, forestry; *Commerce and business*: cooperatives, domestic commerce, exports, imports, services, tourism; *Finance*: banking and credit, money supply, securities; *Income and expenditure*: consumption, prices; *Industry*: communication, construction, energy, manufacturing, mining, transportation, water; *National accounts*: balance of payments, gross domestic product; *Public finance*: government expenditures, government revenue, loans from intergovernmental organizations.

POLITICAL AFFAIRS
Electoral registration.

SOCIAL AND CULTURAL AFFAIRS
Cultural and scientific activities: books and journals, computers, museums and galleries, newspapers, radio, television; *Education*: enrollments, literacy of registered voters, school attendance by age groups; *Health*: hospitals, medical personnel, public health; *Housing*; *Justice*: correctional institutions, courts, crimes; *Labor*: employment, underemployment and unemployment, occupations, salaries and wages; *Religion*; *Social security*; *Recreation*.

Most data are for 1982. Time series of varying lengths are provided. In addition to the national level, data are included for zones, provinces, cities, and the following external territories: Argentine Antarctic Territory and Malvinas Islands (Falkland Islands). There is a chapter devoted to comparative statistics for selected foreign countries.

Explanatory notes are provided at the end of the volume. Notes accompanying most of the tables indicate the names of the agencies furnishing the data. The last chapter includes a list of the principal censuses (national and provincial) and a description of the national statistical system.

Historical statistics. Historical statistics with comparative data for Brazil, Mexico, Canada, Australia and the U.S.A. may be found in: Vásquez-Presedo, Vicente. *Estadísticas argentinas (comparadas), Primera parte 1875-1914, Segunda parte, 1914-1939*. Buenos Aires: Ediciones Macchi, 1971, 1976.

Available from the agency, Alsina 1924, 1207 Buenos Aires. Price: $A1,500.

Available in microform: CH: 1944-50, 1957 and *Anuario de la Dirección General de Estadística,* 1893-96, 1898-1907, 1909-12. CIS: 1973. IDC: 1948-50, 1957.

114. *Boletín estadístico trimestral* [Quarterly statistical bulletin]. 1956- Buenos Aires: Instituto Nacional de Estadística y Censos. Frequency varies. Spanish.

Agency varies: Earlier issues by the Dirección Nacional de Estadística y Censos.

July-Dec., 1982 edition, 192 p., contains statistical data in the following areas:

DEMOGRAPHY
Population: arrivals and departures, households and families.

ECONOMIC AFFAIRS
Agriculture and food: farming, fishing; *Commerce and business*: domestic commerce, exports, imports; *Finance*: banking and credit; *Income and expenditure*: prices; *Industry*: communication, construction, manufacturing, transportation.

SOCIAL AND CULTURAL AFFAIRS
Labor: salaries and wages.

Most data are monthly or quarterly for 1982 and annual for the preceding 2 years. Notes accompanying the tables indicate the names of the agencies furnishing the data.

Available from the address in entry 113. Price: $A130 per issue; $U.S.30 per issue.

BAHAMAS

115. *Statistical abstract.* 1969- Nassau: Department of Statistics.

1980 edition, published July, 1982, 204 p., contains statistical data in the following areas:

PHYSICAL ENVIRONMENT
Climatology: precipitation, temperature; *Geography*: area and use of land, maps.

DEMOGRAPHY
Population: arrivals and departures, census results from 1838-1980, distribution by age and sex, distribution by geographic/administrative area, external migration, households and families, internal migration, population estimates; *Vital statistics*: births, including illegitimate births, causes of death, deaths, divorces, infant mortality, marriages.

ECONOMIC AFFAIRS
Agriculture and food: farming, fishing, forestry; *Commerce and business*: exports, imports, tourism; *Finance*: banking and credit, money supply; *Income and expenditure*: consumption, personal income, prices; *Industry*: communication, construction, energy, transportation; *National accounts*: balance of payments; *Public finance*: government expenditures, government revenue.

POLITICAL AFFAIRS
Elections.

SOCIAL AND CULTURAL AFFAIRS
Education: enrollments, teaching staff; *Health*: disease, hospitals, medical personnel, public health; *Housing*; *Justice*: correctional institutions, courts, crimes, police; *Labor*: occupations, salaries and wages.

Most data are for 1980 and the preceding 4 years. There are time series to the early 1970s. In addition to the national level, data are included for regions and islands.

Explanatory notes are provided in the introduction. Notes accompanying the tables indicate the names of the agencies furnishing the data.

Available from the agency, PO Box, N3904, Nassau NP. Priced. Available in microform: CIS: 1978-79. IDC: 1969-70, 1972-76.

116. **Quarterly statistical summary.** 1971- Nassau: Department of Statistics.

4th qtr., 1981 edition, 88 p., contains statistical data in the following areas:

PHYSICAL ENVIRONMENT
Climatology: precipitation, temperature.

DEMOGRAPHY
Population: population estimates; *Vital statistics*: births, deaths.

ECONOMIC AFFAIRS
Agriculture and food: farming, fishing, forestry; *Commerce and business*: companies, exports, imports, tourism; *Finance*: banking and credit; *Income and expenditure*: prices; *Industry*: construction, energy, transportation.

SOCIAL AND CULTURAL AFFAIRS
Health: disease; *Justice*: correctional institutions, courts; *Labor*: employment, occupations.

Most data are monthly or quarterly for 1981 and 1980 and annual for 4 years. Notes accompanying the tables indicate the names of the agencies furnishing the data.

Available from the address given in entry 115. Priced.

BARBADOS

117. **Barbados economic report.** 1962- Bridgetown: Ministry of Finance and Planning.

Continues: *Barbados economic surveys,* 1962-?1976, published by Economic Planning Unit.

1983 edition, published April, 1984, 89 p., contains statistical data in the following areas:

DEMOGRAPHY
Population: households and families; *Vital statistics*: births, deaths, infant mortality.

ECONOMIC AFFAIRS
Agriculture and food: farming, fishing; *Commerce and business*: exports, imports, tourism; *Finance*: banking and credit, money supply; *Income and expenditure*: consumption, prices; *Industry*: energy, manufacturing, quarrying, water; *National accounts*: balance of payments, gross domestic product; *Public finance*: government expenditures, government revenue.

SOCIAL AND CULTURAL AFFAIRS
Housing; *Labor*: employment and unemployment, labor force, salaries and wages.

Most data are for 1983 and varying numbers of earlier years. Commentaries are intermixed with statistics. Notes accompanying the tables indicate the names of the agencies furnishing the data. There is a detailed list of tables at the beginning of the volume.

Available from the Office of the Prime Minister and Ministry of Finance and Planning, Government Headquarters, Bay St., Bridgetown.

118. **Abstract of statistics.* 1956-69. Bridgetown: Statistical Service.

119. **Monthly digest of statistics.** 1956- Bridgetown: Barbados Statistical Service.

    Title and frequency vary: Earlier, *Quarterly digest of statistics*.

    No. 16, Sept., 1982 edition, 42 p., contains statistical data in the following areas:

    #### DEMOGRAPHY
    Population: arrivals and departures; *Vital statistics*: births, deaths, marriages.

    #### ECONOMIC AFFAIRS
    Agriculture and food: farming, fishing, forestry; *Commerce and business*: exports, imports, tourism; *Finance*: banking and credit, money supply; *Income and expenditure*: prices; *Industry*: energy, manufacturing, transportation; *Public finance*: government expenditures, government revenue.

    Most data are monthly or quarterly for the current and preceding years, plus some earlier years. Notes accompanying the tables indicate the names of the agencies furnishing the data.

    Available from the agency, 3rd Floor, National Insurance Building, Fairchild Street, Bridgetown. Priced.

BELIZE

120. **Abstract of statistics.** 1961- Belmopan: Central Statistical Office.

    Title varies slightly: Some years as *Annual abstract of statistics*. Country name and agency vary: 1961-1980 by British Honduras, Central Planning Unit.

1982 edition, published July, 1983, 82 p., contains statistical data in the following areas:

PHYSICAL ENVIRONMENT
Climatology: precipitation, temperature; *Geography*: area of land.

DEMOGRAPHY
Population: arrivals and departures, census results from 1921-1980, distribution by age, distribution by sex, distribution by geographic/administrative area, ethnic groups; *Vital statistics*: births, including illegitimate births, causes of death, deaths, marriages.

ECONOMIC AFFAIRS
Agriculture and food: farming; *Commerce and business*: exports, imports, tourism; *Finance*: banking and credit; *Income and expenditure*: consumption; *Industry*: communication, energy, transportation, water; *National accounts*: gross domestic product; *Public finance*: government expenditures, government revenue, planning and economic development.

SOCIAL AND CULTURAL AFFAIRS
Education: enrollments, teaching staff; *Health*: hospitals, medical personnel, public health; *Justice*: traffic accidents; *Religion*.

Most data are for 1982 and varying numbers of earlier years. In addition to the national level, data are included for districts and sub-divisions.

Notes accompanying the tables indicate the names of the agencies furnishing the data. There is a detailed list of tables at the beginning of the volume.

Available from the Chief Statistician, Central Statistical Office, Belmopan. Price: $U.S.5.00, plus postage.
Available in microform: CIS: 1970/72. IDC: 1961-63, 1965-69.

No general statistical bulletin is currently published for Belize.

BERMUDA

121. **Bermuda digest of statistics.** 1973- Hamilton: Statistical Department.

1983 edition, 86 p., contains statistical data in the following areas:

PHYSICAL ENVIRONMENT
Climatology: precipitation, temperature.*Geography* area and use of land.

DEMOGRAPHY
Population: arrivals and departures, census results from 1931-1980, distribution by age and sex, distribution by geographic/administrative area, ethnic groups, population estimates and projections; *Vital statistics*: births, including illegitimate births, deaths, infant mortality, marriages.

ECONOMIC AFFAIRS
Agriculture and food: farming; *Commerce and business*: businesses registered, exports, imports, tourism; *Finance*: banking and credit, money supply; *Income and expenditure*: consumption, prices; *Industry*: construction, energy, transportation; *National accounts*: balance of payments, gross domestic and gross national product, national income; *Public finance*: government expenditures and government revenue for central government, Hamilton, and St. George.

SOCIAL AND CULTURAL AFFAIRS
Education: enrollments, teaching staff; *Health*: hospitals, medical personnel, public health; *Housing*; *Justice*: correctional institutions, courts, crimes, traffic accidents; *Labor*: employment and unemployment, foreign workers, labor-management relations, occupations, salaries and wages.

Most data are for 1982. Time series may be provided to 1970. In addition to the national level, data are included for parishes.

Notes accompanying the tables indicate the names of the agencies furnishing the data. There is a detailed list of tables at the beginning of the volume.

Available from the agency, PO Box 177, Hamilton. Price: $2.50.

Available in microform: CIS: 1973-74. IDC: 1973-74.

No general statistical bulletin is currently published for Bermuda.

BOLIVIA

122. ***Resumen estadístico*** [Statistical summary]. 1982- La Paz: Instituto Nacional de Estadística. Spanish.

The 1983 edition, published July, 1984, 122 p., contains statistical data in the following areas:

PHYSICAL ENVIRONMENT
Geography: maps.

DEMOGRAPHY
Population: census results from 1976, distribution by age and sex, distribution by geographic/administrative area, ethnic groups, households and families, internal migration, population estimates and projections; *Vital statistics*: birth rate, death rate, fertility, infant mortality, life expectancy.

ECONOMIC AFFAIRS
Agriculture and food: farming; *Commerce and business*: establishments, exports, imports; *Finance*: banking and credit, money supply; *Income and expenditure*: prices; *Industry*: communication, construction, energy, manufacturing, mining, transportation; *National accounts*: balance of payments, gross domestic product; *Public finance*: government expenditures, government revenue.

SOCIAL AND CULTURAL AFFAIRS

Education: educational attainment, enrollments, literacy; *Health*: hospitals, medical personnel, public health; *Housing*; *Labor*: labor force, occupations, salaries and wages.

Most data are for 1983 or 1984. In addition to the national level, data are included for regions, departments and principal cities.

Notes accompanying the tables indicate the names of the agencies furnishing the data.

Available from the agency, Plaza Mario Guzmán Aspiazu No. 1, La Paz.

123. ***Bolivia en cifras*** [Bolivia in figures]. 1972- La Paz: Instituto Nacional de Estadística. Spanish.

1980 edition, published 1981, 311 p., contains statistical data in the following areas:

PHYSICAL ENVIRONMENT
Geography: maps.

DEMOGRAPHY
Population: census results from 1976, distribution by age and sex, distribution by geographic/administrative area, ethnic groups, households and families, internal migration, population estimates and projections; *Vital statistics*: birth rate, death rate, fertility, infant mortality, life expectancy.

ECONOMIC AFFAIRS
Agriculture and food: farming; *Commerce and business*: establishments, exports, imports; *Finance*: banking and credit, money supply; *Income and expenditure*: prices; *Industry*: communication, construction, energy, manufacturing, mining, transportation; *National accounts*: balance of payments, gross domestic product; *Public finance*: government expenditures, government revenue.

SOCIAL AND CULTURAL AFFAIRS
Education: educational attainment, enrollments, literacy; *Health*: hospitals, medical personnel, public health; *Housing*; *Labor*: labor force, occupations, salaries and wages.

Most data are for 1979 and the preceding 2 to 4 years. In addition to the national level, data are included for regions, departments, and principal cities.

Notes accompanying the tables indicate the names of the agencies furnishing the data. Special features include a chronology of historical events and a map and list of ethnic groups and languages spoken.

Historical statistics. Statistics for earlier periods are found in *Extracto estadístico de Bolivia*, 1936, published by Dirección General de Estadística y Censos, and *Anuario nacional estadístico y geográfico de Bolivia*, 1917 and *Anuario geográfico y estadístico de la Republica de Bolivia*, 1919, both published by the Dirección General de Estadística y Estudios Geográficos.

Available from the agency, Plaza Mario Guzmán Aspiazu No. 1, La Paz.

Available in microform: CH: 1973; *Anuario nacional estadístico y geográfico de Bolivia*,

1917 and *Anuario geográfico y estadístico de la República de Bolivia*, 1919, both published by the Dirección General de Estadística y Estudios Geográficos.

124. **Boletín estadístico** [Statistical bulletin]. 1901- La Paz: Instituto Nacional de Estadístico. Frequency varies; currently quarterly. Spanish.

    Agency varies: Earlier issues by Dirección General de Estadística y Censos.

    Subject coverage in individual issues varies. V.6, nos. 48 and 49, April and May, 1980, 6p. and 4 p., respectively, contain statistical data in the following areas:

    DEMOGRAPHY
    Population: census results from 1976, distribution by age and sex; *Vital statistics*: life expectancy.

    ECONOMIC AFFAIRS
    Agriculture and food: farming; *Commerce and business*: imports; *Finance*: banking and credit, money supply; *Industry*: energy, mining, transportation; *National accounts*: gross domestic product.

    SOCIAL AND CULTURAL AFFAIRS
    Labor: employment, labor force.

    Most data are for 1979 or 1978. Latest data are for Feb., 1980. In addition to the national level, data are included for departments and some cities. Notes accompanying the tables indicate the names of the agencies furnishing the data.

    Available from the address given in entry 122.

BRAZIL

125. **Anuário estatístico do Brasil** [Statistical yearbook of Brazil]. 1908/12- Rio de Janeiro: Fundação Instituto Brasileiro de Geografia e Estatística (IBGE), Departamento de Divulgação Estatística. Portuguese.

    Not published 1913-1935. V. 1 covers 1908/12; v. 5, 1939/40; and v. 6, 1941/48.

    Agency varies: 1908/12 issued by Diretoria Geral de Estatística do Ministério da Agricultura, Industria y Commercio; 1934-36 by Instituto Nacional de Estatística; 1936-67 by Instituto Brasileiro de Geografia e Estatística, Conselho Nacional de Estatística, Diretoria de Documentação e Divulgação; 1967-69 by Fundação Instituto Brasileiro de Geografia e Estatística, Instituto Brasileiro de Estatística, Diretoria de Documentação e Divulgação; 1969-73 by Fundação Instituto Brasileiro de Geografia e Estatística, Instituto Brasileiro de Estatística, Departamento de Divulgação Estatística.

    V. 43, 1982, 899 p., contains statistical data in the following areas:

    PHYSICAL ENVIRONMENT
    Climatology: precipitation, sunshine, temperature; *Environmental quality*: national parks and reserves; *Geography*: area of land, maps.

DEMOGRAPHY

Population: census results from 1872-1980, distribution by age and sex, distribution by geographic/administrative area, external migration, internal migration, population estimates and projections; *Vital statistics*: births, causes of death, deaths, divorces, fertility, infant mortality, life expectancy, marriages.

ECONOMIC AFFAIRS

Agriculture and food: farming, fishing, forestry; *Commerce and business*: domestic commerce, exports, imports, services, tourism; *Finance*: banking and credit, money in circulation, securities; *Income and expenditure*: consumption, prices; *Industry*: communication, construction, energy, manufacturing, mining, transportation; *National accounts*: balance of payments, gross domestic product, national income; *Public finance*: government expenditures and government revenue for federal, state and municipal level, planning and economic development.

POLITICAL AFFAIRS

Elections.

SOCIAL AND CULTURAL AFFAIRS

Cultural and scientific activities: books and journals, cinema and performing arts, museums and galleries, newspapers, radio, television; *Education*: degrees conferred, enrollments, literacy, teaching staff; *Health*: disease, hospitals, medical personnel, public health; *Housing*; *Justice*: correctional institutions, courts, crimes; *Labor*: labor force, occupations, salaries and wages; *Religion*; *Social security*; *Sports and recreation*.

Most data are for 1981 and the preceding 2 years. In addition to the national level, data are included for states.

Commentaries which include discussions of sources are provided at the beginnings of chapters. Notes accompanying the tables indicate the names of the agencies furnishing the data. There is a detailed list of tables at the beginning of the volume and an alphabetical subject index at the end.

Historical statistics. Historical statistics may be found in *Brazil: a handbook of historical statistics* by Armin K. Ludwig, Boston: G.K. Hall, 1985, and in Colloque International sur l'Histoire Quantitative de Brésil, Paris, 11-15 oct. 1971, *L'Histoire quantitative de Brésil de 1800 à 1930* (Colloques internationaux du Centre National de la Recherche Scientifique no. 543), Paris: CNRS, 1973, 488 p. V. 1 of the IBGE's *Brasil: séries estatísticas retrospectivas*, published in 1970, offers statistics for the period from 1959 to the date of publication.

Latest edition published: 1983, 988 p. Available from the Fundação Instituto Brasileiro de Geografia e Estatístico, Avenida Brasil, 15.671, Lucas, 21.241, Rio de Janeiro, R.J. Price: $ U.S.50.00.

Available in microform: CH: 1908/12, 1936-37, 1939/40-45, 1947-69. CIS: 1970-76.

126. **Boletim estatístico** [Statistical bulletin]. 1943- Rio de Janeiro: Fundação Instituto Brasileiro de Geografia e Estatística, Departamento de Divulgação. Quarterly. Portuguese.

Publication suspended in 1978.

For agency variations, see entry 125.

V. XXXV, no. 137, Jan./March, 1977, 185 p., contains 4 sections of statistics: national, regional, municipal and international. The first offers statistics on foreign commerce, banking and credit, prices and consumption, industry, transportation, public finance and public health, while the second is devoted to agricultural statistics. The municipal section covers vital statistics, prices, energy consumption, construction, labor force and salaries. The last section contains a selection of comparative statistics for a number of countries. Figures are monthly or quarterly for 1 year, and annual for the 2 preceding years, with the latest data covering the dates of the issue.

Back copies available from the address in entry 125. Price: $U.S.8.00.

BRITISH VIRGIN ISLANDS

127. ***Statistical abstract of the British Virgin Islands.*** 1974- Tortola: Statistical Division. Irregular.

Agency varies: 1974 by Statistics Office.

No. 2, 1980, published Nov., 1983, 235 p., contains statistical data in the following areas:

PHYSICAL ENVIRONMENT
Climatology: precipitation.

DEMOGRAPHY
Population: arrivals and departures, census results from 1717-1980, distribution by age and sex, distribution by geographic/administrative area, ethnic groups; *Vital statistics*: births, causes of death, deaths, divorces, infant mortality, marriages.

ECONOMIC AFFAIRS
Agriculture and food: farming; *Commerce and business*: exports, imports, tourism; *Finance*: banking and credit; *Income and expenditure*: consumption, prices; *Industry*: communication, energy, transportation, water; *Public finance*: government expenditures, government revenue.

SOCIAL AND CULTURAL AFFAIRS
Cultural and scientific activities: libraries; *Education*: educational attainment, enrollments, examination results, literacy, teaching staff; *Health*: family planning, hospitals, medical personnel, public health; *Housing*; *Justice*: correctional institutions, courts, crimes, police, traffic accidents; *Labor*: employment and unemployment, labor force, salaries and wages; *Religion*; *Social security*.

Most data are for 1980 or 1981 and varying numbers of earlier years. There are some monthly data. In addition to the national level, data are included for islands/towns and enumeration districts.

Sources of tables are indicated by numbers accompanying the tables; a key to source numbers is found in the front of the volume. There is a detailed list of tables at the beginning of the volume and a chronology of events from 1493 to 1967 is provided.

Available from Statistical Division, Planning Unit, Chief Minister's Office, Road Town, Tortola. Price: $10.00.

No general statistical bulletin has been found for the British Virgin Islands.

CANADA

128. *Canada yearbook: a review of economic, social and political developments in Canada.* 1905- Ottawa: Statistics Canada. Irregular. French edition also available.

Subtitle varies slightly. Agency varies: 1905-1916/17 by Dominion Census and Statistical Office; 1918-71 by Dominion Bureau of Statistics. Continues: *Year-book and almanac of Canada: an annual statistical abstract for the Dominion,* 1867-1885, published by the Montreal Printing and Publishing Co., Montreal, and *Statistical yearbook of Canada,* 1886-1904, published by the Department of Agriculture.

1980/81 edition, published April, 1981, 1004 p., contains statistical data in the following areas:

PHYSICAL ENVIRONMENT
Climatology: precipitation, temperature; *Geography*: area of land, maps.

DEMOGRAPHY
Population: census results from 1851-1976, distribution by age and sex, distribution by geographic/administrative area, ethnic groups, external migration, households and families, internal migration, population estimates and projections; *Vital statistics*: births, causes of death, deaths, divorces, fertility, infant mortality, life expectancy, marriages.

ECONOMIC AFFAIRS
Agriculture and food: farming, fishing, forestry; *Commerce and business*: corporations, domestic commerce, exports, imports, services, tourism; *Finance*: banking and credit, money supply; *Income and expenditure*: consumption, personal income, prices; *Industry*: communication, construction, energy, manufacturing, mining, transportation; *National accounts*: balance of payments, gross domestic product, national income; *Public finance*: government expenditures and government revenue at federal, provincial, territorial and local levels (local aggregated by province or territory).

POLITICAL AFFAIRS
Defense; *Elections*; *Foreign aid.*

SOCIAL AND CULTURAL AFFAIRS
Cultural and scientific activities: books and journals, cinema and performing arts, libraries, newspapers, radio, television, science and research; *Education*: degrees conferred, enrollments; *Health*: disease, hospitals, medical personnel, public health *Housing*; *Justice*: correctional institutions, courts, crimes, traffic accidents; *Labor* employment and unemployment, labor force, labor-management relations, occupations, salaries and wages; *Religion*; *Social assistance*; *Social security.*

Most data are for 1979 or 1978 and the preceding 1 to 7 years. Time series of varying lengths are provided. In addition to the national level, data are included for provinces and cities of 50,000 or more.

Commentaries, which include a discussion of sources, are provided at the beginnings of chapters. There is a list of tables at the beginning of each chapter and an alphabetical subject index at the end. Special features include: a description of the constitutional and legal system; a government organization manual and directory; a list of laws passed in the last session of Parliament before publication; a chronology of economic events; a bibliography of books about Canada; and a list of special articles contained in earlier editions of this series.

Historical statistics. Historical statistics for the period from Confederation to the mid-1970's are available in *Historical statistics of Canada,* 2nd ed., 1983, v.p., edited by F. H. Leacy, and published by Statistics Canada in joint sponsorship with the Social Science Federation of Canada, (CS 11-516 E), $Can 60.00, (also available in a French edition).

Latest edition published: 1985, 894 p. Available from the agency, Ottawa, Ontario, KIA OT6. Price: $Can70.00, foreign.

Available in microform: Micromedia Ltd.: 1867-1980/81.

129. ***Canadian statistical review.*** 1926- Ottawa: Statistics Canada. Monthly. Separate French edition.

Annual bilingual supplement. Weekly supplements ceased April, 1984.

Agency varies: See entry 128 for agency variations.

Each issue has articles as well as regularly published statistical tables, which include selected economic indicators. Nov.,1983 edition, 127 p., contains statistical data in the following areas:

DEMOGRAPHY
Population: distribution by geographic/administrative areas, external migration; *Vital statistics*: births, deaths, marriages.

ECONOMIC AFFAIRS
Agriculture and food: farming; *Commerce and business*: domestic commerce, exports, imports; *Finance*: banking and credit, securities; *Income and expenditure*: consumption, personal income, prices; *Industry*: construction, energy, manufacturing, mining; *National accounts*: balance of payments, gross domestic and national product, national income; *Public finance*: government expenditures, government revenue.

SOCIAL AND CULTURAL AFFAIRS
Housing; *Labor*: employment and unemployment, labor force, labor-management relations, salaries and wages.

Most data are monthly or quarterly for the current year and the preceding 2 or 3 years. The latest data are for a month before the date of the issue. The annual supplements have quarterly figures to 1950 for a number of topics. In addition to the national level, data are included for provinces. Notes accompanying the tables indicate the names of the agencies furnishing the data.

Available from the address in entry 128. Price: $Can3.85 per issue; $Can38.50 per year.

Available in microform: Micromedia Ltd.: 1926-79.

CAYMAN ISLANDS

130. ***Statistical abstract of the Government of the Cayman Islands.*** 1975- Grand Cayman: Government Statistics Unit. Annual.

V. 2, no. 4, n.s., 1983, 104 p., contains statistical data in the following areas:

PHYSICAL ENVIRONMENT
Climatology: precipitation, temperature; *Geography*: area of land.

DEMOGRAPHY
Population: census results from 1960-1979, distribution by age, distribution by sex, distribution by geographic/administrative area, households and families; *Vital statistics*: births, deaths, marriages.

ECONOMIC AFFAIRS
Agriculture and food: farming; *Commerce and business*: companies, exports, imports, tourism; *Finance*: banking and credit, currency in circulation; *Income and expenditure*: consumption, prices; *Industry*: communication, construction, energy, manufacturing, transportation; *Public finance*: government expenditures, government revenue.

POLITICAL AFFAIRS
Elections.

SOCIAL AND CULTURAL AFFAIRS
Education: enrollments, teaching staff; *Health*: hospitals, public health; *Housing*; *Justice*: traffic accidents; *Labor*: employment, foreign workers, occupations.

Most data are for 1983 and varying numbers of earlier years. In addition to the national level, data are included for districts.

Notes accompanying the tables indicate the names of the agencies furnishing the data. There is a detailed list of tables at the beginning of the volume.

Latest edition published: 1984, published June, 1985, 106 p. Available from Statistics Unit, Department of Finance and Development, Government Administration Building, Grand Cayman. Priced.

CHILE

131. ***Compendio estadístico*** [Statistical compendium]. 1971- Santiago: Instituto Nacional de Estadísticas (INE). Spanish.

Not published 1972, 1975.

1982 edition, 210 p., contains statistical data in the following areas:

PHYSICAL ENVIRONMENT
Climatology: precipitation, temperature; *Geography*: area and use of land, maps.

DEMOGRAPHY
Population: arrivals and departures, census results from 1952, 1960, 1970 and 1982 (prelim.), distribution by age and sex, distribution by geographic/administrative area, households and families, internal migration, population estimates; *Vital statistics*: annulments, births, causes of death, deaths, infant mortality, life expectancy, marriages.

ECONOMIC AFFAIRS
Agriculture and food: farming, fishing, forestry; *Commerce and business*: domestic commerce, exports, imports, tourism; *Finance*: banking and credit; *Income and expenditure*: consumption, prices; *Industry*: communication, construction, energy, manufacturing, mining, transportation; *National accounts*: balance of payments, gross domestic product,*Public finance*: government expenditures for social purposes.

SOCIAL AND CULTURAL AFFAIRS
Cultural and scientific activities: books and journals, cinema and performing arts, libraries, newspapers, radio, television, science and research; *Education*: enrollments; *Health*: hospitals, medical personnel, public health; *Housing*; *Justice*: correctional institutions, courts, crimes, police, traffic accidents; *Labor*: employment and unemployment, labor force, salaries and wages; *Social security*.

Most data are for 1981 or 1980 and preceding periods of varying length, usually 2 to 4 years. There are some monthly and quarterly figures. In addition to the national level, data are included for regions and municipalities.

The introduction includes a description of the geography, climate and political/administrative organization of the country. Notes accompanying the tables indicate the names of the agencies furnishing the data. There is a detailed list of tables at the beginning of the volume.

Historical statistics. Statistics for earlier periods are available in *Historical statistics of Chile*, by Markos G. Mamalakis, Westport, Conn., Greenwood Press, 1980, 2 volumes. Dates covered vary for different topics; many tables have figures for the mid-19th century or earlier. Time series from 1960, or earlier, to 1981 may be found in *Chile series estadísticas 1981*, 160 p., published by the INE in 1981.

Available from the agency, Casilla 7597, Correo 3, Santiago. Priced.

Available in microform: CIS: *Compendio estadístico,*1971, 1973-74, 1976-77.

132. **Anuario estadístico de Chile** [Statistical yearbook of Chile]. 1848/58-1976? Santiago: Servicio Nacional de Estadística y Censos. Irregular.

Title varies: 1928-33 as *Estadística anual*. Agency varies: 1848/58-1926 by Oficina Central de Estadística; 1928-59 by Dirección [Servicio] General de Estadística; 1960-69 by Dirección de Estadística y Censos. Continued by a number of separate series.

Covers most of same topics as entry 131.

Available from the agency, Casilla 7597, Correo 3, Santiago. Priced.

Available in microform: CH: *Anuario estadístico,* 1848/58-59,1864-70, 1883-90, 1896, 1909-16, 1920-35, 1937. (Some parts of these years are missing.)

133. *Sinopsis estadística* [Statistical summary]. 1882-1969/70. Santiago: Oficina Central de Estadística.

From 1940 to 1969, the *Sinopsis* was published each year in the Jan.-Dec. issue of the *Boletín* or its predecessor, *Estadística chilena* (see continuation note in entry 134).

For agency name variations, see entry 132.

Covers most of the same topics as entry 131.

Available in microform: CH: *Sinopsis estadística,* 1882-85, 1891, 1893-96, 1898-1907, 1912-13, 1915-22, 1924-28, 1933,1940-58, 1960-64, 1966-69/70. CIS: 1969/70.

134. **Síntesis estadística** [Statistical synthesis]. 1971- Santiago: Instituto Nacional de Estadísticas. Monthly. Spanish.

Continues: *Estadística chilena,* 1940-Jan./Febr.,1961, and *Boletín,* 1961-69, published by Dirección [Servicio] General de Estadística, 1940-59 and by Dirección de Estadística y Censos, 1960-69.

Each issue contains special statistical studies in addition to regular tables. The Dec., 1972 issue, 20 p., contains statistical data in the following areas:

DEMOGRAPHY
Population: population estimates; *Vital statistics*: births, deaths, infant mortality, marriages.

ECONOMIC AFFAIRS
Agriculture and food: farming; *Commerce and business*: domestic commerce, exports, imports, tourism; *Finance*: banking and credit, securities; *Income and expenditure*: prices; *Industry*: construction, energy, manufacturing, mining, transportation.

SOCIAL AND CULTURAL AFFAIRS
Cultural and scientific activities: cinema and performing arts; *Justice*: police, traffic accidents.

Most data are monthly or quarterly for the current year and the preceding 2 years. Latest data are for the date of the issue.

Available from the address in entry 131.

COLOMBIA

135. *Colombia estadística* [Statistics Colombia]. 1979- Bogota: Departamento Administrativo Nacional de Estadística (DANE). Spanish.

1982 edition, 375 p., contains statistical data in the following areas:

PHYSICAL ENVIRONMENT
Geography: area and use of land, maps.

DEMOGRAPHY
Population: arrivals and departures, census results from 1770-1973, distribution by age and sex, distribution by geographic/administrative area, population estimates and projections; *Vital statistics*: births, deaths, infant mortality, marriages.

ECONOMIC AFFAIRS
Agriculture and food: farming; *Commerce and business*: domestic commerce, exports, imports, tourism; *Finance*: banking and credit, money supply; *Income and expenditure*: consumption, prices; *Industry*: communication, construction, energy, manufacturing, mining, transportation; *National accounts*: balance of payments, gross domestic product, national income; *Public finance*: government expenditures, government revenue.

POLITICAL AFFAIRS
Elections.

SOCIAL AND CULTURAL AFFAIRS
Cultural and scientific activities: cinema and performing arts, radio, television; *Education*: enrollments (post-secondary only), literacy, teaching staff (post-secondary only); *Health*: hospitals, public health; *Housing*; *Justice*: courts, crimes; *Labor*: underemployment and unemployment, labor force, labor-management relations, salaries and wages; *Sports and recreation*.

Most data are for 1981 or 1980 and the preceding 3 to 6 years. The first edition published in 1979 covered 1970-79. In addition to the national level, data are included for departments and municipalities. There are comparative statistics for a number of Latin American countries in the last chapter.

Commentaries are provided at the beginnings of some chapters. Notes accompanying the tables indicate the titles of sources from which the data were taken. There are lists of tables at the beginnings of chapters.

Historical statistics. Statistics to the first third of the 19th century or earlier are found in *Estadísticas históricas*, 200 p., published by DANE in 1975.

Latest edition published: 1985, 580 p. Available from the agency, Centro Administrativo Nacional, via Eldorado, Bogotá DE. Priced.

36. *Anuario general de estadística* [General statistical yearbook]. 1905, 1915-1968. Bogotá: Departamento Administrativo Nacional de Estadística. Spanish.

Not published 1906-14.

Title varies: 1905: *Estadística anual de la República de Colombia*; 1915-27: *Anuario estadístico*; 1928: *Anuario general de estadística*; 1929-34: *Anuario de estadística general*. Agency varies: 1905-34 by Dirección General de Estadística; 1935-50 by Dirección Nacional de Estadística. Continues *Anuario estadístico*, 1875-76, 1882-3, published by the Oficina de Estadística Nacional.

Some years issued in multiple parts. Contains statistics on geography and climatology, demography, economic, social and cultural affairs.

Available in microform: CH: 1905, 1915-17, 1929-34, 1936-54, 1956-57, 1959-62, 1964-69.

137. *Boletín mensual de estadística* [Monthly bulletin of statistics]. 1951- Bogotá: Departamento Administrativo Nacional de Estadística. Spanish. Title varies: 1951-July, 1952 as *Boletín informativo*. Agency varies: Earlier by Dirección Nacional de Estadística.

In addition to a small number of tables which appear in every issue, there are a number of special topics treated in each issue. No. 359, June, 1981, published Aug., 1981, 159 p., contains statistical data in the following areas:

ECONOMIC AFFAIRS
Commerce and business: companies, domestic commerce, imports; *Income and expenditure*: prices; *Industry*: construction, manufacturing, transportation.

SOCIAL AND CULTURAL AFFAIRS
Labor: unemployment, labor force, salaries and wages.

Most data are monthly or quarterly for the current and preceding year, with annual figures for as many as 5 years. Latest data are advance statistics for the month in which issue was published. Notes accompanying the tables indicate the names of the agencies furnishing the data.

Available from the agency, Centro Administrativo Nacional, via Eldorado, Bogotá. Priced.

COSTA RICA

138. *Anuario estadístico* [Statistical yearbook]. 1883- San Jośe: Dirección General de Estadística y Censos. Spanish.

Not published 1894-1906, 1946-47. Title varies slightly. Agency name varies: 1883-1913 by Oficina Nacional de Estadística. 1914-50 by Dirección General de Estadística.

1977 edition, 248 p., contains statistical data in the following areas:

PHYSICAL ENVIRONMENT
Climatology: precipitation, temperature; *Geography*: area of land, maps.

DEMOGRAPHY
Population: distribution by geographic/administrative area, internal migration; *Vital statistics*: births, causes of death, deaths, divorces, infant mortality, marriages.

ECONOMIC AFFAIRS
Agriculture and food: farming; *Commerce and business*: domestic commerce, exports, imports, tourism; *Finance*: banking and credit; *Income and expenditure*: consumption, prices; *Industry*: communication, construction, energy, manufacturing, transportation; *National accounts*: balance of payments, gross domestic and gross national product, national income; *Public finance*: government expenditures, government revenue.

SOCIAL AND CULTURAL AFFAIRS

Education: degrees conferred, enrollments; *Health*: disease, hospitals, public health; *Justice*: correctional institutions, courts, traffic accidents; *Labor*: underemployment, labor force, occupations, salaries and wages; *Social security*.

Most data are for 1977 and the preceding 3 or 4 years. There are some monthly figures. Time series of varying lengths are provided. In addition to the national level, data are included for provinces, cantones y distritos [cantons and districts], and capitals of provinces.

Sources and methodology are discussed on pages 31-49. Some tables are accompanied by notes indicating the names of the agencies furnishing the data. There is a detailed list of tables at the beginning of the volume. Special features include the text of the basic law on statistics and the annual report of the Dirección General de Estadística y Censos for 1976/77.

Available from the agency, Apartado 10163, San José.

Available in microform: CH: 1888-89, 1907, 1909, 1911-16, 1918-38, 1940-45, 1951-69. CIS: 1970-75. IDC: 1937-45, 1948-76.

No general statistical bulletin is currently published by Costa Rica.

CUBA

139. ***Anuario estadístico de Cuba*** [Statistical yearbook of Cuba]. 1914, 1952, 1956- Havana: Comité Estatal de Estadísticas. Irregular. Spanish.

Title varies: 1964-71 as *Boletín estadístico*. Agency varies: Before 1975 by Dirección General de Estadística.

1982 edition, 591 p., contains statistical data in the following areas:

PHYSICAL ENVIRONMENT
Climatology: precipitation, temperature; *Geography*: area of land.

DEMOGRAPHY
Population: census results, 1899-1981, distribution by age and sex, distribution by geographic/administrative area, external migration, internal migration, population estimates; *Vital statistics*: births, causes of death, deaths, divorces, infant mortality, life expectancy, marriages.

ECONOMIC AFFAIRS
Agriculture and food: farming, fishing; *Commerce and business*: domestic commerce, exports, imports, services, tourism; *Income and expenditure*: consumption, prices; *Industry*: communication, construction, energy, manufacturing, transportation; *National accounts*: gross domestic product.

SOCIAL AND CULTURAL AFFAIRS
Cultural and scientific activities: books and journals, cinema and performing arts, libraries, museums and galleries, newspapers, radio, science and research, television;

Education: degrees conferred, educational attainment of workers, enrollments, teaching staff; *Health*: disease, hospitals, medical personnel, public health; *Labor*: employment, labor force, occupations, salaries and wages; *Social security*; *Sports and recreation*.

Most data are for 1982 and varying numbers of earlier years. In addition to the national level, data are included for provinces. There is a section of comparative statistics for selected foreign countries.

Commentaries are provided at the beginnings of sections. There is an alphabetical subject index at the end.

Available from the agency, Calle 46, No. 307, Gaveta Postal 6016, Miramar, Havana.

Historical statistics. Cuba, a handbook of historical statistics by Susan Schroeder, Boston: G.K. Hall, 1982, 589 p., includes data to 1511 in some series.

Available in microform: CH: 1952, 1956-57, 1964-65, 1968, 1971, 1972-74. CIS: 1971-73. IDC: 1952, 1956-57, 1972-73.

140. **Cuba en cifras** [Cuba in figures]. 1980- Havana: Comité Estatal de Estadística. Spanish.

Title varies: Some years as *Compendio del anuario estadístico de la República de Cuba*. Continues: *Compendio estadístico de Cuba* [Statistical compendium of Cuba], 1965-78, published by the same agency in English, Spanish, and Russian editions.

Contains less detailed data on most of the same topics as entry 139.

Available from the agency, Calle 46, No. 307, Gaveta Postal 6016, Miramar, Havana.

Available in microform: CH: 1965-66, 1968, 1976 eds. of *Compendio estadístico de Cuba*.

141. ***Boletín mensual de estadísticas*** [Statistical bulletin]. 1945-55. Havana: Dirección General de Estadística. Irregular. Spanish.

DOMINICA

142. **Statistical digest.** 1963- Roseau: Statistical Division. Irregular.

Publication suspended 1973-1979.

No. 5, 1970-78, published May, 1980, 71 p., contains data in the following areas:

PHYSICAL ENVIRONMENT
Climatology: precipitation, temperature.

DEMOGRAPHY
Population: arrivals and departures, census results, 1871-1970, distribution by age and sex, distribution by geographic/administrative area, ethnic groups, external migration, households; *Vital statistics*: births, causes of death, deaths, infant mortality.

ECONOMIC AFFAIRS
Agriculture and food: farming; *Commerce and business*: exports, imports, tourism; *Finance*: banking and credit; *Income and expenditure*: household income, prices; *Industry*: communication, energy, manufacturing, transportation; *National accounts*: gross domestic product; *Public finance*: government expenditure and government revenue.

POLITICAL AFFAIRS
Elections.

SOCIAL AND CULTURAL AFFAIRS
Education: educational attainment, enrollments, examination results, teaching staff; *Health*: disease, hospitals; *Housing*; *Labor*: labor force; *Justice*: crimes, traffic accidents; *Religion*.

Most data are for 1970 through 1978, with some figures for earlier years. In addition to the national level, data are given for parishes, towns and selected villages.

Sources are noted at the foot of tables. There is a detailed list of tables at the beginning.

Latest edition published: 1985, 150 p. Available from the agency, 22 Bath Road, Roseau. Price: $20.00.

No general statistical bulletin has been found for Dominica.

DOMINICAN REPUBLIC

143. ***República Dominicana en cifras*** [Dominican Republic in figures]. 1964- Santo Domingo: Oficina Nacional de Estadística.

Continues: *Anuario estadístico*, 1936-54, published by the Dirección General de Estadístico y Censos.

V. IX, 1980, published Feb., 1980, 382 p., contains statistical data in the following areas:

PHYSICAL ENVIRONMENT
Climatology: precipitation, temperature; *Geography*: area and use of land.

DEMOGRAPHY
Population: census results from 1920-70, distribution by age and sex, distribution by geographic/administrative area, population estimates; *Vital statistics*: births, causes of death, deaths, infant mortality, marriages.

ECONOMIC AFFAIRS
Agriculture and food: farming; *Commerce and business*: cooperatives, domestic commerce, exports, imports, tourism; *Finance*: banking and credit, money supply; *Income and expenditure*: consumption, prices; *Industry*: communication, construction, energy, manufacturing, mining, transportation; *National accounts*: balance of payments, gross domestic and gross national product; *Public finance*: government expenditures, government revenue.

SOCIAL AND CULTURAL AFFAIRS
Education: educational attainment, enrollments, number of graduates; *Labor*: labor force, occupations, salaries and wages; *Social assistance*; *Social security*.

Most data are for 1979 or 1978 and the preceding 1 to 4 years. In addition to the national level, data are included for provinces and municipalities. Notes accompanying the tables indicate the names of the agencies furnishing the data. There is a detailed list of tables at the beginning of the volume.

Historical statistics. Statistics for 1936-1956 are available in *21 años de estadísticas dominicanas,* published by the Dirección General de Estadística in 1957.

Latest edition published: v. 11, 1984, published Sept., 1985, 424 p. Available from the agency, Apartado de Correos No. 1342, Santo Domingo, D.N.

Available in microform: CH: 1964-65, 1967-69. CIS: 1970-71, 1975, 1978. IDC: 1964-69. In addition, the *Anuario estadístico* is available as follows: CH: 1936-54. IDC: 1937-54 (some parts of some years lacking). CH also offers *21 años* in film.

No general statistical bulletin is currently published for the Dominican Republic.

ECUADOR

144. ***Boletín anuario*** [Annual bulletin]. 1977- Quito: Banco Central del Ecuador.

No. 7, 1984, 223 p., contains statistical data in the following areas:

DEMOGRAPHY
Population: census results from 1950-1982 (prelim.), distribution by age, distribution by geographic/administrative area.

ECONOMIC AFFAIRS
Agriculture and food: farming; *Commerce and business*: exports, imports; *Finance*: banking and credit, money supply, securities; *Income and expenditure*: consumption, prices; *Industry*: construction, energy, manufacturing, mining; *National accounts*: balance of payments; *Public finance*: government expenditures, government revenue.

SOCIAL AND CULTURAL AFFAIRS
Education: enrollments, literacy, percent of age group in school, teaching staff; *Housing*; *Labor*: employment, underemployment, and unemployment, labor force, salaries and wages.

Most data are for 1983 and varying numbers of earlier years. Time series to 1967 are provided wherever data are available. In addition to the national level, data are included for provinces.

Notes accompanying the tables indicate the names of the agencies responsible for the collection and presentation of the data.

Available on an exchange basis from the Secretaria General, Banco Central de Ecuador, Casilla 339, Quito.

145. *Serie estadística* [Statistical series]. 1967/1972- Quito: Instituto Nacional de Estadística. Irregular. Spanish.

Continues: *Anuario de estadística* [Statistical yearbook], 1963/68- 1966/71.

1968/73 edition, published 1976, 195 p., contains statistical data in the following areas:

PHYSICAL ENVIRONMENT
Climatology: precipitation, temperature; *Geography*: area of land, maps.

DEMOGRAPHY
Population: census results from 1950, 1962, distribution by geographic/administrative area, population estimates and projections; *Vital statistics*: births, deaths, divorces, infant mortality, marriages.

ECONOMIC AFFAIRS
Agriculture and food: farming; *Commerce and business*: establishments, domestic commerce, exports, imports, services; *Finance*: banking and credit, money supply; *Income and expenditure*: prices; *Industry*: communication, construction, energy, manufacturing, mining, transportation; *National accounts*: gross domestic and gross national product; *Public finance*: government expenditures and government revenue for the central government and provincial and municipal councils (aggregate only).

SOCIAL AND CULTURAL AFFAIRS
Cultural and scientific activities: radio, television; *Education*: degrees conferred, educational attainment, enrollments, literacy, teaching staff; *Health*: disease, hospitals; *Housing*; *Labor*: employment, labor force, occupations, salaries and wages.

Most data are for 1973 and the preceding 2 to 5 years. In addition to the national level, data are included for regions and provinces.

Notes accompanying the tables indicate the names of the agencies furnishing the data. There is a detailed list of tables at the beginning of the volume.

Historical statistics. For statistics for earlier periods, see *Síntesis estadística del Ecuador*, 1955/60-1955/62, published by the Dirección General de Estadística y Censos and *Ecuador en cifras, 1938 a 1942*, published by the Dirección General de Estadística in 1944.

Available in microform: CH: 1967/72-1968/73, plus the following: *Anuario*, 1963/68-1966/71, *Síntesis estadística*, 1955/60-1955/62, *Ecuador en cifras, 1938 a 1942*. CIS: *Anuario*, 1970.

No general statistical bulletin is currently published by Ecuador.

EL SALVADOR

146. *Anuario estadístico* [Statistical yearbook]. 1911- San Salvador: Dirección General de Estadística y Censos. Spanish.

Not published 1924-26.

Agency varies: 1911-34 by Dirección General de Estadística y Observatorio Nacional; 1935-49 by Dirección General de Estadística.

1979 edition, consisted of 10 volumes published between Aug., 1980 and Feb., 1981. (Vols. 2,3, and 6 were not available for examination; descriptions for these volumes are based on the 1976 ed.) Statistical data were provided in the following areas:

PHYSICAL ENVIRONMENT
Climatology: precipitation, sunshine, temperature; *Geography*: area of land, maps.

DEMOGRAPHY
Population: arrivals and departures, census results from 1950-1971, distribution by age and sex, distribution by geographic/administrative area, population estimates; *Vital statistics*: births, including illegitimate births, causes of death, deaths, divorces, infant and maternal mortality, marriages.

ECONOMIC AFFAIRS
Agriculture and food: farming, fishing, forestry; *Commerce and business*: domestic commerce, exports, imports, tourism; *Finance*: banking and credit; *Income and expenditure*: consumption, prices; *Industry*: construction, energy, manufacturing, transportation; *National accounts*: balance of payments; *Public finance*: government expenditures, government revenue.

SOCIAL AND CULTURAL AFFAIRS
Cultural and scientific activities: cinema and performing arts, libraries, newspapers, radio; *Education*: enrollments, examination results, literacy, teaching staff; *Health*: family planning, hospitals, medical personnel, public health; *Housing*; *Justice*: courts, crimes, police, traffic accidents; *Labor*: labor force, labor-management relations, occupations, salaries and wages; *Social assistance*; *Social security*; *Sports and recreation*.

Most data are for 1979 and the preceding 4 years. In addition to the national level, data are included for departments and judicial districts.

Commentaries, including discussions of sources, are provided at the beginnings of sections. Notes accompanying some of the tables indicate the names of the agencies furnishing the data. Special features include a list of official statistical materials published by the Dirección at the end of each volume and a description of the educational system in v. 9.

Available from the agency, Calle Arce No. 953, San Salvador.

Available in microform: CH: 1911-14, 1916-17, 1919-22, 1925-35, 1937-65 (lacking parts of 1945 and 1963). CIS: 1970-71. IDC: 1931, 1934-70, 1972-77 (lacking parts of 1940, 1968-74, 1977).

147. *Boletín estadístico* [Statistical bulletin]. 1935- San Salvador: Dirección General de Estadística y Censos. Quarterly. Spanish.

Publication suspended after first qtr., 1935 until May, 1937.

No. 123, July-Dec., 1980, 81 p., contains statistical data in the following areas:

AMERICAS : FRENCH GUIANA

DEMOGRAPHY
Population: external migration, population estimates; *Vital statistics*: births, causes of death, deaths, divorces, marriages.

ECONOMIC AFFAIRS
Agriculture and food: farming, fishing; *Commerce and business*: domestic commerce, exports, imports; *Finance*: banking and credit; *Income and expenditure*: consumption, prices; *Industry*: construction, manufacturing, transportation. *Public finance*: government expenditures and government revenue.

SOCIAL AND CULTURAL AFFAIRS
Cultural and scientific activities: cinema and performing arts, libraries, newspapers, radio; *Justice*: courts, crimes, traffic accidents; *Labor*: salaries and wages; *Sports and recreation*.

Most data are monthly for 15 months and annual for 4 years. Latest data are for the date of the issue. Explanations are provided at the beginning of the volume. Notes accompanying a few of the tables indicate the names of the agencies furnishing the data.

Available from the address given in entry 146.

FRENCH GUIANA

148. ***Annuaire statistique de la Guyane*** [Statistical yearbook of French Guiana]. 1947/52- Paris: Institut National de la Statistique et des Etudes Economiques (France), Service Interrégional Antilles Guyane. Irregular. French.

1977/81 edition, published 1983, 193 p., contains statistical data in the following areas:

PHYSICAL ENVIRONMENT
Climatology: precipitation, sunshine, temperature; *Geography*: area of land, maps.

DEMOGRAPHY
Population: arrivals and departures, census results from 1677-1982, distribution by age and sex, distribution by geographic/administrative area, migration; *Vital statistics*: births, including illegitimate births, deaths, divorces, infant mortality, marriages.

ECONOMIC AFFAIRS
Agriculture and food: farming, fishing, forestry; *Commerce and business*: exports, imports; *Finance*: banking and credit, money supply; *Income and expenditure*: consumption, prices; *Industry*: communication, construction, energy, mining, transportation; *Public finance*: government expenditures and government revenue.

POLITICAL AFFAIRS
Elections.

SOCIAL AND CULTURAL AFFAIRS
Education: enrollments, examination results, teaching staff; *Health*: disease, hospitals, medical personnel, public health; *Housing*; *Justice*: traffic accidents; *Labor*: employment

and unemployment, labor force, salaries and wages; *Social assistance*; *Social security*; *Sports and recreation*.

Most data are for 1977-1981. In addition to the national level, data are included for communes.

Commentaries are provided at the beginnings of chapters. Notes accompanying the tables indicate the names of the agencies furnishing the data. There is a detailed list of tables at the end of the volume.

Available from INSEE, Observatoire Economique de Paris, Tour Gamma A, 195 rue de Bercy, 75582, Paris, Cedex 12 or INSEE, Service Départementale de la Guyane, 81 rue Christophe Colomb, 97306, Cayenne. Price: F70.

Available in microform: CH: 1953/57.

149. ***Bulletin statistique de la Guyane*** [Statistical bulletin of French Guiana]. 1974- Cayenne: Institut National de la Statistique et des Etudes Economiques (France), Service Régional de la Guyane. Quarterly. French.

Title varies: Earlier, *Bulletin de statistiques.*

No. 2/3 of 1984, 31 p., contains statistical data in the following areas:

PHYSICAL ENVIRONMENT
Climatology: precipitation, sunshine, temperature; *Geography*: maps.

DEMOGRAPHY
Population: census results from 1974, 1982, distribution by age and sex, migration; *Vital statistics*: births, including illegitimate births, deaths, divorces, infant mortality, marriages.

ECONOMIC AFFAIRS
Agriculture and food: farming, fishing, forestry; *Commerce and business*: exports, imports; *Finance*: banking and credit, money supply; *Income and expenditure*: prices; *Industry*: communication, construction, energy, mining, transportation; *Public finance*: government expenditures and government revenue.

SOCIAL AND CULTURAL AFFAIRS
Labor: employment, foreign workers, labor force, salaries and wages; *Social assistance*; *Social security*.

Most data are monthly for the current and 2 preceding years. Latest data are for the date of the issue. Notes accompanying the tables indicate the names of the agencies furnishing the data. There is a list of tables at the beginning of the issue.

Available from INSEE, Observatoire Economique de Paris, Tour Gamma A, 195 rue de Bercy, 75582, Paris, Cedex 12 or INSEE, Service Départementale de la Guyane, 81 rue Christophe Colomb, 97306, Cayenne. Price: F30 per issue.

GRENADA

150. ***Abstract of statistics.*** 1978- St. George's: Central Statistics Office.

1979 edition, 146 p., contains statistical data in the following areas:

PHYSICAL ENVIRONMENT
Climatology: precipitation, sunshine, temperature; *Geography*: area and use of land.

DEMOGRAPHY
Population: arrivals and departures, census results from 1844-1970, distribution by age and sex, distribution by geographic/administrative area, ethnic groups, population estimates; *Vital statistics*: births, including illegitimate births, causes of death, deaths, divorces, marriages.

ECONOMIC AFFAIRS
Agriculture and food: farming, fishing; *Commerce and business*: exports, imports, tourism; *Finance*: banking and credit; *Income and expenditure*: consumption, personal income, prices; *Industry*: communication, energy, transportation; *National accounts*: balance of payments, gross domestic product; *Public finance*: government expenditures, government revenue.

SOCIAL AND CULTURAL AFFAIRS
Cultural and scientific activities: cinema and performing arts, libraries, radio; *Education*: educational attainment, enrollments, teaching staff; *Health*: disease, hospitals, medical personnel; *Housing*; *Justice*: correctional institutions, courts, crimes; *Labor*: employment; *Religion*.

Most data are for 1979. There are time series of varying lengths. In addition to the national level, data are included for parishes. Notes accompanying the tables indicate the names of the agencies furnishing the data.

Available from the agency, Ministry of Finance, St. George's.

No statistical bulletin has been found for Grenada.

GUADELOUPE

151. ***Bilan statistique annuel de la Guadeloupe*** [Annual statistical account of Guadeloupe]. 1979?- Pointe-à-Pitre: Institut National de la Statistique et des Etudes Economiques (France), Service Interrégional Antilles Guyane. French.

1980 edition, published Oct., 1981, 62 p., contains statistical data in the following areas:

DEMOGRAPHY
Population: population estimates; *Vital statistics*: births, deaths.

ECONOMIC AFFAIRS
Agriculture and food: farming; *Commerce and business*: exports, imports, tourism; *Finance*: banking and credit, money supply; *Income and expenditure*: consumption, prices; *Industry*: construction, energy, transportation; *Public finance*: government expenditures, government revenue, planning and economic development.

SOCIAL AND CULTURAL AFFAIRS
Labor: underemployment and unemployment, salaries and wages; *Social assistance*; *Social security*.

Most data are for 1980 and varying numbers of earlier years. Explanatory notes are provided at the beginnings of chapters. Some tables have notes indicating the agencies furnishing the data. There is a list of tables at the beginning of the volume.

Latest edition published: 1983, 70p. (*Conjoncture* no. 6, Nov., 1984). Available from INSEE (Institut National de la Statistique et des Etudes Economiques), Observatoire Economique de Paris, Tour Gamma A, 195 rue de Bercy, 75582, Paris, Cedex 12; INSEE, Service Départemental de la Guadeloupe, Chemin du Petit- Paris, BP 96, 97102 Basse-Terre, Guadeloupe, or INSEE, Service Interrégional Antilles Guyane, BP 863, 97175, Pointe-à-Pitre, Guadeloupe. Price: F15.

152. ***Annuaire statistique de la Guadeloupe*** [Statistical yearbook of Guadeloupe]. 1949/53- Paris: Institut National de la Statistique et des Etudes Economiques (France). Irregular. French.

1971/76 edition, 180 p., contains statistical data in the following areas:

PHYSICAL ENVIRONMENT
Climatology: precipitation, sunshine, temperature; *Geography*: area and use of land, maps.

DEMOGRAPHY
Population: census results from 1954, 1961, 1967, 1974, distribution by age and sex, distribution by geographic/administrative area, migration, population estimates; *Vital statistics*: abortions, births, including illegitimate births, causes of death, deaths, divorces, infant mortality, marriages.

ECONOMIC AFFAIRS
Agriculture and food: farming, fishing, forestry; *Commerce and business*: exports, imports, tourism; *Finance*: banking and credit, money supply; *Income and expenditure*: consumption, prices; *Industry*: communication, construction, energy, manufacturing, transportation; *National accounts*: gross domestic product.

POLITICAL AFFAIRS
Elections.

SOCIAL AND CULTURAL AFFAIRS
Education: enrollments, examination results, teaching staff; *Health*: disease, hospitals, medical personnel, public health; *Housing*; *Justice*: courts, crimes, traffic accidents; *Labor*: employment and unemployment, labor force, salaries and wages; *Social assistance*; *Social security*; *Sports and recreation*.

Most data are for 1976 and 3 to 6 preceding years. In addition to the department level, data are included for communes. Explanatory notes are provided at the beginnings of some chapters. Notes accompanying the tables indicate the names of the agencies furnishing the data. There is a detailed list of tables at the beginning of the volume.

Available from the addresses in entry 150. Price: F35.

Available in microform: CH: 1953/57-1967/70. CIS: 1967/70.

153. ***Bulletin statistique de la Guadeloupe*** [Statistical bulletin of Guadeloupe]. Pointe-à-Pitre: Institut National de la Statistique et des Etudes Economiques (France). Service Interrégional Antilles Guyane. Quarterly and monthly editions. French.

No. 1, 1984, 22 p., contains statistical data in the following areas:

PHYSICAL ENVIRONMENT
Climatology: precipitation, sunshine, temperature; *Geography*: maps.

DEMOGRAPHY
Population: population estimates; *Vital statistics*: births, including illegitimate births, divorces, marriages.

ECONOMIC AFFAIRS
Agriculture and food: farming,*Commerce and business*: exports, imports, tourism; *Finance*: banking and credit, money supply; *Income and expenditure*: prices; *Industry*: communication, construction, energy, mining, transportation.

SOCIAL AND CULTURAL AFFAIRS
Labor: employment offices, salaries and wages; *Social assistance*; *Social security*.

Most data are monthly or quarterly and annual for 2 years. Latest data are for the month before the date of the issue. Notes accompanying the tables indicate the names of the agencies furnishing the data. There is a list of tables at the beginning of the volume.

Available from the addresses in entry 151. Price: F25 per issue for the quarterly; F80 per year, domestic, and F100, foreign, for the quarterly; F25 per year for the monthly.

GUATEMALA

154. ***Anuario estadístico*** [Statistical yearbook]. 1970- Guatemala City: Dirección General de Estadística. Spanish.

Continues: *Guatemala en cifras*, 1955-69.

1980 edition, published April, 1983, 183 p., contains statistical data in the following areas:

PHYSICAL ENVIRONMENT
Climatology: precipitation, temperature; *Geography*: maps.

DEMOGRAPHY
Population: arrivals and departures; *Vital statistics*: births, deaths, divorces, infant and maternal mortality, marriages.

ECONOMIC AFFAIRS
Agriculture and food: farming; *Finance*: banking and credit, money in circulation; *Income and expenditure*: prices; *Industry*: construction, energy, manufacturing, transportation; *National accounts*: balance of payments, gross national product.

SOCIAL AND CULTURAL AFFAIRS
Cultural and scientific activities: cinema; *Education*: enrollments, teaching staff; *Health*: hospitals, public health; *Justice*: crimes; *Social assistance*; *Social security*.

Most data are for 1980, with time series of varying lengths. In addition to the national level, data are included for departments. Notes accompanying the tables indicate the names of the agencies furnishing the data. There is a detailed list of tables at the beginning of the volume.

Historical statistics. Statistics for earlier periods are available in *Anuario de la Dirección General de Estadística*, 1898, and *República de Guatemala: sintesis geográfico-estadística*, 1948.

Latest edition published: 1981, 229 p.

Available from the agency, 8A Calle 9-55, Zona 1, Guatemala City. Price: Q3.50.

Available in microform: CH: 1970. CIS: 1970-71, 1973-74. IDC: 1970, 1974, 1976. *Guatemala en cifras*: CH: 1955-66, 1969. IDC: 1955-66, 1968-69. CH also offers the 1898 and 1948 titles in microfiche.

155. ***Boletín estadístico*** [Statistical bulletin]. 1946- Guatemala City: Dirección General de Estadística. Semi-annual. Spanish.

2nd half-year, 1976 edition, published June, 1978, 130 p., contains statistical data in the following areas:

PHYSICAL ENVIRONMENT
Climatology: precipitation, temperature; *Geography*: maps.

DEMOGRAPHY
Population: arrivals and departures, ethnic groups; *Vital statistics*: births, deaths, divorces, infant mortality, marriages.

ECONOMIC AFFAIRS
Agriculture and food: farming; *Commerce and business*: exports, imports, tourism; *Finance*: banking and credit, money supply; *Income and expenditure*: prices; *Industry*: construction, transportation; *Public finance*: government expenditures, government revenue.

SOCIAL AND CULTURAL AFFAIRS
Cultural and scientific activities: cinema; *Health*: hospitals, public health; *Social security*.

Most data are monthly or quarterly for 2 years and annual for 5 years. The latest data are for Dec., 1976. In addition to the national level, data are included for departamentos.

Commentaries are provided at the beginnings of chapters. Notes accompanying the tables indicate the names of the agencies furnishing the data. There is a detailed list of tables at the beginning of the volume.

Available from Dirección General de Estadística, 8a Calle 9-55, Zona 1, Guatemala City. Price: Q2 per issue; Q4 per year.

GUYANA

156. ***Annual statistical abstract.*** 1970- Georgetown: Statistical Bureau.

Not published 1973.

1974 edition, 305 p., contains statistical data in the following areas:

PHYSICAL ENVIRONMENT
Climatology: precipitation, sunshine, temperature.

DEMOGRAPHY
Population: arrivals and departures, census results from 1841-1970, distribution by age and sex, distribution by geographic/administrative area, ethnic groups, external migration, population estimates; *Vital statistics*: births, causes of death, deaths.

ECONOMIC AFFAIRS
Agriculture and food: farming; *Commerce and business*: cooperatives, domestic commerce, exports, imports; *Finance*: banking and credit; *Income and expenditure*: personal income, prices; *Industry*: communication, energy, mining, transportation; *National accounts*: balance of payments, gross domestic product, national income; *Public finance*: government expenditures, government revenue.

SOCIAL AND CULTURAL AFFAIRS
Education: degrees conferred, enrollments, teaching staff; *Housing*; *Justice*: crimes, traffic accidents; *Labor*: employment, labor-management relations.

Most data are for 1974, with time series to 1965 or 1957. Notes accompanying the tables indicate the names of the agencies furnishing the data. There is a detailed list of tables at the beginning of chapters and a list of official statistical materials published by the Statistical Bureau at the end of the volume.

Available from the agency, Avenue of the Republic and Brickdam, PO Box 542, Georgetown.

Available in microform: CH: 1970-71, 1974. CIS: 1971. CH also provides Great Britain, Colonial Office, *British Guiana: blue books of statistics*, 1843-1943; *Berbice: blue books of statistics*, 1821-24, 1826-29, 1831-42, and *Demerara and Essequibo: bluebooks of statistics*, 1821-24, 1826-42.

157. ***Quarterly statistical digest.*** 1960- Georgetown: Statistical Bureau.

July-Sept., 1977 edition, 62 p., contains statistical data in the following areas:

PHYSICAL ENVIRONMENT
Climatology: precipitation, sunshine, temperature.

ECONOMIC AFFAIRS
Commerce and business: domestic commerce, exports, firms, imports; *Income and expenditure*: prices; *Industry*: communication, energy, manufacturing, transportation.

SOCIAL AND CULTURAL AFFAIRS
Labor: employment, salaries and wages.

Most data are quarterly for the current and preceding year and annual for 5 years. The latest data are for the quarter of issue. Notes accompanying the tables indicate the names of the agencies furnishing the data.

Available from the address given in the entry 156. Priced.

HAITI

158. ***Bulletin de statistique: supplément annuel*** [Bulletin of statistics: annual supplement]. 1967- Port-au-Prince: Institut Haïtien de Statistique et d'Informatique. French.

    No. 11, 1979, 71 p., contains statistical data in the following areas:

    DEMOGRAPHY
    Population: census results from 1971, distribution by age and sex, population estimates; *Vital statistics*: births, deaths, infant mortality.

    ECONOMIC AFFAIRS
    Agriculture and food: farming, fishing; *Commerce and business*: establishments, exports, imports; *Finance*: banking and credit; *Income and expenditure*: consumption; *Industry*: communication, energy, manufacturing, mining, transportation; *National accounts*: balance of payments, gross domestic product, national income; *Public finance*: government expenditures, government revenue.

    SOCIAL AND CULTURAL AFFAIRS
    Education: enrollments, examination results, graduates of higher education institutions, teaching staff; *Health*: hospitals, public health; *Housing*; *Labor*: employment (in public sector only), salaries and wages; *Social security*.

    Most data are for 1979 and varying numbers of earlier years. In addition to the national level, data are included for departments. Notes accompanying the tables indicate the names of the agencies furnishing the data.

    Latest edition published: 1980/1982, 233 p. Available on an exchange basis from the agency, Cité de l'Exposition, Boulevard Harry Truman, Port-au-Prince.

159. ***Bulletin trimestriel de statistique*** [Quarterly bulletin of statistics]. 1951- Port-au-Prince: Institut Haïtien de Statistique et d'Informatique. French.

    No. 123, 3rd qtr, 1981, 123 p., contains statistical data in the following areas:

PHYSICAL ENVIRONMENT
Climatology: precipitation, sunshine, temperature.

DEMOGRAPHY
Population: external migration; *Vital statistics*: births, infant mortality, marriages.

ECONOMIC AFFAIRS
Commerce and business: domestic commerce, exports, imports, tourism; *Finance*: banking and credit, money supply; *Income and expenditure*: consumption, cost of living, prices; *Industry*: communication, construction, energy, manufacturing, transportation.

SOCIAL AND CULTURAL AFFAIRS
Cultural and scientific activities: cinema, libraries; *Housing*; *Justice*: correctional institutions (minors imprisoned only), courts, crimes, police; *Labor*: labor-management relations; *Social security*.

Most data are monthly and/or quarterly for the date of issue, quarterly for the 3 preceding quarters and annual for the 2 preceding years. In addition to the national level, data are included for departments. Notes accompanying the tables indicate the names of the agencies furnishing the data.

Available on an exchange basis from the address in entry 158.

HONDURAS

160. **Anuario estadístico** [Statistical yearbook]. 1952- Tegucigalpa: Dirección General de Estadística y Censos. Spanish.

1979 edition, published 1981, 211 p., contains statistical data in the following areas:

DEMOGRAPHY
Population: arrivals and departures, census results from 1881-1974, distribution by age, distribution by sex, distribution by geographic/administrative area, population estimates; *Vital statistics*: births, causes of death, deaths, divorces, infant mortality, marriages.

ECONOMIC AFFAIRS
Agriculture and food: farming; *Commerce and business*: tourism; *Finance*: banking and credit, money supply; *Income and expenditure*: prices; *Industry*: communication, energy and water, transportation; *Public finance*: government expenditures, government revenue.

SOCIAL AND CULTURAL AFFAIRS
Education: degrees conferred, enrollments, teaching staff; *Health*: hospitals, public health; *Social security*.

Most data are for 1979, with time series of varying lengths. In addition to the national level, data are included for departments. Commentaries, which include discussions of sources, are provided at the beginnings of chapters.

Available from the agency, 6ª Ave. and 8ª Calle, Comayaguela.

Available in microform: CH: 1952-68. CIS: 1972-73, 1975. IDC: 1952-77, lacking parts of 1969 and 1970.

No general statistical bulletin is currently published by Honduras.

JAMAICA

161. *Statistical yearbook.* 1973- Kingston: Department of Statistics.

Agency name changed to the Statistical Institute of Jamaica on April 9, 1984. 1982 edition, published March, 1984, 692 p., contains statistical data in the following areas:

PHYSICAL ENVIRONMENT
Climatology: precipitation, sunshine, temperature; *Geography*: area of land, maps.

DEMOGRAPHY
Population: census results from 1844-1970, distribution by age and sex, distribution by geographic/administrative area, ethnic groups, external migration and indenture immigration 1834-1914; *Vital statistics*: births, including illegitimate births, causes of death, deaths, divorces, infant mortality, life expectancy, marriages.

ECONOMIC AFFAIRS
Agriculture and food: farming, fishing, forestry; *Commerce and business*: cooperatives, exports, factories, imports, tourism; *Finance*: banking and credit, money supply, securities; *Income and expenditure*: consumption, personal income, prices; *Industry*: communication, construction, energy, manufacturing, mining, transportation, water; *National accounts*: balance of payments, gross domestic product, national income; *Public finance*: government expenditures and government revenue for central government and parishes (aggregate only).

POLITICAL AFFAIRS
Elections.

SOCIAL AND CULTURAL AFFAIRS
Cultural and scientific activities: libraries, radio, television; *Education*: educational attainment, enrollment, examination results, graduates of University of West Indies, literacy, teaching staff; *Health*: disease, family planning, hospitals, medical personnel, public health; *Housing*; *Justice*: correctional institutions, courts, crimes, police, traffic accidents; *Labor*: employment and unemployment, Jamaicans on overseas contract work schemes, labor force, labor-management relations; *Religion*; *Social assistance*; *Social security*.

Most data are for 1981 and varying numbers of earlier years. In addition to the national level, data are included for parishes.

Commentaries, which include discussions of sources, are provided at the beginnings of chapters. Notes accompanying the tables indicate the names of the agencies furnishing the data. Special features include a list of official statistical materials, and chapters on the physiography, history and governmental system of the country. There is a detailed list of tables at the beginning of the volume.

Available from the Statistical Institute of Jamaica, 9 Swallowfield Rd, Kingston 5. Priced.

162. **Statistical abstract.** 1947- Kingston: Department of Statistics.

Title varies: 1947-51 as *Quarterly digest of statistics*; 1952-57 as *Digest of statistics*; 1958-67 as *Abstract of statistics*; 1968 as *Annual abstract of statistics*. Agency varies: Name changed to the Statistical Institute of Jamaica on April 9, 1984; 1947-53 issued by the Central Bureau of Statistics.

1980 edition, published Feb., 1982, 194 p., contains statistical data in the following areas:

DEMOGRAPHY
Population: census results from 1970, distribution by age and sex, distribution by geographic/administrative area, external migration, population estimates; *Vital statistics*: births, deaths, divorces, infant mortality, marriages.

ECONOMIC AFFAIRS
Agriculture and food: farming; *Commerce and business*: registered factories, exports, imports, tourism; *Finance*: banking and credit, securities; *Income and expenditure*: prices; *Industry*: communication, energy, manufacturing, mining, transportation; *National accounts*: gross domestic product; *Public finance*: government expenditures, government revenue;

SOCIAL AND CULTURAL AFFAIRS
Cultural and scientific activities: libraries; *Education*: degrees conferred, educational attainment, enrollments, examination results, teaching staff; *Health*: disease, family planning, hospitals, medical personnel, public health; *Housing*; *Justice*: courts, crimes, traffic accidents; *Labor*: employment and unemployment, Jamaicans on overseas contract work schemes, labor force, labor-management relations, occupations; *Social security*.

Most data are for 1980 and the preceding year. In addition to the national level, data are included for parishes. Notes accompanying the tables indicate the names of the agencies furnishing the data.

Available from the address in entry 161. Priced.

Available in microform: CH: 1948-68, 1972-76. IDC: 1947-68, lacking parts of 1947 and 1948.

163. **Quarterly abstract of statistics.** 1961- Kingston: Department of Statistics.

April-June, 1979, published July,1980, 65p., contains statistical data in the following areas:

PHYSICAL ENVIRONMENT
Climatology: precipitation, temperature.

DEMOGRAPHY
Population: arrivals and departures, distribution by geographic/administrative area, external migration; *Vital statistics*: births, deaths, divorces, infant mortality, marriages.

ECONOMIC AFFAIRS
Commerce and business: establishments, exports, imports, tourism; *Finance*: banking and credit; *Income and expenditure*: prices; *Industry*: communication, manufacturing, transportation.

SOCIAL AND CULTURAL AFFAIRS
Health: disease, family planning, hospitals; *Housing*; *Justice*: traffic accidents; *Labor*: employment, occupations, salaries and wages.

Most data are quarterly for 2 quarters and annual for 3 years. Latest data are for the date of the issue. In addition to the national level, data are included for parishes. Notes accompanying the tables indicate the names of the agencies furnishing the data.

Available from the address in entry 161. Priced.

MARTINIQUE

164. ***Annuaire statistique de la Martinique*** [Statistical yearbook of Martinique]. 1952/56- Paris: Institut National de la Statistique et des Etudes Economiques (France); Pointe-à-Pitre: Institut National de la Statistique et des Etudes Economiques (France), Service Interrégional Antilles-Guyane. Irregular. French.

1977/80 edition, published 1983, 178 p., contains statistical data in the following areas:

PHYSICAL ENVIRONMENT
Climatology: precipitation, sunshine, temperature; *Geography*: area and use of land, maps.

DEMOGRAPHY
Population: census results from 1954-1974, distribution by age and sex, distribution by geographic/administrative area, external migration; *Vital statistics*: abortions, births, including illegitimate births, causes of death, deaths, divorces, infant mortality, marriages.

ECONOMIC AFFAIRS
Agriculture and food: farming, fishing, forestry; *Commerce and business*: exports, imports, tourism; *Finance*: banking and credit, money supply; *Income and expenditure*: consumption, prices; *Industry*: communication, construction, energy, manufacturing, transportation; *National accounts*: balance of payments, gross domestic product; *Public finance*: government expenditures and government revenue for the department and communes (aggregate only).

POLITICAL AFFAIRS
Elections.

SOCIAL AND CULTURAL AFFAIRS
Education: enrollments, examination results, teaching staff; *Health*: disease, hospitals, medical personnel, public health; *Justice*: courts, crimes, traffic accidents; *Labor*: employment and unemployment, labor force, salaries and wages; *Social assistance*; *Social security*; *Sports and recreation.*

Most data are for 1980 and the preceding 3 years. In addition to the department level, data are included for communes.

Commentaries are provided at the beginnings of some of the chapters. Notes accompanying the tables indicate the names of the agencies furnishing the data. There is a list of tables at the beginning of the volume.

Available from Institut National de la Statistique et des Etudes Economiques (France), Service Interrégional Antilles-Guyane, Tour Faidherbe 4, Bd. Chanzy, BP 863, 97175, Pointe-à-Pitre or Service Régional de la Martinique, Lotissement Pointe de Jaham Schoelcher, BP 605, 97621, Fort-de-France. Price: F40.

Available in microform: CH: 1952/56-1969/72.

165. *Bulletin statistique* [Statistical bulletin]. 1962- Pointe-à-Pitre: Institut National de la Statistique et des Etudes Economiques (France), Service Interrégional Antilles-Guyane. Quarterly. French.

Title varies slightly.

No. 1, 1984, 24 p., contains statistical data in the following areas:

PHYSICAL ENVIRONMENT
Climatology: precipitation, sunshine, temperature; *Geography*: maps.

DEMOGRAPHY
Population: population estimates; *Vital statistics*: births, including illegitimate births, deaths, divorces, marriages.

ECONOMIC AFFAIRS
Agriculture and food: farming; *Commerce and business*: exports, imports, tourism; *Finance*: banking and credit, money supply; *Income and expenditure*: prices; *Industry*: communication, construction, energy, manufacturing, transportation.

SOCIAL AND CULTURAL AFFAIRS
Labor: employment office activity, salaries and wages; *Social assistance*; *Social security.*

Most data are monthly or quarterly and annual for 2 years. Latest data are for the last month before the date of the issue. Notes accompanying the tables indicate agencies furnishing the data.

Available from the address in entry 164. Price: F25 per issue.

MEXICO

166. *Anuario estadístico de los Estados Unidos Mexicanos* [Statistical yearbook of the United States of Mexico]. 1893- Mexico City: Instituto Nacional de Estadística Geografía e Informática. Spanish.

None published for 1908-24, 1926-29, 1931-37.

Title varies: 1893-1907: *Anuario estadístico de la República Mexicana*; 1925, 1930: *Anuario estadístico*. Agency varies: 1893-1907, 1938-73 by Dirección General de Estadística; 1925, 1930 by Departamento [Autónomo] de la Estadística Nacional; 1974-80 by Coordinación General del Sistema Nacional de Información.

1980 edition, published Jan., 1982, 988 p., is divided into two parts, with the first containing data for the national level and the second data for states. Included in the first part are data in the following areas:

PHYSICAL ENVIRONMENT
Geography: area of land.

DEMOGRAPHY
Population: census results from 1900-1970, distribution by age and sex, external migration; *Vital statistics*: births, causes of death, deaths, divorces, infant mortality, marriages.

ECONOMIC AFFAIRS
Agriculture and food: farming, fishing, forestry; *Commerce and business*: exports, imports, tourism; *Finance*: banking and credit, money in circulation; *Income and expenditure*: consumption, prices; *Industry*: communication, energy, transportation; *National accounts*: balance of payments, gross domestic product; *Public finance*: government expenditures, government revenue.

SOCIAL AND CULTURAL AFFAIRS
Cultural and scientific activities: cinema and performing arts, museums and galleries; *Education*: enrollments, teaching staff; *Housing*; *Justice*: courts, traffic accidents; *Labor*: labor force, labor-management relations, salaries and wages.

Part II offers data on the same topics for individual states, with the following additions: climatological data, internal migration, planning and economic development, and population distribution by geographic area. Omitted are courts, distribution of population by age and sex, energy, exports, external migration, imports, labor force, marriages, money in circulation, national accounts, prices.

Most data are for 1980 and the preceding 4 years, with time series of varying lengths. Notes accompanying the tables indicate the names of the agencies furnishing the data. There is a detailed list of tables at the beginning of each part.

Latest edition published: 1984, 520 p. Available from the Dirección General de Integración y Análisis de la Información, Instituto Nacional de Estadística Geografía e Informática, Secretaría de Programación y Presupuesto, Centeno 670, Col. Granjas México, Delegación Iztacalco, CP 08400, México, D.F. Price: Pesos 2,100.00.

Available in microform: CH: 1893-1904, 1906-07, 1930, 1938-45, 1951-69.

167. *Agenda estadística* [Statistical agenda]. 1966- Mexico City: Instituto Nacional de Estadística Geografía e Informática. Annual. Spanish.

Covers most of the same topics as entry 166.

Latest edition: 1984, 237 p. Available from the address in entry 166. Price: Pesos 340.00.

168. **Anuario estadístico compendiado de los Estados Unidos Mexicanos* [Annual statistical compendium of the United Mexican States]. 1964-75. Mexico City: Dirección General de Estadística. Biennial after 1966. Spanish.

Title varies slightly.

Less detailed coverage of the same topics as entry 166.

Available in microform: CIS: 1970/71, 1972. IDC: 1941-76.

No general monthly or quarterly statistical bulletin is currently published by Mexico.

MONTSERRAT

169. *Statistical digest.* 1973- Plymouth: Statistics Office. Irregular.

No. 8, 1979 edition, published Dec., 1980, 167 p., contains statistical data in the following areas:

PHYSICAL ENVIRONMENT
Climatology: precipitation, sunshine, temperature.

DEMOGRAPHY
Population: arrivals and departures, census results from 1871-1970, distribution by age and sex, distribution by geographic/administrative area, external migration, households and families, population estimates, race.*Vital statistics*: births, causes of death, deaths, fertility, infant mortality, life expectancy, marriages.

ECONOMIC AFFAIRS
Agriculture and food: farming, fishing; *Commerce and business*: exports, imports, tourism; *Finance*: banking and credit, money supply; *Income and expenditure*: consumption, prices; *Industry*: communication, energy, transportation, water; *National accounts*: gross domestic product; *Public finance*: government expenditures, government revenue.

SOCIAL AND CULTURAL AFFAIRS
Education: educational attainment, enrollments, examination results; *Health*: hospitals; *Housing*; *Justice*: courts, crimes, traffic accidents; *Labor*: employment, labor-management relations, occupations; *Religion*.

Most data are for 1979 and the preceding 9 years. In addition to the central government data are provided by parish.

Notes accompanying the tables indicate the names of the agencies furnishing the data. A list of official statistical materials and a detailed list of tables are provided at the beginning of the volume. The Constitution, judicial and financial system, religion, and mass media of the country are described in the introductory section.

Available from the agency. Government Headquarters, PO Box 292, Plymouth. Available in microform: CH: 1974-76.

No general statistical bulletin for Montserrat has been found.

NETHERLANDS ANTILLES

170. ***Statistical yearbook.*** 1956-74; 1981- Willemstad: Centraal Bureau voor de Statistiek. English.

Not published 1962, 1964.

1981 edition, published Nov., 1982, 71 p., contains statistical data in the following areas:

PHYSICAL ENVIRONMENT
Climatology: precipitation, sunshine, temperature; *Geography*: area of land.

DEMOGRAPHY
Population: arrivals and departures, census results from 1972, distribution by age, distribution by geographic/administrative area, external migration, population projections.*Vital statistics*: births, causes of death, deaths, divorces, life expectancy, marriages.

ECONOMIC AFFAIRS
Commerce and business: exports, imports, tourism; *Finance*: banking and credit; *Income and expenditure*: prices; *Industry*: communication, construction, transportation; *National accounts*: balance of payments; *Public finance*: government revenue.

POLITICAL AFFAIRS
Elections.

SOCIAL AND CULTURAL AFFAIRS
Cultural and scientific activities: radio, television; *Education*: educational attainment of unemployed only, enrollments, teaching staff; *Health*: disease, family planning, hospitals, medical personnel; *Housing*; *Justice*: crimes, traffic accidents; *Labor*: employment and unemployment, labor-management relations, salaries and wages; *Religion*; *Social security*.

Most data are for 1980 and the preceding 2 to 6 years. In addition to the national level, data are included for islands. There is a section of comparative statistics from selected foreign countries.

Notes accompanying the tables indicate the names of the agencies furnishing the data. A detailed list of tables and a list of official statistical materials are provided at the beginning of the volume.

Available from the agency, Plaza Piar, Willemstad, Curacao. Price NAf10.

Available in microform: CH: 1956-71, 1965-71. CIS: 1970-71, 1974.

171. **Statistische Mededelingen** [Statistical Information]. 1952- Willemstad: Centraal Bureau voor de Statistiek. Monthly. Dutch, with a list of table headings in English and Spanish.

V. 31, no.4, 1983, 76 p., contains statistical data in the following areas:

PHYSICAL ENVIRONMENT
Climatology: precipitation, temperature.

DEMOGRAPHY
Population: distribution by geographic/administrative area; *Vital statistics*: births, deaths, divorces, marriages.

ECONOMIC AFFAIRS
Agriculture and food: farming; *Commerce and business*: exports, imports, tourism; *Finance*: banking and credit, money supply; *Income and expenditure*: prices; *Industry*: construction, energy, transportation, water; *Public finance*: government revenue.

SOCIAL AND CULTURAL AFFAIRS
Health: disease; *Housing*; *Justice*: crimes, traffic accidents.*Social security*.

Most data are monthly for current and preceding year and annual for 11 years. Latest data are for 3 months before the date of the issue. In addition to the national level, data are included for islands. There is also a section of comparative data for selected countries.

Explanatory notes are provided at the end of the issue in Dutch, English and Spanish. Notes accompanying the tables indicate the names of the agencies furnishing the data. There is a detailed list of tables at the beginning of the issue and publications of the agency are listed at the end of the issue.

Available from the address in entry 170. Price: NAf30 per annum.

NICARAGUA

172. **Anuario estadístico de Nicaragua** [Statistical yearbook of Nicaragua]. 1938- Managua: Instituto Nacional de Estadística y Censos. Spanish.

Not published 1948-67.

Agency varies: 1938-68: Dirección General de Estadística [y Censos]; 1969-73: Ministerio de Economía, Industria y Commercio and Banco Central de Nicaragua; 1974-79: Oficina Ejecutiva de Encuestas y Censos.

1982 edition, published Aug., 1983, 259 p., contains statistical data in the following areas:

PHYSICAL ENVIRONMENT
Climatology: precipitation, temperature; *Geography*: area and use of land.

DEMOGRAPHY
Population: census results from 1778-1971, distribution by age and sex, distribution by geographic/administrative area, external migration, population estimates and projections; *Vital statistics*: births, deaths, divorces, infant mortality, marriages.

ECONOMIC AFFAIRS
Agriculture and food: farming, fishing, forestry; *Commerce and business*: domestic commerce, exports, imports; *Finance*: banking and credit; *Income and expenditure*: consumption, prices; *Industry*: communication, construction, energy, manufacturing, mining, transportation, water; *National accounts*: gross domestic product; *Public finance*: government expenditures, government revenue.

SOCIAL AND CULTURAL AFFAIRS
Cultural and scientific activities: cinema and performing arts, libraries; *Education*: degrees conferred, enrollments, teaching staff; *Health*: hospitals, medical personnel, public health; *Justice*: courts, crimes, traffic accidents; *Labor*: employment, labor force, labor-management relations, salaries and wages; *Social assistance*; *Social security*; *Sports and recreation*.

Most data are for 1982 and varying numbers of earlier years. In addition to the national level, data are included for departments and municipalities.

Commentaries are provided at the beginnings of chapters. Notes accompanying the tables indicate the names of the agencies furnishing the data. There is a detailed list of tables at the beginning of the volume and an alphabetical subject index at the end.

Historical statistics. Statistics for earlier periods may also be found in two compilations, *Compendio estadístico, 1965-1974* [Statistical compendium, 1965-1974], 487 p., published by the Oficina Ejecutiva de Encuestas y Censos in 1976; and *Resumen estadístico, 1950-1960,* [Statistical summary, 1950-1960], published by the Dirección General de Estadística y Censos in 1960.

Latest edition published: 1983. Available from the agency, Apartado 4031, Managua. Price: $U.S.40.00.

Available in microform: CH: 1939-45, 1947. IDC: 1939-47, 1968, 1971-72.

173. **Boletín de estadística** [Bulletin of statistics]. 1944- Managua: Dirección General de Estadística y Censos. Frequency varies. Spanish.

For agency variations, see entry 172.

Jan.-June, 1970, 147 p., contains statistical data in the following areas:

PHYSICAL ENVIRONMENT
Climatology: precipitation, sunshine, temperature; *Geography*: area of land.

DEMOGRAPHY
Population: distribution by sex, distribution by geographic/administrative area.

ECONOMIC AFFAIRS
Agriculture and food: farming; *Commerce and business*: exports, imports; *Finance*: banking and credit, money in circulation; *Income and expenditure*: consumption, prices; *Industry*: communication, construction, energy, mining, transportation; *Public finance*: government expenditures, government revenue.

SOCIAL AND CULTURAL AFFAIRS
Education: enrollments, teaching staff; *Labor*: labor force, salaries and wages.

Most data are monthly or quarterly for the dates of the issue and the preceding year. In addition to the national level, data are included for departments and municipalities. There is a detailed list of tables at the beginning of each section.

Available from the address given in entry 172.

PANAMA

174. **Panamá en cifras** [Panama in figures]. 1953- Panama: Dirección de Estadistística y Censo. Spanish.

Title varies: 1953, 1958 as *Nuestro progreso en cifras*. Some years subtitled *Compendio estadístico*.

1982 edition, published Nov., 1983, 259 p., contains statistical data in the following areas:

PHYSICAL ENVIRONMENT
Climatology: precipitation, temperature.

DEMOGRAPHY
Population: arrivals and departures, census results from 1911-1980, distribution by age and sex, distribution by geographic/administrative area, external migration, internal migration; *Vital statistics*: births, causes of death, deaths, divorces, infant mortality, life expectancy, marriages.

ECONOMIC AFFAIRS
Agriculture and food: farming, fishing; *Commerce and business*: domestic commerce, establishments, exports, imports, services; *Finance*: banking and credit, securities; *Income and expenditure*: consumption, personal income, prices; *Industry*: communication, construction, energy, manufacturing, transportation; *National accounts*: balance of payments, gross domestic product, national income; *Public finance*: government expenditures and government revenue for central and local government (latter aggregated by province).

POLITICAL AFFAIRS
Elections.

SOCIAL AND CULTURAL AFFAIRS
Education: educational attainment, enrollments, graduates at all levels, literacy, teaching staff; *Health*: disease, hospitals, medical personnel, public health; *Housing*; *Justice*:

courts, crimes, traffic accidents; *Labor*: employment, underemployment and unemployment, labor force, occupations, salaries and wages; *Social assistance*; *Social security*. Most data are for 1982 and the preceding 4 years. In addition to the national level, data are included for provinces and cities.

Notes accompanying the tables indicate the names of the agencies furnishing the data. There is a detailed list of tables at the beginning of the volume.

Historical statistics. Statistics for earlier periods may be found in *Estadística anual*, 1908-11; *Compendio estadístico descriptivo de la República de Panamá...*, 1917, 220 p., published by the Dirección General de Estadística (the latter offers figures for 1914-1916 with time series to 1907 or 1908 in some cases); and *Extracto estadístico de la República de Panamá*, 1941/43-1953/54, published by the Dirección de Estadística y Censos.

Latest edition published: 1983, 275 p. Available from the agency, Contraloría General de la República, Apartado 5213, Panama 5. Price: B 0.75; $ U.S. 0.75.

Available in microform: CH: 1958/62-1968/72. CIS: 1970-75, 1977-79. IDC: 1955-76. CH also offers *Estadística anual*, 1908-10, by the Dirección General de Estadística and *Compendio estadístico descriptivo de la República de Panamá...*, published by the Dirección General de Estadística. Both CH and IDC offer the *Extracto estadístico de la República de Panamá*, 1941/43-1953/54, by the Dirección de Estadística y Censos (1953/54 lacking from CH).

No general statistical bulletin is currently published by Panama.

PARAGUAY

175. **Anuario estadístico del Paraguay** [Statistical yearbook of Paraguay]. 1886- Asunción: Dirección General de Estadística y Censos. Spanish.

Title varies: 1886-1913 as *Memoria*. Agency varies: 1886-1926 by Oficina General de Estadística; 1925/26-1946/47 by Dirección General de Estadística.

1979 edition, published Nov., 1980, 140 p., contains statistical data in the following areas:

PHYSICAL ENVIRONMENT
Climatology: precipitation, sunshine, temperature; *Geography*: area of land, maps.

DEMOGRAPHY
Population: census results from 1972, distribution by age and sex, distribution by geographic/administrative area, external migration, population estimates and projections; *Vital statistics*: births, including illegitimate births, deaths, infant mortality, marriages.

ECONOMIC AFFAIRS
Agriculture and food: farming, forestry; *Commerce and business*: domestic commerce, exports, imports, tourism; *Finance*: banking and credit, money supply; *Income and*

expenditure: consumption; *Industry*: communication, construction, energy, manufacturing, transportation, water.

SOCIAL AND CULTURAL AFFAIRS
Education: degrees conferred, enrollments, examination results, literacy, teaching staff; *Health*: disease, hospitals, public health; *Justice*: correctional institutions, courts, crimes, traffic accidents; *Labor*: employment; *Social security*.

Latest data are for 1979. Time series of varying lengths are provided. In addition to the national level, data are included for departments and municipalities.

Notes accompanying the tables indicate the names of the agencies furnishing the data and sometimes include titles of sources. There is a list of tables at the beginning of the volume.

Available from the agency, Humaitá 473, Asunción.

Available in microform: CH: 1916-17, 1928-29, 1935-69. CIS: 1970-74, 1976.

176. *Boletín estadístico del Paraguay* [Statistical bulletin of Paraguay]. 1957- Asunción: Dirección General de Estadístico y Censos. Semi-annual; earlier quarterly. Spanish. July-Dec., 1971 edition, published Jan., 1973, 54 p., contains statistical data in the following areas:

PHYSICAL ENVIRONMENT
Climatology: precipitation, temperature; *Geography*: maps.

DEMOGRAPHY
Population: external migration, population estimates and projections; *Vital statistics*: births, including illegitimate births, deaths, infant mortality, marriages.

ECONOMIC AFFAIRS
Commerce and business: exports, imports, tourism; *Finance*: banking and credit, money supply; *Income and expenditure*: prices; *Industry*: communication, energy, transportation.

SOCIAL AND CULTURAL AFFAIRS
Education: enrollments, literacy, teaching staff; *Justice*: correctional institutions.

Most data are monthly for the dates of the issue. Time series of varying lengths are provided. In addition to the national level, data are included for departments. Notes accompanying the tables indicate the names of the agencies furnishing the data.

Available from the address given in entry 175.

PERU

177. *Compendio estadístico* [Statistical compendium]. 1982?- Lima: Oficina Nacional de Estadística y Censos. Spanish.

1982 edition, published July, 1983, 124 p., contains statistical data in the following areas:

PHYSICAL ENVIRONMENT
Geography: area and use of land, maps.

DEMOGRAPHY
Population: census results from 1961-1981, distribution by age and sex, distribution by geographic/administrative area, population estimates; *Vital statistics*: births, deaths, fertility, infant mortality, life expectancy.

ECONOMIC AFFAIRS
Agriculture and food: farming, fishing; *Commerce and business*: exports, imports, tourism; *Finance*: banking and credit, money supply; *Income and expenditure*: consumption, prices; *Industry*: communication, energy, manufacturing, mining, transportation; *National accounts*: balance of payments, gross domestic product; *Public finance*: government expenditures, government revenue.

SOCIAL AND CULTURAL AFFAIRS
Cultural and scientific activities: libraries, museums and galleries; *Education*: enrollments, teaching staff; *Health*: hospitals, medical personnel, public health; *Housing*; *Justice*: correctional institutions, traffic accidents; *Labor*: employment, underemployment and unemployment, labor force, labor-management relations, salaries and wages; *Social security*; *Sports and recreation*.

Most data are for 1982 and varying numbers of earlier years. In addition to the national level, data are included for departments and provinces. Commentaries are provided at the beginnings of chapters. Notes accompanying the tables indicate the names of the agencies furnishing the data and there is a detailed list of tables at the beginning of the volume.

Available from the agency, avenida 28 de julio 1056, Lima 1. Price: $U.S.15.00.

178. **Anuario estadístico del Perú** [Statistical yearbook of Peru]. 1919- Lima: Oficina Nacional de Estadística y Censos. Irregular. Spanish.

Agency varies: 1949-54 by Dirección Nacional de Estadística. Continues *Extracto estadístico del Perú*, 1918-1943, published y the Dirección de Estadística.

V. 29 (13A of new series), 1971, edition, 3 v., with economic and financial statistics in v. 1, social statistics in v. 2 and geographic data in v. 3. Included are statistical data in the following areas:

PHYSICAL ENVIRONMENT
Climatology: precipitation, temperature; *Geography*: area of land, maps.

DEMOGRAPHY
Population: census results from 1940-1972, distribution by age and sex, distribution by geographic/administrative area, external migration, internal migration; *Vital statistics*: births, deaths.

ECONOMIC AFFAIRS
Agriculture and food: farming, fishing, forestry; *Commerce and business*: domestic commerce, exports, imports, tourism; *Finance*: banking and credit, securities; *Industry*: communication, construction, energy, mining, transportation; *National accounts*: bal-

ance of payments, gross domestic and gross national product, national income; *Public finance*: government expenditures and government revenue for the central government and municipalities.

SOCIAL AND CULTURAL AFFAIRS
Cultural and scientific activities: journals, libraries, museums and galleries, newspapers, radio, television; *Education*: enrollments, literacy, teaching staff; *Health*: disease, hospitals, medical personnel, public health; *Housing*; *Justice*: crimes; *Labor*: employment and unemployment, labor force, labor-management relations, occupations; *Social security*.

Most data are for 1971 and 1970, plus varying numbers of earlier years. In addition to the national level, data are included for departments, provinces, districts and municipalities.

Notes accompanying some of the tables indicate the names of the agencies furnishing the data. There are detailed lists of tables at the beginning of the first 2 volumes.

Available in microform: CH: 1944/45-1965, and 1923-24, 1926-43 of *Extracto estadístico*, of the Dirección de Estadística.

179. ***Informe estadístico*** [Statistical report]. ?1965- Lima: Oficina Nacional de Estadística. Quarterly. Spanish.

Continues: *Boletín de estadística peruana*, 1958-64?, published by the Dirección Nacional de Estadística.

Segundo trimestre [second quarter], 1984, 102 p., contains statistical data in the following areas:

DEMOGRAPHY
Vital statistics: births, deaths, fertility, infant mortality, life expectancy.

ECONOMIC AFFAIRS
Agriculture and food: farming, fishing; *Commerce and business*: domestic commerce, exports, imports; *Finance*: banking and credit, money supply; *Income and expenditure*: prices; *Industry*: construction, energy, manufacturing, mining; *National accounts*: balance of payments, gross domestic product; *Public finance*: government expenditures, government revenue.

SOCIAL AND CULTURAL AFFAIRS
Education: enrollments; *Health*: hospitals, public health; *Labor*: employment, unemployment and under-employment, labor force, labor-management relations, salaries and wages.

Most data are quarterly or monthly for the current year and varying numbers of earlier years. Latest data are for the date of the issue. In addition to the national level, data are included for departments.

Notes accompanying the tables indicate the names of the agencies furnishing the data. There is a detailed list of tables at the end of the issue.

Available from the address given in entry 177. Priced.

Available in microform: CH: 1958-62 of *Boletín de estadística Peruana*.

PUERTO RICO

180. ***Anuario estadístico*** [Statistical yearbook]. 1948/49-1976. San Juan: Junta de Planificación/ Planning Board, Negociado de Analisis y Proyecciones Económicas/ Bureau of Economic Analysis and Projections. Spanish and English.

Agency varies: Earlier years by Bureau of Economics and Statistics, Economic Development Administration, and Department of Agriculture and Commerce.
1976 edition, published Nov., 1977, 209 p., contains statistical data in the following areas:

PHYSICAL ENVIRONMENT
Climatology: precipitation, temperature.

DEMOGRAPHY
Population: arrivals and departures, census results from 1940-1975, distribution by age and sex, distribution by geographic/administrative area, population estimates; *Vital statistics*: births, including illegitimate births, causes of death, deaths, divorces, infant mortality, marriages.

ECONOMIC AFFAIRS
Agriculture and food: farming; *Commerce and business*: cooperatives, domestic commerce, establishments, exports, imports, tourism; *Finance*: banking and credit; *Income and expenditure*: consumption, personal income, prices; *Industry*: communication, construction, energy, manufacturing, transportation, water; *National accounts*: balance of payments, gross national product, national income; *Public finance*: government expenditures, government revenue.

SOCIAL AND CULTURAL AFFAIRS
Education: enrollments; *Health*: disease, hospitals, medical personnel, public health; *Housing*; *Justice*: crimes, police, traffic accidents; *Labor*: employment, labor force, labor-management relations, salaries and wages; *Social assistance*; *Social security*.

Most data are for 1976 and the preceding 2 years. Time series of varying lengths are provided. In addition to the Commonwealth, data are included for municipalities.

Notes accompanying the tables indicate the names of the agencies furnishing the data. There is a detailed list of tables at the beginning of the volume and an alphabetical subject index at the end.

Historical statistics. Historical statistics may be found in *Anuario estadístico: estadísticas históricas /Statistical yearbook, historical statistics,* 396 p., published by the Bureau of Economics and Statistics in 1959. Most tables include figures from the 1940s to 1955/56, with some time series to 1900 included.

A new edition extending coverage through 1981 is in process of preparation and will be available from the Junta de Planificación, Negociado de Estadísticas, Apartado 41119, San Juan, 00940-9985.

Available in microform: CH: 1948/49-64, 1966-70. IDC: 1948/49-52, 1954, 1956-62, 1964.

No general statistical bulletin is currently published for Puerto Rico.

See also entries under UNITED STATES.

SAINT CHRISTOPHER AND NEVIS

181. ***Annual digest of statistics.*** 1965?- Basseterre: Statistical Office Planning Unit.

1981 edition, published Aug., 1982, 87 p., contains statistical data in the following areas:

PHYSICAL ENVIRONMENT
Climatology: precipitation, temperature.

DEMOGRAPHY
Population: arrivals and departures, census results from 1871-1980, distribution by age and sex, distribution by geographic/administrative area, population estimates; *Vital statistics*: births, deaths, infant mortality.

ECONOMIC AFFAIRS
Agriculture and food: farming; *Commerce and business*: exports, imports, tourism; *Finance*: banking and credit; *Income and expenditure*: consumption, prices; *Industry*: communication, energy, manufacturing, transportation; *National accounts*: gross domestic product; *Public finance*: government expenditures, government revenue.

SOCIAL AND CULTURAL AFFAIRS
Education: enrollments; *Justice*: traffic accidents; *Labor*: employment.

Most data are for 1981 and varying numbers of earlier years. In addition to the national level, data are included for islands and parishes.

Notes accompanying the tables indicate the names of the agencies furnishing the data and there is a detailed list of tables at the beginning of the volume.

Available from the agency, Basseterre. Price: $U.S.10.00

No general statistical bulletin has been found for Saint Christopher and Nevis.

SAINT LUCIA

182. ***Annual statistical digest.*** 1966- Castries: Development, Planning and Statistics Division.

Agency name varies: Current name is Statistical Department.

1975 edition, 57 p., contains statistical data in the following areas:

PHYSICAL ENVIRONMENT
Climatology: precipitation, temperature; *Geography*: area and use of land, maps.

DEMOGRAPHY
Population: arrivals and departures, census results from 1843-1970, distribution by age and sex, population estimates.*Vital statistics*: births, including illegitimate births, causes of death, deaths, divorces, infant mortality, marriages.

ECONOMIC AFFAIRS
Agriculture and food: farming, forestry; *Commerce and business*: exports, imports; *Finance*: banking and credit; *Income and expenditure*: consumption, prices; *Industry*: communication, construction, energy, manufacturing, transportation; *Public finance*: government expenditures, government revenue.

SOCIAL AND CULTURAL AFFAIRS
Education: enrollments, examination results, teaching staff; *Health*: disease, hospitals, medical personnel, public health; *Housing*; *Justice*: correctional institutions, crimes, traffic accidents; *Labor*: employment, foreign workers, labor force, occupations, salaries and wages.

Most data are for 1975 and varying numbers of earlier years. Some monthly data are provided. Notes accompanying the tables indicate the names of the agencies furnishing the data and there is a detailed list of tables at the beginning of the volume.

Latest edition published: 1983. Available from the Government Printing Office, Castries. Priced.

Available in microform: CH: 1966-71, 1974. CIS: 1971, 1974.

No general statistical bulletin has been found for Saint Lucia.

SAINT VINCENT AND THE GRENADINES

183. ***Digest of statistics.*** 1959- St. Vincent: Statistical Unit.

Title varies: 1959-61 as *Quarterly digest of statistics.*

No. 32, 1984, published April, 1984, 63 p., contains statistical data in the following areas:

PHYSICAL ENVIRONMENT
Climatology: precipitation, temperature.

DEMOGRAPHY
Population: arrivals and departures, population estimates; *Vital statistics*: births, causes of death, deaths.

ECONOMIC AFFAIRS
Agriculture and food: farming; *Commerce and business*: exports, imports, tourism; *Income and expenditure*: prices; *Industry*: construction, energy, manufacturing; *National accounts*: gross domestic product; *Public finance*: government expenditures, government revenue.

POLITICAL AFFAIRS
Elections.

SOCIAL AND CULTURAL AFFAIRS
Education: enrollments, examination results, teaching staff; *Health*: hospitals; *Justice*: correctional institutions, crimes, traffic accidents.

Most data are for 1982 and the preceding 4 years. Some data by major census division are presented. Notes accompanying most of the tables indicate the names of the agencies furnishing the data.

Available from the agency, Kingstown.

Available in microform: CH: 1960, 1962-63, 1965, 1967-73.

No general statistical bulletin is currently published for Saint Vincent and the Grenadines.

SURINAM

184. ***Vijf en twintig jaren Centrale Bank van Suriname**: Verslag over 1981 tevens Jubileum-verslag 1957-1982* [Twenty-five years of the Central Bank of Surinam...]. Paramaribo: Centrale Bank van Suriname, 1982. 213 p. and annexes. Dutch.

Part II contains statistical data in the following areas:

DEMOGRAPHY
Population: census results from 1964-1980, distribution by age and sex, external migration; *Vital statistics*: births, deaths.

ECONOMIC AFFAIRS
Agriculture and food: farming, forestry; *Commerce and business*: exports, imports; *Finance*: banking and credit, money supply; *Income and expenditure*: prices; *Industry*: mining; *National accounts*: balance of payments, gross domestic and gross national product; *Public finance*: government expenditures, government revenue, planning and economic development.

SOCIAL AND CULTURAL AFFAIRS
Education: literacy; *Health*: disease, medical personnel, public health; *Labor*: labor market.

Most data are for 1957-1982. Commentaries are intermixed with data. Notes accompanying the tables indicate the names of the agencies furnishing the data. There is a detailed list of tables at the beginning of Part II.

Available from the Bank, Waterkant, Paramaribo.

185. **Jaarcijfers voor Suriname* [Statistical yearbook of Surinam]. 1956/60-1961/65. Paramaribo: Algemeen Bureau voor de Statistiek. Dutch and English.

The 1956-60 edition covers area and climate, population, economic affairs, education, health, housing, justice, labor, religion and social assistance. Data are for the years in the title. Breakdowns by district are included and sources are noted at the foot of tables.

Available in microform: CH: 1956-65.

No general statistical bulletin is currently published by Surinam.

TRINIDAD AND TOBAGO

186. *Annual statistical digest.* 1935/51- Port of Spain: Central Statistical Office.

No. 28, 1981, 227 p., contains statistical data in the following areas:

PHYSICAL ENVIRONMENT
Climatology: precipitation, sunshine, temperature; *Geography*: area and use of land.

DEMOGRAPHY
Population: arrivals and departures, census results from 1851-1970, distribution by age and sex, distribution by geographic/administrative area, ethnic groups, external migration, households and families, internal migration, population estimates and projections; *Vital statistics*: births, including illegitimate births, causes of death, deaths, divorces, infant mortality, life expectancy, marriages.

ECONOMIC AFFAIRS
Agriculture and food: farming, forestry; *Commerce and business*: companies, exports, imports, tourism; *Finance*: banking and credit, money supply; *Income and expenditure*: prices; *Industry*: communication, construction, energy, manufacturing, mining, transportation, water; *National accounts*: balance of payments, gross domestic product; *Public finance*: government expenditures, government revenue.

POLITICAL AFFAIRS
Elections.

SOCIAL AND CULTURAL AFFAIRS
Cultural and scientific activities: cinema and performing arts, newspapers; *Education*: educational attainment, enrollments, examination results, literacy, teaching staff, University of West Indies graduates; *Health*: disease, hospitals, public health; *Housing*; *Justice*: correctional institutions, courts (juvenile only), crimes, traffic accidents; *Labor*: employment and unemployment, labor force, labor-management relations, productivity, salaries and wages; *Religion*; *Social assistance*; *Social security*.

Most data are for 1981, with 10-year time series wherever possible. In addition to the national level, data are included for administrative areas. Tables are accompanied by symbols indicating the names of the agencies furnishing the data; the key to the symbols is found at the beginning of the volume. There is a detailed list of tables at the beginning of the volume.

Available from the agency, Textel Building, 1 Edward St., PO Box 98, Port of Spain. Priced.

Available in microform: CH: 1935/51-1973/74. CIS: 1970-1973/74, 1976/77.

No general statistical bulletin is currently published for Trinidad and Tobago.

UNITED STATES

187. **Statistical abstract of the United States.** 1878- Washington, D. C.: Bureau of the Census. Annual, except 1982 and 1983 published in 1 volume.

Agency varies: 1878-1902 by the Bureau of Statistics (Treasury Dept.); 1903-11 by the Bureau of Statistics (Dept. of Commerce and Labor); 1912-37 by the Bureau of Foreign and Domestic Commerce.

105th ed., 1985, 991 p. [Supt. of Docs. no.: C 3.134], contains statistical data in the following areas:

PHYSICAL ENVIRONMENT
Climatology: precipitation, sunshine, temperature; *Environmental quality*: air quality, endangered species, national parks, pesticide use, pollution abatement expenditure, river quality, solid waste disposal; *Geography*: area of land and water, use of land, maps.

DEMOGRAPHY
Population: census results from 1790-1980, distribution by age and sex, distribution by geographic/ administrative area, ethnic groups and ancestry, external migration, households and families, internal migration, population estimates and projections, refugees; *Vital statistics*: abortions, births, including illegitimate births, causes of death, deaths, divorces, fertility, infant and maternal mortality, life expectancy, marriages.

ECONOMIC AFFAIRS
Agriculture and food: farming, fishing, forestry; *Commerce and business*: companies, including multinationals, domestic commerce, exports, imports, services, tourism; *Finance*: banking and credit, money supply, securities; *Income and expenditure*: consumption, family, household, and personal income, poverty status, prices; *Industry*: communication, construction, energy, manufacturing, mining, transportation, water; *National accounts*: balance of payments, gross domestic and gross national product, national income; *Public finance*: government expenditures and government revenue for federal government, states and local governments.

POLITICAL AFFAIRS
Defense; *Elections*; *Foreign aid*.

SOCIAL AND CULTURAL AFFAIRS
Cultural and scientific activities: books and journals, cinema and performing arts, computers, copyright and patents, libraries, museums and galleries, newspapers, radio, television, science and research; *Education*: degrees conferred, educational attainment, enrollments, examination results, literacy, teaching staff; *Health*: alcohol, drug and cigarette use, average heights and weights, disease, family planning, hospitals, medical personnel, public health; *Housing*; *Justice*: correctional institutions, courts, crimes, police, traffic accidents; *Labor*: employment and unemployment, foreign workers, labor force, labor-management relations, occupations, productivity, salaries and wages; *Religion*; *Social assistance and philanthropy*; *Social security*; *Sports and recreation*.

Most data are for 1983 and varying numbers of earlier years. In addition to the national level, many tables include data for one or more of the following: regions; states; selected cities and metropolitan areas; outlying areas; foreign countries. The following special sections for geographical areas are also provided: (1) Section 32: outlying areas of the U.S. (American Samoa, Guam, Northern Marianas, Puerto Rico, Trust Territory of the Pacific Islands and the Virgin Islands); (2) Section 33: selected foreign countries; (3) Appendix V: states (presents rankings for 50 data items selected from tables published elsewhere in the *Abstract*, with citations to tables furnishing the original information); (4) Appendix II: metropolitan areas (included are definitions of the various types of metropolitan areas, metropolitan statistical areas (MSAs), consolidated metropolitan areas (CMSAs) and primary metropolitan statistical areas (PSMAs), and an alphabetical list of MSAs and their components as of June 30, 1984, together with their population as of July 1, 1983).

Explanations at the beginnings of sections offer definitions of concepts, descriptions of sources, and methodological notes. Notes accompanying the tables give authors and titles of published sources and names of agencies furnishing unpublished data. Information on methodology and sources is also found in Appendixes III and IV. The former contains a table describing the principal sample surveys and censuses used as sources. Included are the name of the survey or census and the agency responsible for it, the frequency with which it is conducted, the numbers of the *Abstract* tables for which it served as a source, the types of data it includes and the universe it covers, and the types of data collection operations and procedures it utilizes. In addition, the table includes information on errors and sources for additional information. Arrangement is by broad subject category. Appendix IV lists the authors and titles of the primary sources of statistics in the U.S., both official and non-official, in alphabetical subject arrangement. Appendix IV lists the most recent statistical abstract or equivalent published for each state since 1974.

There is a detailed list of tables at the beginning of the volume; selected tables added in this edition are noted in the preface. A comprehensive alphabetical subject index is also provided.

Other special features include a section at the beginning of the volume, entitled 'Recent trends', offering tables, charts and graphs with data from selected years from 1970 to 1983 on major topics. Titles and prices of supplements to the *Abstract* are listed inside the back cover and include three supplements offering more geographic and historical detail, the *County and city data book* (latest ed., 1983); *State and metropolitan area data book* (latest ed., 1982, with a new edition scheduled for publication in late 1985), and the historical statistics supplement described below. Other supplements are: *Pocket data book, U.S.A.* (latest edition, 1979); a monthly 3» by 5 card, *U.S.A. statistics at a glance*,; and a leaflet distributed with the abstract, but also available separately, *USA Statistics in brief.*

Historical statistics. Statistics for earlier periods are found in *Historical statistics: Colonial times to 1970,* 1975, 2 v. (House document 93-78, 93rd Congress, 1st Session). Notes at the heads of tables in the *Abstract* indicate where earlier information may be found in *Historical statistics,* and Appendix I of the *Abstract* indicates where information updating time series in *Historical statistics*, may be found in the *Abstract*, in cases where comparable or related data exist for one or more years later than 1970.

Latest edition published: 1986, 985 p. Available from GPO, Washington, D.C. 20402. Paper: $22.00 domestic; $27.50 foreign. Cloth: $27.00, domestic; $33.75, foreign.

Available in microform: Brookhaven Press: 1878-1972. University Microfilms: 1878- . Princeton Microfilm Corp.: 1878-1973. William S. Hein: 1878-1973.

No general statistical bulletin is published for the United States.

URUGUAY

188. ***Anuario estadístico*** [Statistical yearbook]. 1884- Montevideo: Dirección General de Estadística y Censos. Irregular. Spanish.

Not published 1971-1980, 1982.

Title varies: 1844-1944 as *Anuario estadístico de la República Oriental del Uruguay*. Agency varies: 1884-96 by Dirección de Estadística General; 1897-1944 by Dirección General de Estadística.

1983 edition, v. p., contains statistical data in the following areas:

PHYSICAL ENVIRONMENT
Climatology: precipitation, sunshine, temperature; *Geography*: area of land.

DEMOGRAPHY
Population: census results from 1908, 1963, 1975, distribution by age and sex, distribution by geographic/administrative area, external migration, internal migration, population estimates and projections; *Vital statistics*: births, including illegitimate births, causes of death, deaths, divorces, infant mortality, life expectancy, marriages.

ECONOMIC AFFAIRS
Agriculture and food: farming, fishing; *Commerce and business*: establishments, exports, imports, tourism; *Finance*: banking and credit, money supply, securities; *Income and expenditure*: consumption, prices; *Industry*: communication, construction, energy, manufacturing, mining, transportation, water; *National accounts*: balance of payments, gross domestic and gross national product, national income; *Public finance*: government expenditures and government revenue for central government and for municipalities (aggregate for each department), planning and urban development.

POLITICAL AFFAIRS
Elections.

SOCIAL AND CULTURAL AFFAIRS
Cultural and scientific activities: cinema and performing arts, libraries, museums and galleries, radio, television; *Education*: degrees conferred, educational attainment, enrollments, literacy, teaching staff; *Health*: disease, hospitals, public health; *Housing*; *Justice*: crimes, traffic accidents; *Labor*: employment and unemployment, labor force, salaries and wages; *Social assistance*; *Social security*; *Sports and recreation*.

Most data are for 1979-82 and varying numbers of earlier years. The 1981 edition provided figures for the period 1970-1978. In addition to the national level, data are included for departments and municipalities. Notes accompanying the tables indicate the names of the agencies furnishing the data. There are detailed lists of tables at the beginning of each section.

Available from the agency, Cuareim, 2052, Montevideo.

Available in microform: CH: 1884-89, 1891-1901, 1904-42, 1945-1967/69.

No general statistical bulletin is currently published for Uruguay.

VENEZUELA

189. ***Anuario estadístico*** [Statistical yearbook]. 1877-1912, 1938- Caracas: Oficina Central de Estadística e Informática. Irregular. Spanish.

    Not published 1879-83, 1885-86, 1888, 1890, 1892-93, 1895-1907.

    Agency varies: 1877-91 by Dirección de Estadística, 1894 by Dirección de Estadística y Immigración, 1908-48 by Dirección General de Estadística.

    1981 edition was to have 9 volumes with following titles: I. Situación física; II. Situación demografía; III-VI. Situación económica; VII. Situación social; VIII. Situación cultural, ciencia y tecnología; IX. Situación politica, administrativa y justicia. The only volume available for examination was v. 8, published Sept., 1982, 86 p.,which contains statistical data in the following areas:

    DEMOGRAPHY
    Population: census results from 1971, distribution by age and sex.

    SOCIAL AND CULTURAL AFFAIRS
    Cultural and scientific activities: television, science and research; *Education*: enrollments, literacy, teaching staff; *Sports and recreation*.

    Most data are for 1981.

    Available from the agency, Apartado de Correos 4593, San Martín, Caracas 101.

    Available in microform: CH: 1877, 1894, 1908-12, 1938-40, 1942-69. CIS: 1970-74.

190. ***Boletín mensual*** [Monthly bulletin]. 1941?- Caracas: Oficina Central de Estadística e Informatica.

    Available from the address in entry 189.

ASIA

AFGHANISTAN

191. ***Statistical yearbook.*** 1978/79- Kabul: Central Statistics Office. Separate editions in English and Dari.

Continues: *Statistical information of Afghanistan*, 1975/78, published by the Central Statistics Office and *Statistical pocketbook*, 1971/72-1974/75?, published by the Department of Statistics.

1981/82 edition, published May, 1983, 160 p., contains statistical data in the following areas:

PHYSICAL ENVIRONMENT
Climatology: precipitation, temperature; *Geography*: area and use of land.

DEMOGRAPHY
Population: distribution by age and sex, distribution by geographic/administrative area, population estimates.

ECONOMIC AFFAIRS
Agriculture and food: farming; *Commerce and business*: exports, imports; *Income and expenditure*: personal income, prices; *Industry*: communication, construction, energy, manufacturing, mining, transportation; *National accounts*: gross national product, national income; *Public finance*: government expenditure, government revenue, planning and economic development.

POLITICAL AFFAIRS
Foreign aid.

SOCIAL AND CULTURAL AFFAIRS
Cultural and scientific activities: books and journals, cinema and performing arts, libraries, museums and galleries, newspapers, radio, television; *Education*: enrollments, graduates by field of study, literacy, teaching staff; *Health*: family planning, hospitals, medical personnel, public health; *Labor*: labor force.

Most data are for March, 1981-March, 1982 and the preceding 2 years. In addition to the national level, data are included for provinces and cities. The volume opens with a review of economic conditions in 1981/82.

Available from the agency, Micro-Rayon, Block No. 4, PO Box 2002, Kabul.

Available in microform: CIS and IDC: 1971/72 of *Statistical pocketbook*.

192. *Survey of progress.* 1966/67-1970/71. Kabul: Department of Statistics.

Statistical tables cover such subjects as education, health, labor force and employment, and precipitation in addition to economic affairs. Most tables appear in Part III, the statistical appendix, but some are interspersed with narrative sections in Parts I and II.

No general statistical bulletin is published by Afghanistan.

BAHRAIN

193. **Statistical abstract.** 1967- Manama: Central Statistics Organisation. English and Arabic.

Agency varies: Earlier, Directorate of Statistics.

1982 edition, published August, 1983, 269 p., contains statistical data in the following areas:

PHYSICAL ENVIRONMENT
Climatology: precipitation, temperature; *Geography*: area of land, maps.

DEMOGRAPHY
Population: census results from 1941-1981, distribution by age and sex, distribution by geographic/administrative area, households, population estimates and projections; *Vital statistics*: births, causes of death, deaths, divorces, infant mortality, marriages.

ECONOMIC AFFAIRS
Agriculture and food: farming; *Commerce and business*: establishments, exports, imports, tourism; *Finance*: banking and credit, money supply; *Income and expenditure*: consumption; *Industry*: communication, construction, energy, manufacturing, transportation, water.

SOCIAL AND CULTURAL AFFAIRS
Cultural and scientific activities: cinema and performing arts, libraries; *Education*: educational attainment, enrollments, examination results, literacy, teaching staff; *Health*: disease, hospitals, public health; *Housing*; *Justice*: courts, crimes, traffic accidents; *Labor*: employment and unemployment, foreign workers, labor force, occupations, salaries and wages; *Religion*; *Social assistance*; *Social security*.

Most data are for 1982. Time series may be provided for periods up to 10 or more years. Some data for regions are offered.

Commentaries are provided at the beginning of sections and there is a detailed list of tables at the beginning of the volume. Sources of data are not given.

Available from Public Relations Section, Central Statistics Organisation. PO Box 5835, Manama. Price: Bahrain dinar 3,000.

Available in microform: CIS: 1971-4, 1976, 1979-80.

No general statistical bulletin is published by Bahrain.

BANGLADESH

194. ***Statistical yearbook of Bangladesh.*** 1975- Dacca: Bureau of Statistics. Annual since 1979. Text in English; title, foreword and preface in English and Bengali.

Not published 1976-78.

Title varies: *Statistical digest,* 1970/71-1974. Continues: *Statistical digest of East Pakistan,* 1963-69, published by the Bureau of Statistics of East Pakistan.

1982 edition, published Dec., 1983, 766 p., contains statistical data in the following areas:

PHYSICAL ENVIRONMENT
Climatology: precipitation, sunshine, temperature; *Geography*: area and use of land, maps.

DEMOGRAPHY
Population: census results from 1901-1981, distribution by age and sex, distribution by geographic/administrative area, households and families, internal migration, population estimates and projections, tribal populations; *Vital statistics*: births, deaths, fertility, infant mortality, life expectancy, mean age of marriages.

ECONOMIC AFFAIRS
Agriculture and food: farming, fishing, forestry; *Commerce and business*: cooperatives, exports, factories, imports; *Finance*: banking and credit, money supply; *Income and expenditure*: consumption, prices; *Industry*: communication, energy, manufacturing, transportation, water; *National accounts*: balance of payments, gross domestic product, gross district product; *Public finance*: government expenditures and government revenue for central government and other levels of government (aggregate only), planning and economic development.

POLITICAL AFFAIRS
Foreign aid; *Number of eligible voters*.

SOCIAL AND CULTURAL AFFAIRS
Cultural and scientific activities: books and journals, cinema and performing arts, newspapers; *Education*: enrollments, examination results, literacy, teaching staff; *Health*: family planning, hospitals, medical personnel, public health; *Housing*; *Justice*: crimes, traffic accidents; *Labor*: employment, labor force, labor-management relations, number of workers leaving for employment abroad, occupations, productivity, salaries and wages; *Religion*.

Most data are for 1982 and the preceding 2 to 8 years. In addition to the national level, data are included for districts (some data by division or municipality). There is a section of comparative tables for selected foreign countries.

Notes accompanying the tables indicate the names of the agencies furnishing the data and explanatory notes are provided at the end of the volume. There is a detailed list of tables at the beginning of the volume and an alphabetical subject index at the end. Publications of the Bureau of Statistics are listed at the end of the volume.

A summary of the National Perspective Plan, 1980-2000, and a list of names of government officials are included, along with descriptions of government organization and the national statistical system.

Available from the agency, Bangladesh Secretariat, School Building, Room no. 12, Dacca. Price: TK50.00, domestic; $U.S.25.00, foreign. The agency also offers an abridged edition, entitled *Statistical pocket book*.

Available in microform: IDC: 1970/71-1973, 1975, 1979-80.

195. **Monthly statistical bulletin of Bangladesh.** 1963- Dacca: Bureau of Statistics.

V. 12, no. 8, Aug., 1983, published Sept., 1983, v.p., contains statistical data in the following areas:

PHYSICAL ENVIRONMENT
Climatology: precipitation, temperature; *Geography*: area and use of land.

DEMOGRAPHY
Population: census results from 1974, 1981, distribution by age and sex, distribution by geographic/administrative area, external migration, households and families, population estimates, tribal populations.

ECONOMIC AFFAIRS
Agriculture and food: farming; *Commerce and business*: exports, imports, tourism; *Finance*: banking and credit; *Income and expenditure*: prices; *Industry*: manufacturing, transportation; *National accounts*: gross domestic product; *Public finance*: government revenue.

SOCIAL AND CULTURAL AFFAIRS
Education: literacy; *Housing*; *Labor*: labor-management relations, salaries and wages.

Most data are monthly for the current year and annual for the preceding 5 years. Latest data are for the date of the issue. In addition to the national level, data are included for districts and some municipalities. Notes accompanying the tables indicate the names of the agencies furnishing the data.

Available from the address given in entry 194.

BHUTAN

196. **Statistics at a glance: Bhutan.** 1977- [Thimphu] Central Statistical Organisation.

The 1980-81 edition, 20 p., contains data in the following areas:

PHYSICAL ENVIRONMENT
Climatology: precipitation; *Geography*: area of land.

DEMOGRAPHY
Population: census results 1969, households and families, population estimates; *Vital statistics*: birth rate, death rate, fertility, life expectancy.

ECONOMIC AFFAIRS

Agriculture and food: farming, forestry; *Commerce and business*: exports, imports; *Finance*: banking and credit; *Income and expenditure*: consumption; *Industry*: communication, cottage industries, energy, manufacturing, mining, transportation, water; *National accounts*: national income.

SOCIAL AND CULTURAL AFFAIRS

Cultural and scientific activities: newspapers; *Education*: enrollments, literacy, teaching staff; *Health*: hospitals, medical personnel, public health; *Labor*: employment, foreign workers, labor force.

Most data are for 1977 and 1978.

BRUNEI

197. ***Brunei statistical yearbook.*** 1972/73- Bandar Seri Begawan: Economic Planning Unit.

1979/80 edition, 214 p., contains statistical data in the following areas:

PHYSICAL ENVIRONMENT
Climatology: precipitation, sunshine, temperature; *Geography*: area of land.

DEMOGRAPHY
Population: arrivals and departures, census results from 1911-1971, distribution by age and sex, distribution by geographic/administrative area, population estimates, racial groups; *Vital statistics*: births, causes of death, deaths, divorces, life expectancy, marriages.

ECONOMIC AFFAIRS
Agriculture and food: farming, fishing, forestry; *Commerce and business*: establishments, exports, imports; *Finance*: banking and credit, money supply; *Income and expenditure*: consumption, prices; *Industry*: communication, energy, mining, transportation, water; *National accounts*: gross domestic product; *Public finance*: government expenditures, government revenue.

SOCIAL AND CULTURAL AFFAIRS
Cultural and scientific activities: cinema, libraries, newspapers, radio, television; *Education*: enrollments, examination results, literacy, teaching staff; *Health*: hospitals, medical personnel, public health; *Justice*: crimes, traffic accidents; *Labor*: employment, labor force, labor-management relations, occupations, salaries and wages.

Most data are for 1980 and the preceding 4 to 11 years. Notes accompanying the tables indicate the names of the agencies furnishing the data.

Latest edition published: 1981/82. Available from the agency, Ministry of Finance, Bandar Seri Begawan. Price: $B5.00.

Available in microform: IDC: 1974/76-1978/79.

No general statistical bulletin is published by Brunei.

BURMA

198. *Statistical yearbook.* 1961- Rangoon: Central Statistical Organization. Irregular.

Agency name varies: Earlier by Central Statistical and Economics Department.

1975 edition, 391 p., contains statistical data in the following areas:

PHYSICAL ENVIRONMENT
Climatology: precipitation, temperature.

DEMOGRAPHY
Population: arrivals and departures, distribution by age and sex, distribution by geographic/administrative area, households and families, population estimates; *Vital statistics*: births, causes of death, deaths, infant and maternal mortality, life expectancy.

ECONOMIC AFFAIRS
Agriculture and food: farming, forestry; *Commerce and business*: domestic commerce, exports, imports; *Finance*: banking and credit, money supply; *Income and expenditure*: consumption, personal income, prices; *Industry*: communication, construction, energy, manufacturing, mining, transportation; *National accounts*: gross national output; *Public finance*: government expenditures, government revenue.

SOCIAL AND CULTURAL AFFAIRS
Cultural and scientific activities: books and journals, cinema and performing arts, newspapers, radio; *Education*: enrollments, teaching staff; *Health*: hospitals, public health; *Justice*: crimes; *Labor*: employment; *Social security*.

Most data are for 1975 and the preceding 9 years. Notes accompanying the tables indicate the names of the agencies furnishing the data. There is a detailed list of tables at the beginning of the volume.

Available from the agency, Six Storeyed Building, Strand Road, Rangoon.

Available in microform: CIS: 1971/72, 1975. IDC: 1963, 1965, 1967.

199. *Statistical pocketbook.* 1961- Rangoon: Central Statistical Organization.

Title varies: Some years as *Statistical abstract.* For agency name changes, see preceding entry.

1978 edition, 159 p., contains statistical data in the following areas:

PHYSICAL ENVIRONMENT
Climatology: precipitation, temperature.

DEMOGRAPHY
Population: arrivals and departures, distribution by age and sex, distribution by geographic/administrative area, households and families, population estimates; *Vital statistics*: births, deaths, infant and maternal mortality, life expectancy.

ECONOMIC AFFAIRS
Agriculture and food: farming, forestry; *Commerce and business*: cooperatives, domestic commerce, exports, imports, tourism; *Finance*: banking and credit, money supply; *Income and expenditure*: consumption, personal income, prices; *Industry*: communication, construction, energy, manufacturing, mining, transportation; *National accounts*: gross domestic product; *Public finance*: government expenditures, government revenue.

SOCIAL AND CULTURAL AFFAIRS
Cultural and scientific activities: books and journals, cinema and performing arts, newspapers, radio; *Education*: educational level of manpower, enrollments, teaching staff; *Health*: hospitals, medical personnel, public health; *Justice*: crimes; *Labor*: employment and unemployment, labor force; *Social security*.

Most data are for 1978 and the preceding 3 years, plus 1955 and 1965. There is a section of comparative statistics for selected foreign countries.

Available from the address in entry 198.

200. **Quarterly bulletin of statistics**. 1951- Rangoon, Central Statistical and Economics Department. English and Burmese.

Available from the address in entry 198.

CAMBODIA

See KAMPUCHEA.

CHINA

201. **Statistical yearbook of China.** 1981- Beijing: State Statistical Bureau. English translation of the Chinese edition.

[2nd edition] 1983, published Oct., 1983, 596 p., contains statistical data in the following areas:

PHYSICAL ENVIRONMENT
Climatology: precipitation,*Geography*: area and use of land.

DEMOGRAPHY
Population: census results from 1953-1982, distribution by age and sex, distribution by geographic/administrative area, households and families, minority nationalities, population estimates; *Vital statistics*: birth rate, death rate, divorces, life expectancy, marriages.

ECONOMIC AFFAIRS
Agriculture and food: farming, fishing, forestry; *Commerce and business*: domestic commerce, exports, imports, state enterprises and communes, services, tourism; *Finance*: banking and credit; *Income and expenditure*: consumption, household income, prices; *Industry*: communication, construction, energy, manufacturing, mining, trans-

portation; *National accounts*: total product of society, national income; *Public finance*: government expenditures, government revenue, investment in fixed assets.

POLITICAL AFFAIRS
Members of National People's Congress and Chinese People's Political Consultative Conference.

SOCIAL AND CULTURAL AFFAIRS
Cultural and scientific activities: books and journals, cinema and performing arts, libraries, museums and galleries, newspapers, radio, science and research, television; *Education*: educational attainment, enrollments, graduates of higher education institutions, teaching staff; *Health*: hospitals, medical personnel, public health; *Labor*: employment, labor force, productivity, salaries and wages; *Social assistance*; *Social security*; *Sports and recreation.*

Most data are for 1982 and selected earlier years. Time series for principal indicators are provided to 1949. In addition to the national level, data are included for provinces/ autonomous regions and 17 key cities. Information on the following topics is presented for the 21 minority nationalities: administration, education and culture, investment, main economic indicators, natural resources, and population. Statistics for Taiwan are in Appendix 1 and comparative statistics for selected foreign countries in Appendix 2.

Sources are given for the tables in Appendix 2 only. There are explanatory notes at the end of the volume and a detailed list of tables at the beginning.

Latest edition: 1984. Available from the Economic Information and Agency, Hong Kong. Price: $H.K.160.00

No general statistical bulletin of China is published in a Roman alphabet language.

CHINA (REPUBLIC)

202. **Statistical yearbook of the Republic of China.** 1975- Taipei: Directorate-General of Budget, Accounting and Statistics.

    Continues: *Statistical abstract of the Republic of China,* 1947-1974.

    Numbers of main tables are the same as those in the U.N. *Statistical yearbook,* with additional information provided in supplementary tables following the main tables.

    1984 edition, 503 p., contains statistical data in the following areas:

    PHYSICAL ENVIRONMENT
    Geography: area of land.

    DEMOGRAPHY
    Population: census results from 1956-1980, distribution by age and sex, households and families; *Vital statistics*: births, deaths, divorces, fertility, infant mortality, life expectancy, marriages.

ASIA : CHINA (REPUBLIC)

ECONOMIC AFFAIRS
Agriculture and food: farming, fishing, forestry; *Commerce and business*: companies, domestic commerce, exports, imports, tourism; *Finance*: banking and credit, money supply, securities; *Income and expenditure*: consumption, personal income, prices; *Industry*: communication, construction, energy, manufacturing, mining, transportation; *National accounts*: balance of payments, gross domestic product, national income; *Public finance*: government expenditures and government revenue.

POLITICAL AFFAIRS
Foreign aid.

SOCIAL AND CULTURAL AFFAIRS
Cultural and scientific activities: books and journals, cinema, newspapers, patents; *Education*: educational attainment, enrollments, number of graduates at all levels, literacy, teaching staff; *Health*: disease, hospitals, medical personnel, public health; *Housing*; *Labor*: employment and unemployment, labor force, occupations, productivity, salaries and wages.

Most data are for 1983, with time series of varying length, often to 1952. Most data are for the Taiwan area. There are some breakdowns by locality (county, city, special municipality). Explanatory notes and discussions of sources are provided in Part II. There is a detailed list of tables at the beginning of the volume.

Latest edition published: 1985, published Nov., 1985, 518 p. Available from Li-Ming Cultural Enterprise Co., Ltd., 3rd Floor, Hsin-Yi Rd, Sec. 1, Taipei. Price: $U.S.30.00

Available in microform: CIS: 1975-76, 1978-80. IDC: 1975, 1977-81. Of the *Statistical abstract*: CIS: 1970-74. IDC: 1955-74.

203. **Monthly statistics of the Republic of China,** 1967- Taipei: Directorate-General of Budget, Accounting and Statistics. English and Chinese.

No. 225, Sept., 1984, 245 p., contains statistical data in the following areas:

PHYSICAL ENVIRONMENT
Climatology: precipitation, temperature; *Geography*: area of land.

DEMOGRAPHY
Population: distribution by age and sex, distribution by geographic/administrative area, groups, external migration, internal migration; *Vital statistics*: births, deaths, divorces, marriages.

ECONOMIC AFFAIRS
Agriculture and food: farming, fishing, forestry; *Commerce and business*: enterprises, domestic commerce, exports, imports, tourism; *Finance*: banking and credit, money supply, securities; *Income and expenditure*: prices; *Industry*: communication, energy, manufacturing, mining, transportation; *National accounts*: gross domestic and gross national product, national income; *Public finance*: government expenditures, government revenue.

SOCIAL AND CULTURAL AFFAIRS
Justice: traffic accidents; *Labor*: employment and unemployment, labor force, occupations, salaries and wages; *Social security*.

Most data are monthly for 12 or more months and annual for 4 to 8 years. Latest data are for 2 to 3 months before date of issue. In addition to the Taiwan area, data are included for localities (counties, cities and special municipalities). There is a section of comparative data for selected foreign countries.

Notes accompanying the tables indicate the names of the agencies furnishing the data. There is a detailed list of tables at the beginning of the issue and a list of statistical periodicals published by all levels of government at the end.

Available from China Cultural Service, 4F, No. 106, Chung-Ching South Rd, Sec. 1, Taipei. Price: $NT1,200.00 per year.

204. **Monthly bulletin of statistics.** 1975- Taipei: Directorate-General of Budget, Accounting and Statistics.

This publication has the same format as the United Nations *Monthly bulletin of statistics*. V.9, no. 9, 1983, 24 p., contains statistical data in the following areas:

DEMOGRAPHY
Population: population estimates; *Vital statistics*: births, deaths, marriages.

ECONOMIC AFFAIRS
Agriculture and food: forestry; *Commerce and business*: domestic commerce, exports, imports; *Finance*: banking and credit, money supply, securities; *Income and expenditure*: prices; *Industry*: construction, energy, manufacturing, mining, transportation.

SOCIAL AND CULTURAL AFFAIRS
Labor: employment and unemployment, salaries and wages.

Most data are monthly for the current and preceding year and annual for 8 years. The latest data are for the month of issue. In addition to the national level, data are included for Taiwan Province, Taipei and Kaohsiung municipalities. Explanatory notes and sources are provided in the annex at the end of the issue.

Available from the address in entry 202. Price: $U.S.21.60 per year.

CYPRUS

205. **Statistical abstract.** 1955- Nicosia: Statistics and Research Department.

1982 edition, published 1984, 347 p., contains statistical data in the following areas:

PHYSICAL ENVIRONMENT
Climatology: precipitation, temperature; *Geography*: area and use of land.

DEMOGRAPHY

Population: arrivals and departures, census results from 1881-1976, distribution by age and sex, distribution by geographic/administrative area, external migration, households and families.*Vital statistics*: births, deaths, infant mortality, marriages.

ECONOMIC AFFAIRS

Agriculture and food: farming, fishing, forestry; *Commerce and business*: domestic commerce, exports, imports, tourism; *Finance*: banking and credit, money supply; *Income and expenditure*: consumption, prices; *Industry*: communication, construction, energy, manufacturing, mining, transportation; *National accounts*: balance of payments, gross domestic product; *Public finance*: government expenditures, government revenue, planning and economic development.

SOCIAL AND CULTURAL AFFAIRS

Education: educational attainment, enrollments, examination results, literacy, teaching staff; *Health*: disease, hospitals, medical personnel, public health; *Housing*; *Justice*: correctional institutions, crimes; *Labor*: employment and unemployment, labor force, labor-management relations, salaries and wages; *Religion*; *Social assistance*; *Social security*.

Most data are for 1982 and the preceding 8 to 10 years. In addition to the national level, data are included for districts and municipalities. There is a section of comparative statistics for selected foreign countries.

Commentaries, which include discussions of sources, are provided at the beginnings of chapters. Notes indicating the sources furnishing the data are provided at the end of some tables. There is a bibliography of official and non-official statistical materials at the end of the volume.

Available from the agency, Ministry of Finance, Nicosia. Price: £C4.00.

Available in microform: CIS: 1970, 1972-73, 1975, 1977-78.

206. *****Quarterly statistical digest.** 1968-Dec., 1979. Nicosia: Department of Statistics and Research.

Although devoted mainly to economic statistics, this series included some demographic and climatological data.

HONG KONG

207. **Hong Kong annual digest of statistics.** 1975- Hong Kong: Census and Statistics Department.

1983 edition, 261 p., contains statistical data in the following areas:

PHYSICAL ENVIRONMENT

Climatology: precipitation, sunshine, temperature; *Geography*: area and use of land, maps.

DEMOGRAPHY
Population: arrivals and departures, census results from 1911-1981, distribution by age and sex, distribution by geographic/administrative area, households and families, population estimates; *Vital statistics*: births, causes of death, deaths, infant mortality, marriages.

ECONOMIC AFFAIRS
Agriculture and food: farming, fishing; *Commerce and business*: companies, domestic commerce, exports, imports, services, tourism; *Finance*: banking and credit, money supply, securities; *Income and expenditure*: consumption, prices; *Industry*: communication, construction, energy, manufacturing, mining, transportation, water; *National accounts*: gross domestic product; *Public finance*: government expenditures, government revenue.

SOCIAL AND CULTURAL AFFAIRS
Cultural and scientific activities: journals, cinema and performing arts, libraries, newspapers, radio, television; *Education*: degrees conferred, educational attainment, enrollments, examination results, teaching staff; *Health*: disease, hospitals, medical personnel, public health; *Housing*; *Justice*: correctional institutions, courts, crimes, traffic accidents; *Labor*: employment and unemployment, labor force, labor-management relations, occupations, salaries and wages; *Social assistance*; *Social security*; *Sports and recreation*.

Most data are for 1982 and the preceding 9 years. Data are for Hong Kong, with some breakdowns by census area and by district. Explanatory notes and discussions of sources are provided at the beginning of sections.

Historical statistics. Statistics for earlier periods are found in *Hong Kong statistics, 1947-1967*, 216 p., published by the Census and Statistics Dept. in 1969.

Latest edition published: 1984. Available from the Information Services Dept., Baskerville House, Duddell St., Central, Hong Kong. Price: $H.K.90.

Available in microform: IDC: 1946/47-1956/57, 1958/59-1979.

208. **Hong Kong [year]; a review of [year].** 1946- Hong Kong: Government Information Services.

Title varies: 1960-1977, as *Hong Kong: report for the [year]*; 1946-59 as *Hong Kong annual report*.

In addition to data presented in the narrative sections which make up the bulk of this work, the 1984 edition, 325 p., contains statistical tables in the following areas in the appendix:

PHYSICAL ENVIRONMENT
Climatology: precipitation, sunshine, temperature.

DEMOGRAPHY
Population: arrivals and departures, population estimates; *Vital statistics*: births, causes of death, deaths, infant and maternal mortality.

ECONOMIC AFFAIRS
Agriculture and food: farming, fishing; *Commerce and business*: establishments, exports, imports; *Finance*: banking and credit, money supply; *Income and expenditure*: consumption, prices; *Industry*: communication, energy, mining, transportation, water; *Public finance*: government expenditures, government revenue.

SOCIAL AND CULTURAL AFFAIRS
Education: degrees conferred, enrollments, examination results, staff; *Health*: hospitals, medical personnel, health; *Housing*; *Justice*: correctional institutions, courts, crimes, traffic accidents; *Labor*: employment, *Sports and recreation*.

Most data are for 1983 and the preceding 2 years. There is an alphabetical subject index at the end.

Available from the address in entry 207. Price: $H.K.32.00.

209. **Hong Kong monthly digest of statistics.** 1970?- Hong Kong: Census and Statistics Department.

April, 1984, 111 p., contains statistical data in the following areas:

PHYSICAL ENVIRONMENT
Climatology: precipitation, sunshine, temperature.

DEMOGRAPHY
Vital statistics: births, causes of death, deaths, marriages.

ECONOMIC AFFAIRS
Agriculture and food: food supplies; *Commerce and business*: companies, establishments, exports, imports, tourism; *Finance*: banking and credit, money supply, securities; *Income and expenditure*: consumption, prices; *Industry*: communication, construction, energy, manufacturing, mining, transportation, water; *National accounts*: gross domestic product; *Public finance*: government expenditures, government revenue.

SOCIAL AND CULTURAL AFFAIRS
Health: disease, hospitals; *Housing*; *Justice*: crimes, traffic accidents; *Labor*: employment and unemployment, labor force, labor-management relations, salaries and wages; *Social assistance*.

Most data are monthly for 25 months and annual for the latest complete 6 years. Latest data are for the month before the month of issue.

Explanatory notes, which include discussions of sources, are provided at the end of the issue. There is a detailed list of tables at the beginning of the issue. Tables published on an annual, semi-annual or quarterly basis only are indicated at the end of the table of contents. A list of official statistical materials is printed inside the back cover.

Available from the address in entry 207. Price: $H.K.25.00.

INDIA

210. ***Statistical abstract India.*** 1949- Delhi: Central Statistical Organization.

Continues: *Statistical abstract for British India,* 1911-12/1920-21, 1940/41, published by the Department of Commercial Intelligence and Statistics, and the *Statistical abstract for 1946/47,* published by the Office of Economic Advisers.

New series, no. 25, 1980, published Dec., 1982, 687 p., contains statistical data in the following areas:

PHYSICAL ENVIRONMENT
Climatology: precipitation; *Geography*: area and use of land; map.

DEMOGRAPHY
Population: census results from 1901-1971, distribution by geographic/administrative area, population estimates; *Vital statistics*: life expectancy.

ECONOMIC AFFAIRS
Agriculture and food: farming, fishing, forestry; *Commerce and business*: companies, cooperatives, exports, imports, tourism; *Finance*: banking and credit, money stock, securities; *Income and expenditure*: consumption, prices; *Industry*: communication, construction, energy, manufacturing, mining, transportation; *National accounts*: balance of payments, national and net domestic product; *Public finance*: government expenditures and government revenue for all levels of government, planning and economic development.

POLITICAL AFFAIRS
Elections; *Foreign aid*.

SOCIAL AND CULTURAL AFFAIRS
Cultural and scientific activities: journals, newspapers; *Education*: enrollments, literacy, teaching staff; *Health*: disease, family planning, hospitals, medical personnel, public health; *Housing*; *Justice*: crimes, police, traffic accidents; *Labor*: employment, labor force, labor-management relations, salaries and wages; *Religion*.

According to the preface, data are given for 1950-51, 1955-56, 1960-61, 1965-66, and 1970-71 through 1979-80 for the national level; data for states are for the latest year available. In addition to the national level, data are included for states, districts and cities. Commentaries are provided at the beginnings of chapters and a subject index is provided. Notes accompanying the tables indicate the names of the agencies furnishing the data.

Latest edition published: No. 26, 1982, 671 p. Available from the Government of India, Publications Branch, Civil Lines, Delhi, 110054. Price: RS249; $U.S.49.50.

Available in microform: CIS: 1970. IDC: 1949-65, 1967-78, and *Statistical abstract,* published by the Department of Commercial Intelligence and Statistics, etc. 1911-1939/40, 1946/47.

211. ***Statistical pocketbook of India.*** 1958- Delhi: Central Statistical Organization.

Continues: *Statistical pocketbook of the Indian Union,* 1948-57.

1981 edition, published Aug., 1982, 279 p. included data on most of the topics covered in entry 210, plus the following: 1981 provisional census results, births, cinema, deaths, infant mortality, radio, temperature, traffic accidents. Topics included in the previous entry omitted from it were castes, consumption, construction, housing, and religion.

Most data are for 1981, plus 1980, 1976, 1971, and 1966. Some data for states and cities are presented and there is a section devoted to comparative statistics for selected foreign countries. Explanatory notes appear at the end of the volume and there is a detailed list of tables at the beginning.

Latest edition available: 1983, 275 p. Available from the address in entry 210. Price: Rs34, domestic; £3.97 or $U.S.12.24, foreign.

212. **India, a reference annual.** 1953- Delhi: Ministry of Information and Broadcasting, Publications Division.

Statistical data intermixed with narrative. 1983 edition, published Dec., 1983, 624 p., contains statistical data in the following areas:

PHYSICAL ENVIRONMENT
Geography: area of land, map.

DEMOGRAPHY
Population: census results from 1911-1981, distribution by geographic/administrative area.

ECONOMIC AFFAIRS
Agriculture and food: farming; *Commerce and business*: cooperatives, exports, imports; *Finance*: banking and credit; *Income and expenditure*: consumption, prices; *Industry*: communication, manufacturing, transportation; *Public finance*: government expenditures, government revenue, planning and economic development.

POLITICAL AFFAIRS
Defense.

SOCIAL AND CULTURAL AFFAIRS
Cultural and scientific activities: newspapers, radio, television, science and research; *Education*: enrollments, literacy, teaching staff; *Health*: public health; *Housing*; *Labor*: employment, labor force, occupations, salaries and wages; *Social security*; *Sports and recreation*.

Most data are for 1981 or 1980. There is an alphabetical subject index at the end of the volume and a bibliography of works on India. Chapter 26 contains a brief profile of each state.

Available from the agency, Patiala House, New Delhi, 110001. Price: Rs36.

No general statistical bulletin is published for India.

INDONESIA

213. ***Statistik Indonesia/Statistical yearbook of Indonesia.*** 1957- Jakarta: Biro Pusat Statistik. Indonesian and English.

1983 edition, published January, 1984, 709 p., contains statistical data in the following areas:

PHYSICAL ENVIRONMENT
Climatology: precipitation, temperature; *Geography*: area and use of land, maps.

DEMOGRAPHY
Population: distribution by geographic/administrative area, internal migration.

ECONOMIC AFFAIRS
Agriculture and food: farming, fishing, forestry; *Commerce and business*: cooperatives, exports, imports, tourism; *Finance*: banking and credit; *Income and expenditure*: consumption, prices; *Industry*: communication, construction, energy, manufacturing, mining, transportation, water; *National accounts*: gross domestic product, national income; *Public finance*: government expenditures and government revenue of the central government, provinces and villages, planning and economic development.

SOCIAL AND CULTURAL AFFAIRS
Cultural and scientific activities: cinema and performing arts, libraries, newspapers, radio, television; *Education*: educational attainment, enrollments, percent of school age population in school, teaching staff; *Health*: family planning, hospitals, medical personnel, public health; *Justice*: correctional institutions, courts, crimes, police; *Labor*: employment and unemployment, labor force, occupations; *Religion*; *Sports and recreation*.

Most data are for 1980 and 3 or 4 preceding years. In addition to the national level, data are included for islands and provinces. Comparative data are presented for selected foreign countries in Section 12.

Explanatory notes are provided at the beginning of the volume and notes accompanying the tables indicate the names of the agencies furnishing the data. There is a detailed list of tables and an outline of statistical organization at the beginning of the volume.

Available from the agency, Jalan Dr. Sutomo 8, PO Box 3, Jakarta Pusat. Price: $U.S.16.00.

Available in microform: CIS: 1976.

214. ***Statistik Indonesia/ Statistical pocketbook of Indonesia.*** 1957- Jakarta: Biro Pusat Statistik. Indonesian and English.

A condensed version of the preceding entry.

Available from the address in entry 213.

Available in microform: CIS: 1970/71, 1972/73, 1974/75. IDC: 1941, 1956-69.

215. *Buletin statistik bulanan: Indikator ekonomi/ Monthly statistical bulletin: Economic indicators.* 1970- Jakarta: Biro Pusat Statistik. Indonesian and English.

Sept., 1984, 152 p., contains statistical data in the following areas:

DEMOGRAPHY
Population: distribution by age.

ECONOMIC AFFAIRS
Agriculture and food: farming; *Commerce and business*: exports, imports, tourism; *Finance*: banking and credit, money supply; *Income and expenditure*: prices; *Industry*: communication, energy, manufacturing, mining, transportation; *National accounts*: balance of payments, gross domestic product; *Public finance*: government expenditures, government revenue.

Most data are monthly or quarterly for 1984 and annual for varying numbers of years. Notes accompanying the tables indicate the names of the agencies furnishing the data. There is a detailed list of tables at the beginning of the issue.

Available from the address given in entry 213. Price: $U.S.1.25 per issue.

Available in microform: IDC: Jan., 1970-Sept., 1972.

IRAN

216. **Statistical yearbook of Iran.** 1966- Tehran: Statistical Centre of Iran. Farsi, with English editions published in 1966, 1968, 1970, 1972, 1973/74, and 1982/83.

1973/74 edition, published June, 1976, 517p., contains statistical data in the following areas:

PHYSICAL ENVIRONMENT
Climatology: precipitation, temperature; *Geography*: maps.

DEMOGRAPHY
Population: census results from 1966, distribution by age and sex, distribution by geographic/administrative area, external migration, households and families, internal migration, population estimates; *Vital statistics*: births, deaths, divorces, marriages.

ECONOMIC AFFAIRS
Agriculture and food: farming, fishing, forestry; *Commerce and business*: companies, cooperatives, domestic commerce, establishments, exports, imports, tourism; *Finance*: banking and credit, money supply, securities; *Income and expenditure*: consumption, cost of living, prices; *Industry*: communication, construction, energy, manufacturing, mining, transportation, water; *National accounts*: balance of payments, gross domestic and gross national product, national income; *Public finance*: government expenditures, government revenue, planning and economic development.

POLITICAL AFFAIRS
Elections.

SOCIAL AND CULTURAL AFFAIRS
Cultural and scientific activities: books, cinema and performing arts, libraries, museums and galleries, newspapers, radio, television; *Education*: enrollments, graduates of secondary schools and higher education institutions, literacy, teaching staff; *Health*: disease, family planning, hospitals, medical personnel, public health; *Housing*; *Justice*: courts, crimes, traffic accidents; *Labor*: employment and unemployment, labor force, migrant workers, occupations, salaries and wages; *Religion*; *Social assistance*; *Social security*; *Sports and recreation*.

Most data are for 1352 (March, 1973-March, 1974) or 1351. Time series may be provided for up to 9 years. In addition to the national level, data are included for administrative divisions and cities of 100,000 or over.

Commentaries are provided at the beginnings of chapters. Notes accompanying the tables indicate the names of the agencies furnishing the data.

Abridged editions have been published since 1981. Latest abridged English edition published is 1982/83, titled *A statistical reflection of the Islamic Republic of Iran*. Available from the agency, Dr.Fatemi Avenue, Corner of Rahiye Moayeri, Opp. Sazeman-e Ab, Tehran, 14144. Price: Rls200; $U.S.3.00.

Available in microform: CIS: 1970, 1972/73-1973/74.

No general statistical bulletin is published for Iran.

IRAQ

217. **Annual abstract of statistics.** 1927/36- Baghdad: Central Statistical Organization. Arabic and English.

Agency varies: 1959-66 by Central Bureau of Statistics; before 1958 by Principal Bureau of Statistics.

1978 edition, 298 p., contains statistical data in the following areas:

PHYSICAL ENVIRONMENT
Climatology: precipitation, sunshine, temperature; *Geography*: area of land, map.

DEMOGRAPHY
Population: census results from 1947-1977, distribution by age and sex, distribution by geographic/administrative area, households, population estimates; *Vital statistics*: divorces, marriages.

ECONOMIC AFFAIRS
Agriculture and food: farming; *Commerce and business*: cooperatives, establishments, exports, imports, tourism; *Finance*: banking and credit; *Income and expenditure*: consumption, prices; *Industry*: communication, construction, energy, manufacturing, transportation, water; *National accounts*: gross domestic product, national income; *Public finance*: government expenditures, government revenue, planning and economic development.

SOCIAL AND CULTURAL AFFAIRS
Education: educational attainment, enrollments, graduates of higher education institutions, literacy, teaching staff; *Health*: hospitals, medical personnel, public health; *Housing*; *Justice*: traffic accidents; *Labor*: employment, labor force; *Social security*, *Sports and recreation*.

Most data are for 1978 or 1977, with time series of varying lengths. In addition to the national level, data are included for regions and governorates. Commentaries are provided at the beginnings of sections. Notes accompanying the tables indicate the names of the agencies furnishing the data. A list of tables is provided.

Historical statistics. Statistics for earlier periods are found in the *Statistical handbook of the Republic of Iraq for the years, 1957-1967*, published by the Central Bureau of Statistics in 1968.

Available from the agency, PO Box 8001, Baghdad. Priced.

Available in microform: CIS: 1970. IDC: 1929-35, 1939-40, 1944-74, 1976; and *Statistical handbook of the Republic of Iraq for the years, 1957-1967*.

218. **Statistical pocketbook.** 1957/67- Baghdad: Central Statistical Organization. Separate editions in Arabic and English.

A condensed version of the previous entry.

Available from the address given in entry 217. Priced.

Available in microform: IDC: 1960/70, 1974, 1976.

No general statistical bulletin has been found for Iraq.

ISRAEL

219. **Statistical abstract of Israel.** 1949/50- Jerusalem: Central Bureau of Statistics. Hebrew and English.

No. 34, 1983, published 1983, 923 p., contains statistical data in the following areas:

PHYSICAL ENVIRONMENT
Climatology: precipitation, temperature; *Environmental quality*; pesticide use; *Geography*: area and use of land, map.

DEMOGRAPHY
Population: arrivals and departures, census results from 1948-1972, distribution by age and sex, distribution by geographic/administrative area, ethnic groups, external migration, households and families, internal migration, population estimates and projections; *Vital statistics*: abortions (in hospitals only), births, causes of death, deaths, divorces, fertility, infant mortality, life expectancy, marriages.

ECONOMIC AFFAIRS
Agriculture and food: farming, forestry; *Commerce and business*: establishments, exports, imports, tourism; *Finance*: banking and credit, money supply, securities; *Income and expenditure*: consumption, personal income, prices; *Industry*: communication, construction, energy, manufacturing, mining, transportation, water; *National accounts*: balance of payments, gross domestic and gross national product, national income; *Public finance*: government expenditures and government revenue for central and local governments (aggregate only).

POLITICAL AFFAIRS
Elections.

SOCIAL AND CULTURAL AFFAIRS
Cultural and scientific activities: journals, cinema and performing arts, computers, libraries (in schools only), museums and galleries, newspapers, patents, radio, television, science and research; *Education*: degrees conferred, educational attainment, enrollments, examination results, teaching staff; *Health*: disease, hospitals, public health; *Housing*; *Justice*: correctional institutions, courts, crimes, police, traffic accidents; *Labor*: employment and unemployment, immigrant workers, labor force, labor-management relations, occupations, salaries and wages; *Religion*; *Social assistance*; *Social security*; *Sports and recreation*.

Most data are for 1982 and selected earlier years to 1950. The world Jewish population and the Jewish population in Israel [Palestine before 1948] are reported for the period 1882-1982. In addition to the national level, data are included for district, sub-district, natural region and localities. A chapter is devoted to Judea, Samaria and the Gaza Area.

Commentaries in English in the introduction to the volume include discussions of sources and references for further information. Explanatory notes in Hebrew are provided at the beginning of each section. There is a detailed list of tables with a list of official statistical publications following it.

Latest edition published: 1985, 858 p. Distributed by the Distribution Services of Government Publications, 25 David Elazar St., Hakirya, Tel Aviv, 67673. Priced: $U.S.27.00.

Available in microform: CIS: 1970-76. IDC: 1949-80.

220. **Monthly bulletin of statistics.** 1962- Jersualem: Central Bureau of Statistics. Hebrew and English.

V. 34, no. 7, July, 1983, 127 p., contains statistical data in the following areas:

PHYSICAL ENVIRONMENT
Climatology: precipitation, temperature.

DEMOGRAPHY
Population: arrivals and departures, ethnic groups, external migration; *Vital statistics* births, deaths, divorces, marriages.

ECONOMIC AFFAIRS

Commerce and business: domestic commerce, exports, imports, tourism; *Finance*: banking and credit, money supply; *Income and expenditure*: prices; *Industry*: construction, energy, manufacturing, transportation; *National accounts*: balance of payments, gross domestic product.

SOCIAL AND CULTURAL AFFAIRS

Health: disease; *Justice*: courts, crimes, police, traffic accidents; *Labor*: employment and unemployment, salaries and wages.

In addition to the tables published regularly, a number of supplements providing more detailed statistics on selected subjects are issued each year. Subjects covered by supplements in 1983 included population and vital statistics in 1981; preliminary national accounts for 1982; candidates for first degree in universities 1981/82; energy; balance of payments; and employment.

Most data are monthly or quarterly for the current and preceding year, and annual for 6 years. Latest data are for 2 months before date of issue. There is a list of materials published by the Bureau at the beginning of the issue.

Available from the address given in entry 219. Priced.

JAPAN

221. *Japan statistical yearbook.* 1949- Tokyo: Statistics Bureau. Japanese and English.

Continues the *Statistical yearbook of the Empire of Japan*, 1882-1941, published in Japanese only.

1984 edition, published Oct., 1984, 866 p., contains statistical data in the following areas:

PHYSICAL ENVIRONMENT

Climatology: precipitation, sunshine, temperature; *Environmental quality*: parks, solid waste; *Geography*: area and use of land.

DEMOGRAPHY

Population: census results from 1920-1980, distribution by age and sex, distribution by geographic/administrative area, external migration, households and families, internal migration, population estimates and projections; *Vital statistics*: births, causes of death, deaths, divorces, infant mortality, life expectancy, marriages, reproduction rates.

ECONOMIC AFFAIRS

Agriculture and food: farming, fishing, forestry; *Commerce and business*: cooperatives, domestic commerce, enterprises, establishments, exports, imports; *Finance*: banking and credit, money supply, securities; *Income and expenditure*: consumption, personal income, prices; *Industry*: communication, construction, energy, manufacturing, mining, transportation, water; *National accounts*: balance of payments, gross domestic product, input-output tables, national income; *Public finance*: government expenditures and government revenue for central and local governments.

POLITICAL AFFAIRS
Elections; Foreign aid.

SOCIAL AND CULTURAL AFFAIRS
Cultural and scientific activities: books and journals, cinema and performing arts, libraries, museums and galleries, newspapers, radio, television, science and research, including patents issued, time spent on daily activities; *Education*: educational attainment, enrollments, graduates, teaching staff; *Health*: body measurements, disease, hospitals, medical personnel, public health; *Housing*; *Justice*: correctional institutions, courts, crimes, infringement of human rights, traffic accidents; *Labor*: employment and unemployment, labor force, labor-management relations, migrant workers, occupations, productivity, salaries and wages; *Religion*; *Social assistance*; *Social security*; *Sports and recreation*.

Most data are for 1983 and the preceding 5 years, plus selected earlier years. Time series to 1945 are provided in Appendix 1. In addition to the national level, data are included for prefectures and cities. The last section contains comparative statistics for selected foreign countries.

Explanatory notes which include discussions of sources appear at the beginning of sections and the names of the agencies furnishing the data are given at the foot of the tables. Sources are discussed in more detail in Appendix 2, which is in Japanese only.

There is a detailed list of tables at the beginning of the volume which signals tables appearing for the first time in this edition. Tables appearing in previous editions omitted from this edition are listed at the end of the lists of tables and charts. An alphabetical subject index is provided in Japanese only.

Latest edition published: 1985, 836 p. Available from the Government Publications Service Center, 1-2-1 Kasumigaskei, Chiyodaku, Tokyo. Price: yen 11,500.

Available in microform: CIS: 1970-81. IDC: 1949-81.

222. **Statistical handbook of Japan.** 1958- Tokyo: Statistics Bureau. English.

1984 edition, 158 p., presents statistical tables and charts interspersed with narrative descriptions on most of the topics in entry 221.

Data are for the whole country for 1983 or 1982 and selected earlier years. Notes accompanying tables indicate sources and there is a detailed list of tables and charts at the end of the volume.

Available from the address in entry 221. Price: yen 1,200.

223. **Monthly statistics of Japan.** 1948- Tokyo: Statistics Bureau. English and Japanese.

No. 280, Oct., 1984, 164 p., contains statistical data in the following areas:

PHYSICAL ENVIRONMENT
Climatology: precipitation, temperature.

DEMOGRAPHY
Population: distribution by age, external migration, households and families, population estimates; *Vital statistics*: births, causes of death, deaths, divorces, infant mortality, marriages.

ECONOMIC AFFAIRS
Agriculture and food: farming, fishing, forestry; *Commerce and business*: corporations, domestic commerce, enterprises, exports, imports; *Finance*: banking and credit, money supply, securities; *Income and expenditure*: consumption, personal income, prices; *Industry*: communication, construction, energy, manufacturing, mining, transportation; *National accounts*: balance of payments, gross national product, national income; *Public finance*: government expenditures, government revenue.

SOCIAL AND CULTURAL AFFAIRS
Cultural and scientific activities: books and journals, radio, television; *Health*: disease, hospitals, public health; *Justice*: crimes, traffic accidents; *Labor*: employment and unemployment, labor force, occupations, productivity, salaries and wages; *Social assistance*; *Social security*; *Sports and recreation*.

Most data are monthly or quarterly for 15 months and annual for 7 years. Latest data are for 2 months before the date of issue. There is a section of comparative data for selected foreign countries. Notes accompanying the tables indicate the names of the agencies furnishing the data and a detailed list of tables is provided at the beginning of the issue.

Available from the address in entry 221. Price: yen 950 per issue.

JORDAN

224. **Statistical yearbook.** 1950- Amman: Department of Statistics. Arabic and English.

No. 34, 1983 edition, 254 p., contains statistical data in the following areas:

PHYSICAL ENVIRONMENT
Climatology: precipitation, temperature.

DEMOGRAPHY
Population: census results from 1979, distribution by age and sex, distribution by cities and towns, households, population estimates.*Vital statistics*: births, deaths, divorces, marriages.

ECONOMIC AFFAIRS
Agriculture and food: farming, fishing, forestry; *Commerce and business*: cooperatives, establishments, exports, imports, tourism; *Finance*: banking and credit, currency in circulation; *Income and expenditure*: consumption, prices; *Industry*: communication, construction, energy, manufacturing, transportation; *National accounts*: balance of payments, gross domestic and gross national product, national income; *Public finance*: government expenditures and government revenue for central government and municipalities.

SOCIAL AND CULTURAL AFFAIRS
Education: educational attainment, enrollments, teaching staff; *Health*: hospitals, medical personnel; *Justice*: traffic accidents; *Labor*: employment, labor force.*Religion*.

Most data are for 1983 and varying numbers of earlier years. Some data are included for governorates and municipalities.

Explanatory notes, which include a discussion of sources, are provided after the table of contents. Notes accompanying the tables indicate the names of the agencies furnishing the data. A detailed list of tables and a price list of official statistical publications appear at the beginning of the volume.

Available from the agency, PO Box 2015, Amman. Price: $U.S.20.00; JD5.00.

Available in microform: CIS: 1970-74. IDC: 1950-79.

No general statistical bulletin has been found for Jordan.

KAMPUCHEA

225. **Annuaire statistique du Cambodge* [Statistical yearbook of Cambodia]. 1949/51, 1937/57-1971?. Phnom-Penh: Institut National de la Statistique et des Recherches Economiques. Irregular. French.

Title varies: 1937/57: *Annuaire statistique rétrospectif du Cambodge*. Agency varies: Earlier by Ministère du Plan. Continues in part the *Annuaire statistique de l'Indochine*, 1913/22-1947/48, published by Direction des Affaires Economiques and Service de la Statistique Générale of Indochina.

1963/64 edition, 162 p., contains statistical data in the following areas:

PHYSICAL ENVIRONMENT
Geography: area of land.

DEMOGRAPHY
Population: census results from 1962 (prelim.), distribution by age and sex, distribution by geographic/administrative area; *Vital statistics*: causes of death.

ECONOMIC AFFAIRS
Agriculture and food: farming, fishing, forestry; *Commerce and business*: exports, imports; *Finance*: banking and credit, money supply; *Income and expenditure*: prices; *Industry*: construction, energy, manufacturing, transportation, water; *National accounts*: balance of payments; *Public finance*: government expenditures, government revenue.

SOCIAL AND CULTURAL AFFAIRS
Education: enrollments, examination results, teaching staff; *Health*: disease, hospitals, medical personnel, public health; *Labor*: labor force, occupations.

Most data are for 1963 and 1964, plus varying numbers of earlier years. The retrospective edition contains time series to 1937. In addition to the national level, data are included for provinces, administrative divisions and municipalities.

Notes accompanying the tables indicate the names of the agencies furnishing the data. There is a detailed list of tables at the beginning of the volume.

Available in microform: CIS: 1970-71. IDC: 1949-51, 1962-67.

226. ***Bulletin [mensuel] statistique*** [[Monthly] statistical bulletin]. 1952- Phnom-Penh: Institut National de la Statistique et des Recherches Economiques. Quarterly; earlier monthly. French.

KOREA (NORTH)

No official statistical yearbook or bulletin has been found for North Korea.

KOREA (SOUTH)

227. ***Korea statistical yearbook.*** 1954- Seoul: National Bureau of Statistics. Korean and English.

Agency name varies slightly: Earlier, Bureau of Statistics.

V. 30, 1983, published Dec., 1983, 616 p., contains statistical data in the following areas:

PHYSICAL ENVIRONMENT
Climatology: precipitation, sunshine, temperature; *Geography*: area and use of land.

DEMOGRAPHY
Population: arrivals and departures, census results from 1930-1980, distribution by age and sex, distribution by geographic/administrative area, households and families, internal migration, population estimates; *Vital statistics*: births, including illegitimate births, deaths, divorces, fertility, infant mortality, life expectancy, marriages.

ECONOMIC AFFAIRS
Agriculture and food: farming, fishing, forestry; *Commerce and business*: domestic commerce, enterprises, exports, imports; *Finance*: banking and credit, money supply, securities; *Income and expenditure*: consumption, prices; *Industry*: communication, construction, energy, manufacturing, mining, transportation, water; *National accounts*: balance of payments, gross domestic and gross national product, national income; *Public finance*: government expenditures, government revenue.

SOCIAL AND CULTURAL AFFAIRS
Cultural and scientific activities: libraries, museums and galleries; *Education*: enrollments, graduates of higher education institutions, teaching staff; *Health*: body measurements, disease, family planning, hospitals, medical personnel, public health; *Justice*: courts, crimes; *Labor*: employment and unemployment, labor force, labor-management relations, occupations, productivity, salaries and wages; *Religion*; *Social assistance*; *Social security*.

Most data are for 1982 and the preceding 9 years. Quarterly or monthly data are also often provided for 1982 or 1981. In addition to the national level, data are included for provinces and cities. There is a section of comparative statistics from selected foreign countries.

Notes accompanying some of the tables indicate the names of the agencies furnishing the data. There is a detailed list of tables at the beginning of the volume.

Available from the Government Publications Center, Joong-Koo, 1 ka, Taepyong Rd., Seoul 110 and the National Bureau of Statistics, Economic Planning Board, 90, Gyeongun-Dong, Jongro-Gu, Seoul 110.

Available in microform: CIS: 1971-76. IDC: 1957-65, 1967-73, 1975-78, 1980-81.

228. ***Korea statistical handbook.*** 1954- Seoul: National Bureau of Statistics.

This is an abridged English edition of entry 227.

Latest edition published: 1983. Available from the addresses in entry 227.

229. ***Monthly statistics of Korea.*** 1959- Seoul: National Bureau of Statistics. Korean and English.

V. 24, no. 4, April, 1982, 167 p., contains statistical data in the following areas:

PHYSICAL ENVIRONMENT
Climatology: precipitation, temperature.

DEMOGRAPHY
Population: arrivals and departures, preliminary census results from 1980, distribution by geographic/administrative area, external migration, households and families, population estimates.

ECONOMIC AFFAIRS
Commerce and business: exports, imports; *Finance*: banking and credit, money supply, securities; *Income and expenditure*: consumption, prices; *Industry*: communication, construction, energy, manufacturing, mining, transportation; *National accounts*: balance of payments; *Public finance*: government expenditures, government revenue.

SOCIAL AND CULTURAL AFFAIRS
Labor: employment and unemployment, labor force, occupations, productivity, salaries and wages.

Most data are monthly for the current and preceding year and annual for 5 to 11 years. Latest data are for the month of issue. In addition to the national level, data are included for provinces and cities, with comparative statistics for selected foreign countries. Notes accompanying some of the tables indicate the names of the agencies furnishing the data.

Available from the addresses in entry 227.

KUWAIT

230. ***Annual statistical abstract.*** 1964- Kuwait City: Central Statistical Office. English and Arabic.

Title varies slightly: Some years as *Statistical abstract* or *Annual abstract of statistics.*

No. XXI, 1984, published Oct., 1984, 370 p., contains statistical data in the following areas:

PHYSICAL ENVIRONMENT
Climatology: precipitation, sunshine, temperature; *Geography*: area and use of land.

DEMOGRAPHY
Population: arrivals and departures, census results from 1957-1980, distribution by age and sex, distribution by geographic/administrative area, households and families, population estimates.*Vital statistics*: births, causes of death, deaths, divorces, fertility, infant mortality, marriages.

ECONOMIC AFFAIRS
Agriculture and food: farming, fishing; *Commerce and business*: cooperatives, establishments, exports, imports, tourism; *Finance*: banking and credit, money supply; *Income and expenditure*: consumption, prices; *Industry*: communication, construction, energy, manufacturing, transportation, water; *National accounts*: balance of payments, gross domestic product, national income; *Public finance*: government expenditures, government revenue.

SOCIAL AND CULTURAL AFFAIRS
Cultural and scientific activities: journals, cinema and performing arts, libraries, museums and galleries, newspapers, radio, television; *Education*: educational attainment, enrollments, graduates of higher education institutions, literacy, teaching staff; *Health*: disease, hospitals, medical personnel, public health; *Housing*; *Justice*: crimes, traffic accidents; *Labor*: employment and unemployment, foreign workers, labor force, occupations, salaries and wages; *Religion*; *Social assistance*; *Social security*.

Most data are for 1983, with time series of varying lengths, usually 4 to 9 years. Monthly statistics for 1984 are provided in an appendix. In addition to the national level, data are included for governorates and localities.

Explanatory notes, which include discussions of sources, are provided at the beginnings of chapters. Notes indicating the names of agencies furnishing the data accompany some tables. There is a detailed list of tables at the beginning of the volume.

Available from the agency, PO Box 26188, Safat. Price: KD1.00, plus postage.

Available in microform: CIS: 1970-73; 1977. IDC: 1964-68, 1970-72, 1975-77.

31. ***Monthly digest of statistics.*** 1980- Kuwait City: Central Statistical Office. Arabic and English.

Replaces *Quarterly statistical bulletin,* 1966-74.

V. V, no. 9, Sept., 1984, 88 p., contains statistical data in the following areas:

DEMOGRAPHY
Population: census results from 1957-1980, distribution by geographic/administrative area, population estimates. *Vital statistics*: births, deaths, divorces, marriages.

ECONOMIC AFFAIRS
Agriculture and food: fishing; *Commerce and business*: exports, imports, tourism; *Finance*: banking and credit, money supply; *Income and expenditure*: consumption, prices; *Industry*: communication, construction, energy, manufacturing, transportation, water; *National accounts*: gross domestic product; *Public finance*: government expenditures, government revenue.

SOCIAL AND CULTURAL AFFAIRS
Health: hospitals, public health; *Housing*; *Justice*: traffic accidents.

Most data are monthly for 24 months and annual for 5 years. Latest data are for 3 or 4 months before date of issue. In addition to the national level, data are included for governorates.

Notes accompanying the tables indicate the names of the agencies furnishing the data. There is a detailed list of tables and a list of statistical materials published by the Central Statistical Office.

Available from the address in entry 228. Price: KD0.500, plus postage, per issue; KD9.00 per year.

LAOS

232. **Annuaire statistique* [Statistical yearbook]. 1949/50-1973? Vientiane: Service National de la Statistique. French.

1973 edition, 115 p., contains statistical data in the following areas:

PHYSICAL ENVIRONMENT
Climatology: precipitation, temperature; *Geography*: area of land.

DEMOGRAPHY
Population: distribution by geographic/administrative area, external migration, population estimates; *Vital statistics*: deaths (in hospitals only).

ECONOMIC AFFAIRS
Agriculture and food: farming, forestry; *Commerce and business*: exports, imports, *Finance*: banking and credit, money supply; *Income and expenditure*: prices; *Industry*: communication, construction, energy, manufacturing, mining, transportation; *Public finance*: government expenditures, government revenue.

SOCIAL AND CULTURAL AFFAIRS
Education: enrollments, examination results, teaching staff; *Health*: hospitals, medical personnel; *Justice*: crimes, traffic accidents; *Religion*.

Most data are for 1973 and the preceding 4 or more years. In addition to the national level, data are included for provinces. Notes accompanying the tables indicate the names of the agencies furnishing the data.

Available in microform: CIS: 1972-73. IDC: 1949/50-71, 1973.

233. *Bulletin de statistiques* [Bulletin of statistics]. 1951- Vientiane: Service National de la Statistique. Semi-annual. French.

Title and agency vary slightly.

V.22, no. 2, 1972, 64 p., contains statistical data in the following areas:

PHYSICAL ENVIRONMENT
Climatology: precipitation, temperature; *Geography*: area of land, map.

DEMOGRAPHY
Population: census results from 1973, distribution by age and sex, distribution by geographic/administrative area, external migration; *Vital statistics*: causes of death.

ECONOMIC AFFAIRS
Agriculture and food: farming, forestry; *Commerce and business*: enterprises, establishments, exports, imports, *Finance*: banking and credit, money supply; *Income and expenditure*: prices; *Industry*: communication, construction, mining, transportation; *Public finance*: government expenditures, government revenue.

SOCIAL AND CULTURAL AFFAIRS
Education: enrollments, examination results, teaching staff; *Justice*: crimes, traffic accidents.

Most data are monthly for July-December 1972, with annual figures for varying numbers of earlier years.

LEBANON

234. *Recueil de statistiques libanaises* [Collection of Lebanese statistics]. 1963- Beirut: Direction Centrale de la Statistique. French and Arabic.

Publication suspended?

Continues: *Recueil des statistiques générales*, 1946-48, published by the Service de Statistique Générale.

1972 edition, 475 p., contains statistical data in the following areas:

PHYSICAL ENVIRONMENT
Climatology: precipitation, temperature; *Geography*: maps.

DEMOGRAPHY
Population: arrivals and departures, distribution by age and sex, distribution by geographic/administrative area; *Vital statistics*: births, deaths, divorces, marriages.

ECONOMIC AFFAIRS
Agriculture and food: farming; *Commerce and business*: enterprises, exports, imports, tourism; *Finance*: banking and credit, money supply; *Income and expenditure*: prices; *Industry*: communication, construction, energy, manufacturing, transportation;

National accounts: gross domestic product, national income; *Public finance*: government expenditures, government revenue.

SOCIAL AND CULTURAL AFFAIRS
Cultural and scientific activities: cinema and performing arts, radio, television; *Education*: enrollments, examination results, teaching staff; *Health*: disease, hospitals, medical personnel, public health; *Housing*; *Labor*: employment and unemployment, foreign workers, labor force, occupations.

Most data are for 1972, with time series of varying lengths. The yearbook recapitulates the monthly series published in the the next entry and adds statistics compiled on an annual or less frequent basis. In addition to the national level, data are included for mohafazat and cazas [districts and cities].

Commentaries are provided at the beginnings of chapters. Notes accompanying the tables indicate the names of the agencies furnishing the data. There is a detailed list of tables at the end of the volume.

Statistics for earlier periods may also be found in the *Recueil de statistiques de la Syrie et du Liban* [Collection of statistics of Syria and Lebanon], 1944- , published by the Conseil Supérieur des Intérêts Communs (Syria and Lebanon), Service des Etudes Economiques et Statistiques.

Available in microform: CIS: 1970-72. IDC: 1946-48, 1963-72, and *Recueil de statistiques de la Syrie et du Liban,* 1942/43-47.

235. ***Bulletin statistique mensuel*** [Monthly statistical bulletin]. 1963- Beirut: Direction Centrale de la Statistique. French and Arabic.

Continues: *Bulletin statistique trimestriel,* published by the Service de Statistique Générale, 1950-63.

V. 12, no. 12, Dec., 1974, 81 p., contains statistical data in the following areas:

PHYSICAL ENVIRONMENT
Climatology: precipitation, temperature.

DEMOGRAPHY
Population: arrivals and departures; *Vital statistics*: births, deaths, divorces, marriages.

ECONOMIC AFFAIRS
Agriculture and food: farming; *Commerce and business*: exports, imports, tourism; *Finance*: banking and credit, money supply; *Income and expenditure*: prices; *Industry*: communication, construction, energy, manufacturing, transportation.

SOCIAL AND CULTURAL AFFAIRS
Labor: foreign workers.

Monthly series are provided for 13 months with annual figures for the preceding year. Notes accompanying the tables indicate the agencies furnishing the data. Latest data are for the date of the issue.

MACAO

236. ***Anuário estatístico/ Yearbook of statistics.*** 1951- Macao: Repartição dos Serviços de Estatística. Portuguese, English, Chinese.

1981 edition, published 1982, 296 p., contains statistical data in the following areas:

PHYSICAL ENVIRONMENT
Climatology: precipitation, sunshine, temperature; *Geography*: area of land, maps.

DEMOGRAPHY
Population: census results from 1910-1970, distribution by age and sex, distribution by geographic/administrative area, ethnic groups, external migration; *Vital statistics*: births, causes of death, deaths, divorces, infant mortality, marriages.

ECONOMIC AFFAIRS
Agriculture and food: fishing; *Commerce and business*: exports, imports, tourism; *Finance*: banking and credit, money supply; *Income and expenditure*: consumption, prices; *Industry*: communication, construction, energy, manufacturing, mining, transportation, water; *Public finance*: government expenditures, government revenue.

SOCIAL AND CULTURAL AFFAIRS
Cultural and scientific activities: journals, cinema and performing arts, libraries, museums and galleries, newspapers, radio; *Education*: educational attainment, enrollments, teaching staff; *Health*: medical personnel; *Justice*: correctional institutions, courts, traffic accidents; *Labor*: employment, labor force, occupations; *Religion*; *Social assistance*; *Social security*; *Sports and recreation*.

Most data are for 1981, with time series of varying lengths. In addition to the whole of Macao, data are included for districts and parishes. There is a detailed list of tables at the end of the volume.

Latest edition published: 1982, published 1983, 226 p. Available from the agency, CP 471, Macao.

Available in microform: CIS: 1970-76. IDC: 1958-80.

237. ***Boletim mensal de estatística/ Monthly bulletin of statistics.*** 1929- Macao: Repartição dos Serviços de Estatística. Portuguese, Chinese and English.

No. 10, Oct.,1982, 98 p., contains statistical data in the following areas:

PHYSICAL ENVIRONMENT
Climatology: precipitation, sunshine, temperature.

DEMOGRAPHY
Population: arrivals and departures, external migration; *Vital statistics*: births, causes of death, deaths, infant mortality, marriages.

ECONOMIC AFFAIRS
Commerce and business: domestic commerce, tourism; *Income and expenditure*: consumption, prices; *Industry*: communication, construction, energy, manufacturing,

transportation, water; *Public finance*: government expenditures and government revenue for the central government and municipalities.

SOCIAL AND CULTURAL AFFAIRS
Justice: correctional institutions, traffic accidents; *Social assistance*.

Most data are for the month of issue and the same month of the preceding year. In addition to the whole of Macao, separate data are included for the peninsula of Macao and the islands of Taipa and Coloane. There is a detailed list of tables at the end of the issue.

Available from the address in entry 236.

MALAYSIA

238. ***Malaysia official yearbook.*** 1961- Kuala Lumpur: Federal Department of Information. Irregular.

1974 ed., 519 p., contains statistics intermixed with narrative and a statistical appendix covering the following topics: education, external trade, health, energy, justice, population, radio and television, transportation, vital statistics. Some data are for the whole of Malaysia and some are reported separately for Peninsular Malaysia, Sabah and Sarawak.

Available from the Federal Department of Information. Ministry of Information, Angkasapuri, Kuala Lumpur 2210.

Available in microform: CIS: 1973.

PENINSULAR MALAYSIA

239. ***Siaran perangkaan tahunan Malaysia/ Annual statistical bulletin, Malaysia.*** 1964- Kuala Lumpur: Department of Statistics. Bahasa Malaysia and English.

Title varies: 1964-71: *Annual bulletin of statistics*.

1982, 62 p., contains statistical data in the following areas:

PHYSICAL ENVIRONMENT
Climatology: precipitation, sunshine, temperature; *Geography*: area of land.

DEMOGRAPHY
Population: census results from 1970, 1980, distribution by age and sex, households and families; *Vital statistics*: births, deaths, infant mortality, life expectancy.

ECONOMIC AFFAIRS
Agriculture and food: farming, fishing, forestry; *Commerce and business*: cooperatives exports, imports, tourism; *Finance*: banking and credit; *Income and expenditure*: prices *Industry*: communication, construction, manufacturing, mining, transportation *National accounts*: balance of payments, gross domestic product; *Public finance*: government expenditures, government revenue.

SOCIAL AND CULTURAL AFFAIRS
Education: enrollments, teaching staff; *Health*: disease, hospitals, medical personnel, public health; *Justice*: crimes, traffic accidents; *Labor*: employment, labor force, occupations.

Most data are for 1982 and the preceding 4 years. In addition to Peninsular Malaysia, data are included for its 11 states. Some data are also included for the whole of Malaysia, Sabah and Sarawak.

Available from the agency, Jalan Cenderasari, Kuala Lumpur 10-01. Priced.

Available in microform: CIS: 1970-72, 1976, 1978. IDC: 1964-71.

Another title offering coverage of most of the same topics, *Statistical handbook of Peninsular Malaysia*, apparently ceased publication after the 1978 edition.

240. **Siaran perangkaan tahunan Malaysia/ Monthly statistical bulletin; Peninsular Malaysia.** 1964- Kuala Lumpur: Department of Statistics. Bahasa Malaysia and English.

Title varies: Earlier, *Monthly statistical bulletin of West Malaysia*.

July, 1983, 202 p., contains statistical data in the following areas:

PHYSICAL ENVIRONMENT
Climatology: precipitation, temperature.

DEMOGRAPHY
Population: census results from 1921-1980, distribution by age and sex, ethnic groups, population estimates; *Vital statistics*: births, deaths, infant and maternal mortality.

ECONOMIC AFFAIRS
Agriculture and food: farming, fishing, forestry; *Commerce and business*: exports, imports, tourism; *Finance*: banking and credit; *Income and expenditure*: prices; *Industry*: communication, energy, manufacturing, mining, transportation.

SOCIAL AND CULTURAL AFFAIRS
Cultural and scientific activities: newspapers; *Health*: hospitals, public health; *Justice*: crimes, traffic accidents; *Labor*: employment and unemployment, labor force, salaries and wages.

Most data are monthly for 1983 and the preceding year, and annual for 5 years. Some data are included for individual states of Peninsular Malaysia.

Commentaries are provided at the beginnings of chapters. Notes accompanying the tables indicate the names of the agencies furnishing the data.

Available from the address in entry 239. Priced.

SABAH

241. **Siaran perangkaan tahunan/ Annual bulletin of statistics.** 1964- Kota Kinabalu: Department of Statistics. English, with title and preface also in Bahasa Malaysia.

ASIA : MALAYSIA (SABAH)

1982 edition, published Nov., 1983, 162 p., contains statistical data in the following areas:

PHYSICAL ENVIRONMENT
Climatology: precipitation, sunshine, temperature; *Environmental quality*: sewage disposal.

DEMOGRAPHY
Population: arrivals and departures, distribution by age and sex, distribution by geographic/administrative area, ethnic groups, households and families, population projections; *Vital statistics*: births, deaths, life expectancy.

ECONOMIC AFFAIRS
Agriculture and food: farming, fishing, forestry; *Commerce and business*: companies, domestic commerce, exports, imports, tourism; *Finance*: banking and credit; *Income and expenditure*: prices; *Industry*: communication, construction, energy, manufacturing, transportation; *National accounts*: gross domestic product; *Public finance*: government expenditures and government revenue of state and local governments, planning and economic development.

POLITICAL AFFAIRS
Number of registered voters.

SOCIAL AND CULTURAL AFFAIRS
Cultural and scientific activities: radio, television; *Education*: educational attainment, enrollments, examination results, literacy, teaching staff; *Health*: hospitals, public health; *Housing*; *Justice*: correctional institutions, courts, crimes, traffic accidents; *Labor*: employment, labor force, occupations; *Religion*.

Most data are for 1982 and the preceding 9 years. Notes accompanying the tables indicate the names of the agencies furnishing the data. A condensed version of this series, entitled *Statistical handbook of Sabah,* ceased publication with the 1978 edition.

Available from the agency, 1st Floor, Federal Building, Kota Kinabalu, East Malaysia. Price: $M6.00.

Available in microform: IDC: 1967-73, 1979.

242. ***Monthly statistics of Sabah.*** 1964- Kota Kinabalu: Department of Statistics. English with title and table of contents also in Bahasa Malaysia.

August, 1984 issue, 118 p., contains data in the following areas:

PHYSICAL ENVIRONMENT
Climatology.

DEMOGRAPHY
Population: migration, population estimates; *Vital statistics.*

ECONOMIC AFFAIRS
Commerce and business: exports, imports, tourism; *Income and expenditure*: prices; *Industry*: communication, transportation.

SOCIAL AND CULTURAL AFFAIRS
Labor.

Available from the address in entry 240. Price: $M2.00 per copy.

SARAWAK

243. ***Siaran perangkaan tahunan/ Annual statistical bulletin.*** 1964- Kuching: Department of Statistics. English, with title and preface also in Bahasa Malaysia.

Title varies: 1964-71 as *Annual bulletin of statistics.*

1981 edition, published Dec., 1982, 201 p., contains statistical data in the following areas:

PHYSICAL ENVIRONMENT
Climatology: precipitation, sunshine, temperature; *Geography*: area and use of land.

DEMOGRAPHY
Population: arrivals and departures, census results from 1960, 1970, distribution by age and sex, distribution by geographic/administrative area, ethnic groups, households and families, population estimates; *Vital statistics*: births, causes of death, deaths, infant and maternal mortality.

ECONOMIC AFFAIRS
Agriculture and food: farming, fishing, forestry; *Commerce and business*: companies, cooperatives, exports, imports, tourism; *Finance*: banking and credit; *Income and expenditure*: consumption, prices; *Industry*: communication, energy, manufacturing, mining, transportation; *National accounts*: gross domestic product; *Public finance*: government expenditures and government revenue for the federal government and the state of Sarawak.

SOCIAL AND CULTURAL AFFAIRS
Cultural and scientific activities: newspapers; *Education*: enrollments, literacy, teaching staff; *Health*: disease, hospitals, medical personnel, public health; *Housing*; *Justice*: correctional institutions, courts, crimes, traffic accidents; *Labor*: employment and unemployment, labor force, occupations.

Most data are for 1981 and the preceding 9 years. Notes accompanying the tables indicate the names of the agencies furnishing the data. In addition to the state level, data are included for districts, divisions, and communities.

A condensed version of this series, *Statistical handbook of Sarawak*, ceased publication in 1978.

Available from the agency, Tingkat Lima, Bangunan Tun Datuk Patinggi, Tuanku Haji Bujang, Kuching. Priced.

Available in microform: IDC: 1964-71, 1973, 1976, 1979-80.

244. ***Sarawak quarterly bulletin of statistics.*** 1964- Kuching: Department of Statistics. English.

MALDIVES

245. ***Statistical yearbook of Maldives.*** 1981- Male': Ministry of Planning and Development. English and Dhivehi.

1984, published Oct., 1984, 150 p., contains statistical data in the following areas:

PHYSICAL ENVIRONMENT
Climatology: precipitation, sunshine, temperature; *Geography*: area of land, map.

DEMOGRAPHY
Population: census results from 1967, 1972, 1977, distribution by age and sex, distribution by geographic/administrative area, internal migration, population estimates; *Vital statistics*: births, deaths, divorces, infant mortality, marriages.

ECONOMIC AFFAIRS
Agriculture and food: farming, fishing; *Commerce and business*: exports, imports, tourism; *Finance*: banking and credit; *Industry*: communication, energy, transportation; *National accounts*: balance of payments, gross domestic product; *Public finance*: government expenditures, government revenue.

SOCIAL AND CULTURAL AFFAIRS
Cultural and scientific activities: libraries, radio, television; *Education*: educational attainment, enrollments, literacy, percent of age group attending school; *Health*: disease, hospitals, medical personnel, public health; *Justice*: courts, crimes; *Labor*: employment, labor force, occupation.

Most data are for 1983 and varying numbers of earlier years. In addition to the national level, data are included for administrative units. Notes accompanying the tables indicate the names of the agencies furnishing the data. There is a detailed list of tables at the beginning of the volume in English and at the end of the volume in Dhivehi.

Available from the Ministry of Planning and Development, Ghaazee Building, Male'. Price: Rf27.00.

No general statistical bulletin is published for the Maldives.

MONGOLIA

246. ***National economy of the Mongolian People's Republic for [60] years.*** Ulan Bator: State Central Statistical Board. Decennial? Mongolian and Russian, English and French editions.

1921/1981 edition, 496 p., contains statistical data in the following areas:

PHYSICAL ENVIRONMENT
Climatology: precipitation, temperature; *Geography*: area of land.

DEMOGRAPHY
Population: census results from 1935-1979, distribution by sex, distribution by geographic/administrative area, families; *Vital statistics*: births, deaths, divorces, marriages.

ECONOMIC AFFAIRS
Agriculture and food: farming; *Commerce and business*: cooperatives, domestic commerce, exports, imports, services, tourism; *Income and expenditure*: consumption; *Industry*: communication, construction, energy, mining, manufacturing, transportation; *National accounts*: national income; *Public finance*: government expenditures, government revenue, economic development.

POLITICAL AFFAIRS
Membership of councils.

SOCIAL AND CULTURAL AFFAIRS
Cultural and scientific activities: journals, cinema and performing arts, libraries, newspapers; *Education*: educational attainment, enrollments, graduates of higher education institutions by field, teaching staff; *Health*: hospitals, medical personnel, public health; *Housing*; *Labor*: employment, productivity; *Social assistance*; *Sports and recreation*.

Most data are for 1980 and selected preceding years to 1921. Explanatory notes are provided at the beginnings of some sections. In addition to the national level, data are included for aimaks [provinces] and towns. There is a detailed list of tables at the end of the volume.

Available from the agency, Ulan Bator.

Available in microform: CIS: *50 years of the MPR; statistical collection,* published in 1971.

247. **National economy MPR.** Ulan Bator: State Central Statistical Board. Irregular. Mongolian, with Russian and English editions for some years.

1979 Russian edition, 278 p., covered most of the topics in the preceding entry for the following years: 1979, 1978, 1975, 1970 1965 and 1960.

Available from the address in entry 246.

No general statistical bulletin has been found for Mongolia.

NEPAL

248. **Statistical pocket book.** 1974- Kathmandu: Central Bureau of Statistics. Irregular (1974, 1982 only editions published).

1982 edition, published March, 1982, 240 p., contains statistical data in the following areas:

PHYSICAL ENVIRONMENT
Climatology: precipitation, temperature; *Geography*: area and use of land, maps.

DEMOGRAPHY
Population: census results from 1981 (prelim.), distribution by age and sex, distribution by geographic/administrative area, external migration, households and families, internal migration, population projections; *Vital statistics*: births, deaths, fertility, infant mortality, life expectancy.

ECONOMIC AFFAIRS
Agriculture and food: farming, forestry; *Commerce and business*: cooperatives, establishments, exports, imports, tourism; *Finance*: banking and credit, money supply; *Income and expenditure*: consumption, personal income, prices; *Industry*: communication, cottage industries, energy, transportation, water; *National accounts*: balance of payments, gross domestic product, national income; *Public finance*: government expenditures, government revenue, planning and economic development.

POLITICAL AFFAIRS
Foreign aid.

SOCIAL AND CULTURAL AFFAIRS
Cultural and scientific activities: newspapers; *Education*: enrollments; *Health*: family planning, hospitals, medical personnel, public health; *Justice*: courts, crimes; *Religion*.

Most data in the main text are for 1979 or 1978 and the 4 preceding years; some later data appear in the appendixes. In addition to the national level, data are given for development regions, zones and districts. There are comparative statistics for selected foreign countries.

Explanatory notes are provided at the end of the volume. Notes accompanying the tables indicate the names of the agencies furnishing the data. There is a detailed list of tables and a general description of the country and its administrative organization at the beginning of the volume.

Available from the agency, National Planning Commission Secretariat, Ramshah Path, Thapathali, Kathmandu.

No general statistical bulletin is currently published for Nepal.

OMAN

249. ***Statistical yearbook.*** 1974?- Muscat: Directorate General of National Statistics.

1982 edition, 173 p., contains statistical data in the following areas:

PHYSICAL ENVIRONMENT
Climatology: precipitation, temperature.

ECONOMIC AFFAIRS
Agriculture and food: farming; *Commerce and business*: companies, establishments, exports, imports; *Finance*: banking and credit, money supply; *Income and expenditure*: prices; *Industry*: communication, energy, transportation, water; *National accounts*: balance of payments, gross domestic product; *Public finance*: government expenditures, government revenue.

SOCIAL AND CULTURAL AFFAIRS
Education: enrollments, literacy, teaching staff; *Health*: hospitals, medical personnel, public health; *Housing*; *Justice*: traffic accidents; *Labor*: employment, foreign workers, occupations, salaries and wages.

Most data are for 1982 and the preceding year. Time series of varying lengths are provided. No sources for data are given. There is a detailed list of tables at the beginning of the volume. A description of geographical areas and administrative regions is found at the beginning of the volume.

Available from the agency, PO Box 881, Muscat.

Available in microform: CIS: 1974-75 and 1972 ed. of *Oman at a glance*.

No general statistical bulletin is published for Oman.

PAKISTAN

250. ***Pakistan statistical yearbook.*** 1952- Karachi: Federal Bureau of Statistics.

Not published 1982-83.

Agency varies: 1952-68 by the Central Statistical Office and Statistics Division.

1984 edition, published May, 1984, 594 p., contains statistical data in the following areas:

PHYSICAL ENVIRONMENT
Climatology: precipitation, temperature; *Geography*: use of land.

DEMOGRAPHY
Population: census results from 1951-1981, distribution by age and sex, distribution by geographic/administrative area, households, population estimates.

ECONOMIC AFFAIRS
Agriculture and food: farming, fishing, forestry; *Commerce and business*: companies, cooperatives, exports, imports, tourism; *Finance*: banking and credit, money supply, securities; *Income and expenditure*: consumption, personal income, prices; *Industry*: communication, energy, manufacturing, mining, transportation; *National accounts*: balance of payments, gross and net national product; *Public finance*: government expenditures and government revenue for central and provincial governments, planning and economic development.

POLITICAL AFFAIRS
Foreign aid.

SOCIAL AND CULTURAL AFFAIRS
Cultural and scientific activities: cinema, journals, language usually spoken, newspapers, radio, television; *Education*: educational attainment, enrollments, literacy, teaching staff; *Health*: family planning, hospitals, medical personnel, public health; *Housing*; *Justice*: courts, crimes; *Labor*: employment, labor force, labor-management relations, occupations.*Religion.*

Most data are for 1982 and 1983, plus the preceding 8 years. In addition to the national level, data are included for provinces and municipalities.

Explanatory notes, which include discussions of sources, are provided at the end of the volume. Notes accompanying tables indicate the names of the agencies furnishing the data.

Historical statistics. Statistics for the period 1947-1950 may be found in *Statistical digest of Pakistan,* issued by the Department of Commercial Intelligence and Statistics in 1950. Time series may be found in *25 years of Pakistan in statistics, 1947-1972,* and *10 years of Pakistan in statistics, 1972-1982*, published by the Central Statistical Office in 1972 and 1983, respectively.

Latest edition available: 1985. Available from Federal Bureau of Statistics, l-S.M.C.H. Society, Karachi-3 or the Manager of Publications, Federal Publication Branch, Government of Pakistan, Deputy Controller of Stationery and Forms Building, University Road, Karachi. Price: Rs50.00.

Available in microform: CIS: 1970-74, 1976-80. IDC: 1952-80.

251. **Statistical pocketbook of Pakistan.** 1962- Karachi: Federal Bureau of Statistics.

For agency variations, see entry 250.

This is a condensed version of the yearbook.

Latest edition published: 1985. Available from the address in entry 250. Price Rs10.00.

252. **Monthly statistical bulletin.** 1952- Karachi: Federal Bureau of Statistics.

V. 32, no. 9, Sept., 1984, 364 p., contains statistical data in the following areas:

ECONOMIC AFFAIRS
Agriculture and food: farming; *Commerce and business*: exports, imports, tourism; *Finance*: banking and credit, money supply, securities; *Income and expenditure*: prices; *Industry*: communication, energy, manufacturing, mining, transportation; *National accounts*: balance of payments, gross and net national product.

SOCIAL AND CULTURAL AFFAIRS
Education: educational attainment of job-seekers only; *Justice*: crimes, traffic accidents; *Labor*: salaries and wages, work performed by employment exchanges.

Most data are monthly for 24 months and annual for 4 years. Notes accompanying the tables indicate the names of the agencies furnishing the data. Explanatory notes are provided in the July and January issues only.

Available from the address in entry 250. Price: Rs 20.00.

PHILIPPINES

253. ***Philippine statistical yearbook.*** 1977- Manila: National Economic and Development Authority (NEDA). Irregular.

Continues: *NEDA statistical yearbook of the Philippines,* 1974-76, published by the same agency.

1984 edition, published Aug., 1984, 759 p., contains statistical data in the following areas:

PHYSICAL ENVIRONMENT
Geography: area and use of land, maps.

DEMOGRAPHY
Population: census results from 1799-1980, distribution by age and sex, distribution by geographic/administrative area, households and families, internal migration, population estimates and projections; *Vital statistics*: births, causes of death, deaths, fertility, infant and maternal mortality, life expectancy, marriages.

ECONOMIC AFFAIRS
Agriculture and food: farming, fishing, forestry; *Commerce and business*: companies, establishments, exports, imports, tourism; *Finance*: banking and credit, money supply; *Income and expenditure*: consumption, personal income, prices; *Industry*: communication, construction, energy, manufacturing, mining, transportation, water; *National accounts*: balance of payments, gross domestic and gross national product, national income; *Public finance*: government expenditures and government revenue for central and local governments (aggregate).

SOCIAL AND CULTURAL AFFAIRS
Cultural and scientific activities: radio, television; *Education*: enrollments, examination results, graduates of higher education institutions, literacy, teaching staff; *Health*: disease, family planning, hospitals, nutrition, public health; *Housing*; *Labor*: employment and unemployment, labor force, number of Filipino workers overseas, occupations; *Social assistance*; *Social security*.

Most data are for 1983 with time series of varying lengths. In addition to the national level, data are included for regions and provinces. There is a section of comparative statistics for selected foreign countries.

Sources are discussed at the beginning of the volume and notes accompanying the tables indicate the names of the agencies furnishing the data. There is a detailed list of tables at the beginning of each chapter.

Available from the agency, PO Box 419, Greenhills, Manila. Price: $U.S.55.00, plus postage.

ASIA : PHILIPPINES

Available in microform: IDC: 1974-79.

254. **Statistical pocketbook of the Philippines,** 1979-82. Manila: National Economic and Development Authority (NEDA).

This is a condensed version of entry 253.

Historical statistics. Statistics for earlier periods may be found in a similar compilation published at irregular intervals from 1952 on by the Bureau of the Census and Statistics under the title, *Statistical handbook of the Philippines.* The second edition, 1903/53, offers lengthy time series.

255. **Philippine yearbook.** 1971- Manila: National Census and Statistics Office. Irregular.

Continues: *Yearbook of Philippine statistics,* 1940-66 (published 1940, 1946, 1957, 1958, 1966), and the *Philippine statistics yearbook,* 1969, both published by the Bureau of the Census and Statistics.

1983, 978 p., has statistical data intermixed with narrative. Subject coverage is similar to that of entry 253.

Available from National Census and Statistics Office, PO Box 779, Manila. Priced?

256. **Journal of Philippine statistics.** 1941- Manila: National Census and Statistics Office. Quarterly.

Agency varies: Earlier, the Bureau of the Census and Statistics.
Each issue has an article on statistics, in addition to a selection of statistical tables. V. 32, no. 3, 3rd qtr, 1981, contains statistical data in the following areas:

DEMOGRAPHY
Population: arrivals and departures.

ECONOMIC AFFAIRS
Commerce and business: exports, imports, tourism; *Income and expenditure*: prices; *Industry*: construction, transportation.

SOCIAL AND CULTURAL AFFAIRS
Justice: crime.

Most data are monthly for the current year. Notes accompanying the tables indicate the names of the agencies furnishing the data and explanatory notes appear at the beginnings of sections.

Available from the address in entry 255. Priced.

QATAR

257. **Year book.** 1981/82- Doha: Ministry of Information.
This is a narrative account with statistical data in the text. The 1981-82 edition, 145 p., contains statistical data in the following areas:

PHYSICAL ENVIRONMENT
Geography: maps.

ECONOMIC AFFAIRS
Agriculture and food: farming; *Commerce and business*: companies, exports, imports; *Finance*: banking and credit, currency in circulation; *Industry*: energy and water, manufacturing; *National accounts*: balance of payments; *Public finance*: government expenditures.

SOCIAL AND CULTURAL AFFAIRS
Education: enrollments, teaching staff; *Health*: hospitals, medical personnel, public health; *Labor*: labor inspections; *Social security*.

Most data are for 1982 or 1981 and the preceding 1 to 4 years. There are descriptions of the geography, history, government, and educational system of Qatar, as well as an overview of health and statistical services. A list of Central Statistical Office publications is included.

Available from the Press and Publications Dept. of the Ministry of Information, PO Box 5147, Doha.

No general statistical bulletin is published for Qatar.

SAUDI ARABIA

258. **Statistical yearbook.** 1965- Riyadh: Central Department of Statistics. Arabic and English.

19th Year, 1983 (1403 A.H.) edition, 629 p., contains statistical data in the following areas:

PHYSICAL ENVIRONMENT
Climatology: precipitation, temperature; *Geography*: maps.

DEMOGRAPHY
Vital statistics: births, deaths.

ECONOMIC AFFAIRS
Agriculture and food: farming; *Commerce and business*: companies, cooperatives, establishments, exports, imports, tourism; *Finance*: banking and credit, money supply; *Income and expenditure*: consumption, cost of living, prices; *Industry*: communication, construction, energy, manufacturing, transportation; *National accounts*: balance of payments, gross domestic product; *Public finance*: government expenditures, government revenue.

SOCIAL AND CULTURAL AFFAIRS
Cultural and scientific activities: journals, newspapers; *Education*: enrollments, graduates of universities, teaching staff; *Health*: hospitals, medical personnel, public health; *Justice*: courts, crimes, traffic accidents; *Labor*: employment, foreign workers (workers in oil companies by nationality), professions; *Religion (pilgrims)*; *Social assistance*; *Social security*; *Sports and recreation*.

Most data are for 1402 (1982) or the previous year, plus varying numbers of earlier years, usually 4. There is a table for converting Gregorian and Hijri dates. In addition to the national level, data are included for regions, amirates and cities.

Explanatory notes are provided at the beginnings of chapters and notes accompanying the tables indicate the names of the agencies furnishing the data. There is a detailed list of tables at the beginning of the volume.

Available from the Central Department of Statistics, Ministry of Finance and National Economy, PO Box 3735, Riyadh, 11118. Price: SR30.00.

Available in microform: CIS: 1970-75. IDC: 1965-80.

No general statistical bulletin is published by Saudi Arabia.

SINGAPORE

259. *Yearbook of statistics.* 1967- Singapore: Department of Statistics.

1983/84 edition, 278 p., contains statistical data in the following areas:

PHYSICAL ENVIRONMENT
Climatology: precipitation, sunshine, temperature; *Environmental quality*: air pollution levels; *Geography*: use of land.

DEMOGRAPHY
Population: arrivals and departures, census results from 1901-1980, distribution by age and sex, ethnic groups, population estimates; *Vital statistics*: births, causes of death, deaths, fertility, infant mortality, life expectancy, marriages.

ECONOMIC AFFAIRS
Agriculture and food: farming, fishing; *Commerce and business*: establishments, exports, imports; *Finance*: banking and credit, money supply, securities; *Income and expenditure*: consumption, prices; *Industry*: communication, construction, energy, manufacturing, transportation, water; *National accounts*: balance of payments, gross domestic and gross national product; *Public finance*: government expenditures, government revenue.

SOCIAL AND CULTURAL AFFAIRS
Cultural and scientific activities: books, cinema and performing arts, libraries, newspapers, radio, television; *Education*: enrollments, graduates of higher education institutions, language of instruction, literacy, teaching staff; *Health*: family planning, hospitals, medical personnel, public health; *Housing*; *Justice*: traffic accidents; *Labor*: employment and unemployment, labor force, labor-management relations, occupations, salaries and wages; *Social security*.

Most data are for 1983 and the preceding 10 years. Explanatory notes are found at the beginning of each chapter. Notes accompanying the tables indicate the names of the agencies furnishing the data in cases where the tables have not been compiled by the Department of Statistics.

Latest edition published: 1984/85, 299 p. Available from Singapore National Printers, 10 Anson Road, 01-29 Singapore 0270. Price: $S5.00.

Available in microform: CIS: 1970-1979/80.

260. ***Monthly digest of statistics.*** 1962- Singapore: Department of Statistics.

Sept., 1984, 143 p., contains statistical data in the following areas:

PHYSICAL ENVIRONMENT
Climatology: precipitation, sunshine, temperature; *Environmental quality*: air pollution levels.

DEMOGRAPHY
Population: arrivals and departures, distribution by age and sex, ethnic groups, population estimates; *Vital statistics*: births, deaths, marriages.

ECONOMIC AFFAIRS
Agriculture and food: fishing, livestock slaughtered; *Commerce and business*: exports, imports; *Finance*: banking and credit, money supply, securities; *Income and expenditure*: prices; *Industry*: communication, energy, manufacturing, transportation, water; *National accounts*: gross domestic product; *Public finance*: government expenditures, government revenue.

SOCIAL AND CULTURAL AFFAIRS
Cultural and scientific activities: radio, television; *Health*: family planning; *Justice*: traffic accidents; *Labor*: employment; *Social security*.

Most data are monthly and/or quarterly for 21 months and annual for 5 years.

Available from the address in entry 259. Price: $S4.70.

SRI LANKA

261. ***Statistical abstract of the Democratic Socialist Republic of Sri Lanka.*** 1949- Colombo, Department of Census and Statistics. Separate editions in English, Sinhala and Tamil. Irregular after 1970/71. Title varies: 1949-1970/71 as *Statistical abstract of Ceylon.*

1982 edition, published Sept., 1983, 394 p., contains statistical data in the following areas:

PHYSICAL ENVIRONMENT
Climatology: precipitation, temperature; *Geography*: area of land.

DEMOGRAPHY
Population: arrivals and departures, census results from 1871-1981, distribution by age and sex, distribution by geographic/administrative area, ethnic groups, population estimates and projections; *Vital statistics*: births, causes of death, deaths, infant mortality, life expectancy, marriages.

ECONOMIC AFFAIRS
Agriculture and food: farming, fishing, forestry; *Commerce and business*: companies, cooperatives, exports, imports, tourism; *Finance*: banking and credit, money supply; *Income and expenditure*: consumption, prices; *Industry*: communication, construction, energy, manufacturing, transportation; *National accounts*: balance of payments, gross

national product, national income; *Public finance*: government expenditures and government revenue for central and local governments (aggregate).

POLITICAL AFFAIRS
Elections.

SOCIAL AND CULTURAL AFFAIRS
Cultural and scientific activities: books; *Education*: enrollments, literacy, teaching staff; *Health*: hospitals, medical personnel, public health; *Justice*: correctional institutions, crimes, police, traffic accidents; *Labor*: employment, labor force, labor-management relations, occupations, salaries and wages; *Religion*; *Social assistance*; *Social security*.

Most data are for 1981 and the preceding 4 years. Commentaries are provided at the beginnings of chapters. Notes accompanying the tables indicate the names of the agencies furnishing the data. There is a detailed list of tables at the beginning of the volume and an alphabetical subject index at the end.

Historical statistics. Sri Lanka: a handbook of historical statistics by Patrick Peebles, Boston: G.K. Hall, 1982, 357 p., contains statistics for the 19th and 20th centuries.

Available from the Superintendent, Government Publications Bureau, Colombo 1. Price: Rs32.00, plus postage.

Available in microform: IDC: 1949-79.

262. **Statistical pocketbook of the Democratic Socialist Republic of Sri Lanka.** 1966- Colombo: Department of Census and Statistics. Separate editions in English, Sinhala and Tamil.

Title varies: 1966-71 as *Statistical pocket book of Ceylon*; 1972-77 as *Statistical pocket book of Sri Lanka (Ceylon)*.

This is a concise treatment of most of the same topics as entry 261.

Latest edition published: 1984. Available from the address in entry 261. Price: Rs20.00, plus postage.

Description furnished by the Department of Census and Statistics.

Available in microform: CIS: 1970-75, 1977. IDC: 1966-81.

263. **Sri Lanka yearbook.** 1948- Colombo: Department of Census and Statistics. English, Sinhala and Tamil editions.

Title varies: 1948-1974 as *Ceylon yearbook*. Continues in part the *Annual general report on Ceylon*, 1920-38, and the *Report on the Ceylon blue book*, 1897?-1919, published by Census and Statistics Dept.

Statistics intermixed with narrative. Slightly less detailed coverage of most of the same topics as entry 261. Statistics for the period 1939-1946 are found in the first edition.

Latest edition published: 1982, 267 p. Available from the address in entry 261. Price: Rs21, plus postage.

No general statistical bulletin is published by Sri Lanka.

SYRIA

264. *Statistical abstract.* 1948- Damascus: Central Bureau of Statistics. English and Arabic.

1983 edition, published Aug., 1983, 493 p., contains statistical data in the following areas:

PHYSICAL ENVIRONMENT
Climatology: precipitation, sunshine, temperature; *Geography*: area of land, maps.

DEMOGRAPHY
Population: arrivals and departures, census results from 1960, 1970, 1981 (prelim.), distribution by age and sex, distribution by geographic/administrative area, households and families, population estimates and projections, registered Palestinian refugees; *Vital statistics*: births, deaths, divorces, fertility, life expectancy, marriages.

ECONOMIC AFFAIRS
Agriculture and food: farming; *Commerce and business*: cooperatives, domestic commerce, establishments, exports, imports, tourism; *Finance*: banking and credit, money supply; *Income and expenditure*: consumption, prices; *Industry*: communication, construction, energy, manufacturing, mining, transportation, water; *National accounts*: balance of payments, gross domestic product; *Public finance*: government expenditures, government revenue.

SOCIAL AND CULTURAL AFFAIRS
Cultural and scientific activities: books and journals, cinema and performing arts, newspapers; *Education*: educational attainment, enrollments, graduates of higher education institutions, literacy, teaching staff; *Health*: disease, hospitals, medical personnel, public health; *Justice*: courts, crimes; *Labor*: employment and unemployment, labor force, labor-management relations.

Most data are for 1983 and varying numbers of earlier years. In addition to the national level, data are included for muhafazat [provinces] and cities. Commentaries which include discussions of sources are provided at the beginnings of chapters.

Available from the agency, Abdel-Malek Bin Marwan St., Malki Quarter, Damascus. Available in microform: CIS: 1970-80. IDC: 1949-79.

No general statistical bulletin is published by Syria.

TAIWAN

See CHINA, (REPUBLIC).

THAILAND

265. *Statistical yearbook.* 1916- Bangkok: National Statistical Office.

Not published 1944-52, 1959-62. English and Thai.

No. 32, 1976-1980, 636 p., contains statistical data in the following areas:

PHYSICAL ENVIRONMENT
Climatology: precipitation, temperature; *Geography*: area of land.

DEMOGRAPHY
Population: arrivals and departures, census results from 1911-1970, distribution by age and sex, distribution by geographic/administrative area, external migration, households and families, population projections; *Vital statistics*: births, causes of death, deaths, infant and maternal mortality.

ECONOMIC AFFAIRS
Agriculture and food: farming, fishing, forestry; *Commerce and business*: exports, imports; *Finance*: banking and credit, money supply; *Income and expenditure*: consumption, personal income, prices; *Industry*: communication, energy, mining, transportation; *National accounts*: balance of payments, gross national product, national income; *Public finance*: government expenditures, government revenue.

SOCIAL AND CULTURAL AFFAIRS
Cultural and scientific activities: cinema and performing arts; *Education*: educational attainment, enrollments, graduates of higher education institutions, literacy, teaching staff; *Health*: disease, family planning, hospitals; *Housing*; *Justice*: correctional institutions, courts, crimes, traffic accidents; *Labor*: employment and unemployment, labor force, occupations; *Religion*.

Most data are for 1980 or 1979 and the preceding 4 to 6 years. In addition to the national level, data are included for regions and changwats [provinces]. Comparative statistics for selected countries are found in an appendix.

Commentaries are provided at the beginnings of chapters. Notes accompanying the tables indicate the names of the agencies furnishing the data. There is a detailed list of tables at the beginning of the volume and an alphabetical subject index at the end.

Available from the National Statistical Office, Office of the Prime Minister, Larn Luang Road, Bangkok. Price: $U.S.15.00, plus postage. Available in microform: CIS: 1970/71-1972/73; 1974/75. IDC: 1935/36-1974/75.

266. *Statistical handbook.* 1972?- Bangkok: National Statistical Office.

1983 edition, 211 p., contains statistical data in the following areas:

PHYSICAL ENVIRONMENT
Climatology: precipitation, temperature; *Geography*: area of land.

DEMOGRAPHY
Population: census results from 1980, distribution by age and sex, distribution by geographic/administrative area, households and families, population projections; *Vital statistics*: births, causes of death, deaths, infant and maternal mortality.

ECONOMIC AFFAIRS
Agriculture and food: farming, fishing, forestry; *Commerce and business*: exports, imports, tourism; *Finance*: banking and credit, money supply; *Income and expenditure*: consumption, prices; *Industry*: communication, energy, manufacturing, mining, transportation; *National accounts*: balance of payments, gross national product, national income; *Public finance*: government expenditures, government revenue.

SOCIAL AND CULTURAL AFFAIRS
Cultural and scientific activities: Radio, television; *Education*: educational attainment, enrollments, literacy, teaching staff; *Health*: family planning, hospitals, medical personnel, public health; *Justice*: crimes, traffic accidents; *Labor*: employment and unemployment, labor force, salaries and wages.

Most data are for 1982 and the preceding 2 to 4 years. Data are included for regions as well as the whole kingdom. Explanatory notes are provided at the beginnings of chapters. Notes accompanying the tables indicate the names of the agencies furnishing the data.

Historical statistics. Thailand: a handbook of historical statistics by Constance M. Wilson, Boston: G. K. Hall, 1983, 360 p., includes data from 1850 to 1979.

Available from the address in entry 265. Price: $U.S.1.00, plus postage.

The National Statistical Office also publishes the *Statistical summary of Thailand*. The latest edition, 1984, covers most of the same topics as the *Handbook* and is available free from the issuing agency.

267. **Quarterly bulletin of statistics.** 1952- Bangkok: National Statistical Office. English and Thai.

V. 30, no.1-2, Jan.-June, 1980, 117 p., contains statistical data in the following areas:

PHYSICAL ENVIRONMENT
Climatology: precipitation, temperature; *Geography*: area of land.

DEMOGRAPHY
Population: arrivals and departures, distribution by age and sex, distribution by geographic/administrative area, external migration; *Vital statistics*: births, causes of death, deaths.

ECONOMIC AFFAIRS
Agriculture and food: farming, fishing, forestry; *Commerce and business*: cooperatives, exports, imports; *Finance*: banking and credit, money supply, securities; *Income and expenditure*: prices; *Industry*: communication, energy, manufacturing, mining, transportation; *Public finance*: government expenditures, government revenue.

SOCIAL AND CULTURAL AFFAIRS
Education: enrollments, literacy, teaching staff; *Health*: family planning; *Justice*: correctional institutions, crimes; *Labor*: employment, labor force.

Most data are monthly for current year, quarterly for preceding year and annual for 1 to 11 years. Latest data are for last month named on cover of issue. In addition to the national level, data are included for region, changwat [province] and Bangkok metropolis.

Notes accompanying the tables indicate the names of the agencies furnishing the data. There is a list of official statistical materials at the end of the issue.

Available from the address given entry 265. Price: $U.S.1.25, plus postage.

TURKEY

268. *Türkiye istatistik yilliği/Statistical yearbook of Turkey.* 1928- Ankara: Devlet Istatistik Enstitüsü. Biennial (published in odd-numbered years; alternates with entry 269, which is published in even-numbered years). English and Turkish.

1983 edition, 465 p., contains statistical data in the following areas:

PHYSICAL ENVIRONMENT
Climatology: precipitation, sunshine, temperature; *Geography*: area of land, maps.

DEMOGRAPHY
Population: census results from 1927-1980, distribution by age and sex, distribution by geographic/administrative area, external migration, households and families; *Vital statistics*: causes of death, deaths, divorces, fertility, marriages.

ECONOMIC AFFAIRS
Agriculture and food: farming, fishing, forestry; *Commerce and business*: companies, domestic commerce, exports, imports, services, tourism; *Finance*: banking and credit, money stock; *Income and expenditure*: consumption, personal income, prices; *Industry*: communication, construction, energy, manufacturing, mining, transportation; *National accounts*: balance of payments, gross national product, national income; *Public finance*: government expenditures and government revenue for central and local governments.

POLITICAL AFFAIRS
Elections.

SOCIAL AND CULTURAL AFFAIRS
Cultural and scientific activities: books and journals, performing arts, libraries, newspapers, radio, television; *Education*: degrees conferred, educational attainment, enrollments, graduates of higher education institutions, literacy, teaching staff; *Health*: disease, hospitals, medical personnel, public health; *Justice*: correctional institutions, crimes, traffic accidents; *Labor*: employment and unemployment, labor force, labor-management relations, occupations, salaries and wages; *Social assistance*; *Social security*; *Sports and recreation.*

Most data are for 1982 and the preceding 7 years. Statistics for the period, 1923-1983, are found in a special section at the front of the volume, entitled 'Turkey in figures in the sixtieth anniversary of the Republic'. In addition to the national level, data are included for provinces and cities of 10,000 or more. There is a section of comparative statistics for selected foreign countries.

Commentaries which include discussions of sources are provided at the beginnings of chapters and agencies responsible for furnishing data are listed in an appendix. A few of the tables have notes indicating the names of the agencies furnishing the data. There is a detailed list of tables at the of the volume and a bibliography of official statistical materials.

Available from the agency, 114 Necatibey Caddesi, Bakanliklar, Yenisehir, Ankara.

Available in microform: CIS: 1975, 1977-80.

269. *Türkiye istatistik cep yilliği/Statistical pocket book of Turkey.* 1928- Ankara: Devlet Istatistik. Biennial (published in even-numbered years; alternates with entry 268, which is published in odd-numbered years). Turkish and English.

1982 edition, 287 p., contains statistical data in the following areas:

PHYSICAL ENVIRONMENT
Climatology: precipitation, sunshine, temperature; *Geography*: area and use of land.

DEMOGRAPHY
Population: census results from 1927-1980, distribution by age and sex, distribution by geographic/administrative area, households and families, internal migration; *Vital statistics*: causes of death, deaths, divorces, fertility, marriages.

ECONOMIC AFFAIRS
Agriculture and food: farming, fishing; *Commerce and business*: cooperatives, establishments, domestic commerce, exports, imports, tourism; *Finance*: banking and credit, money stock; *Income and expenditure*: consumption, household income, prices; *Industry*: communication, construction, energy, manufacturing, mining, transportation; *National accounts*: balance of payments, gross national product, national income; *Public finance*: government expenditures and government revenue of the central government and villages (aggregate only).

POLITICAL AFFAIRS
Elections.

SOCIAL AND CULTURAL AFFAIRS
Cultural and scientific activities: books and journals, performing arts, libraries, newspapers; *Education*: educational attainment, enrollments, literacy, teaching staff; *Health*: hospitals, medical personnel; *Justice*: correctional institutions, crimes, traffic accidents; *Labor*: employment and unemployment, labor force, labor-management relations, occupations; *Social security.*

Most data are for 1981 and the preceding 4 years, plus some longer time series. In addition to the national level, data are included for provinces and selected foreign countries.

Notes accompanying the tables indicate the names of the agencies furnishing the data. There is a detailed list of tables at the beginning of the volume.

Available from the address in entry 268.

Available in microform: CIS: 1978, 1980. IDC: 1972, 1974, 1976.

270. *Aylik istatistik bülteni.* [Monthly bulletin of statistics]. 1952- Ankara: Devlet Istatistik Enstitüsü. English and Turkish.

[No.] VII, 1984, 115 p., contains statistical data in the following areas:

ECONOMIC AFFAIRS
Commerce and business: companies, exports, imports; *Finance*: banking and credit, money supply; *Income and expenditure*: prices; *Industry*: communication, construction, energy, manufacturing, mining, transportation; *Public finance*: government revenue.

SOCIAL AND CULTURAL AFFAIRS
Justice: traffic accidents; *Labor*: employment office activity.*Social security*.

Most data are monthly for 12 months and annual for 5 years. There are some quarterly figures. Latest data are for the month before the date of issue. There is a section of comparative data for selected foreign countries.

Explanatory notes are provided at the beginnings of chapters. Notes accompanying the tables indicate the names of the agencies furnishing the data. There is a detailed list of tables at the beginning of the issue.

Available from the address in entry 268.

UNITED ARAB EMIRATES

271. *Annual statistical abstract.* 1973?- Biennial? Abu Dhabi: Central Statistical Office. English and Arabic.

Title varies: Earlier, *Résumé of statistics for the year*.

1979 edition, 507 p., contains statistical data in the following areas:

PHYSICAL ENVIRONMENT
Climatology: precipitation, temperature; *Geography*: area and use of land, maps.

DEMOGRAPHY
Population: arrivals and departures, census results from 1975, distribution by age and sex, distribution by geographic/administrative area, population estimates; *Vital statistics*: births, deaths.

ECONOMIC AFFAIRS
Agriculture and food: farming, fishing; *Commerce and business*: establishments, domestic commerce, exports, imports, tourism; *Finance*: banking and credit, money supply; *Income and expenditure*: prices; *Industry*: communication, construction, energy, manufacturing, transportation, water; *National accounts*: balance of payments, gross domestic

product, national income; *Public finance*: government expenditures, government revenue.

SOCIAL AND CULTURAL AFFAIRS
Cultural and scientific activities: cinema and performing arts, lectures, radio, television; *Education*: educational attainment, enrollments, teaching staff; *Health*: hospitals, medical personnel, public health; *Housing*; *Justice*: courts, crimes, traffic accidents; *Labor*: employment, foreign workers, labor force, occupations, salaries and wages; *Religion*; *Social assistance*; *Sports and recreation*.

Most data are for 1978 and varying numbers of earlier years. In addition to the national level, data are included for individual emirates. Explanatory notes and discussions of sources are provided at the beginnings of chapters, and a detailed list of tables is provided.

Available from the Central Statistical Office, Ministry of Planning, PO Box 904, Abu Dhabi.

ABU DHABI

272. ***Statistical yearbook.*** 1969- Abu Dhabi: Department of Planning. Irregular. English and Arabic.

Agency varies: 1969, 1972 by Directorate General of Planning and Coordination.

1982 edition, published July, 1983, 271 p., contains statistical data in the following areas:

PHYSICAL ENVIRONMENT
Climatology: precipitation, sunshine, temperature.

DEMOGRAPHY
Population: distribution by age and sex, distribution by geographic/administrative area, households and families; *Vital statistics*: births, deaths, divorces, marriages.

ECONOMIC AFFAIRS
Agriculture and food: farming, afforestation; *Commerce and business*: domestic commerce, exports, imports, tourism; *Finance*: banking and credit; *Income and expenditure*: consumption, prices; *Industry*: communication, construction, energy, manufacturing, transportation; *National accounts*: gross domestic product; *Public finance*: government expenditures, government revenue.

SOCIAL AND CULTURAL AFFAIRS
Education: educational attainment, enrollments, graduates of higher education institutions, literacy, teaching staff; *Health*: disease, hospitals, medical personnel, public health; *Justice*: traffic accidents; *Labor*: employment and unemployment, labor force, salaries and wages.

Most data are for 1982 and the preceding 4 years. In addition to Abu Dhabi, some data are included for the United Arab Emirates. Notes accompanying the tables indicate the names of the agencies furnishing the data.

ASIA : UNITED ARAB EMIRATES (ABU DHABI)

Available from the Department of Planning, Abu Dhabi.

Available in microform: IDC: 1969, 1972, 1973/74-77.

No general statistical bulletin has been found for the United Arab Emirates or Abu Dhabi.

VIETNAM

273. ***Statistical data of the Socialist Republic of Viet Nam.*** 1963?- Hanoi: General Statistical Office. Irregular. English and Vietnamese.

1977 edition, published 1978, 71 p., contains statistical data in the following areas:

PHYSICAL ENVIRONMENT
Geography: area and use of land, maps.

DEMOGRAPHY
Population: distribution by sex, distribution by geographic/administrative area.

ECONOMIC AFFAIRS
Agriculture and food: farming, fishing; *Commerce and business*: domestic commerce, exports, imports; *Industry*: construction, energy, manufacturing, transportation; *National accounts*: national income.

SOCIAL AND CULTURAL AFFAIRS
Cultural and scientific activities: books, cinema and performing arts, libraries; *Education*: enrollments, teaching staff; *Health*: hospitals, medical personnel; *Labor*: employment, labor force.

Most data are for 1975-1977. In addition to the national level, data are included for provinces. There is a detailed list of tables at the beginning of the volume.

Historical statistics. Statistics for earlier periods may be found in *Viet Nam statistical yearbook/ Niên-Giám thông-kê Viêt-Nam*, 1949/50-1972, published in Saigon by the National Institute of Statistics.

Available from the agency, Hanoi.

Available in microform: CIS: 1970-72 of *Viet Nam statistical yearbook/ Niên-Giám thông-kê Viêt-Nam*.

No current statistical bulletin has been found for Vietnam.

Historical statistics. Statistics for earlier periods may be found in *Thóg-kê nguyêt-san/ Monthly statistical bulletin of Viet-Nam*, 1957-72, English and Vietnamese, published by the National Institute of Statistics, and *Bulletin statistique mensuel du Nord-Vietnam*, 1954- , published by Nha Kinh-te Bac-viet Thóng-kê Nguyêt-san.

YEMEN

274. Statistical year book. 1970?- Sana'a: Statistics Department of the Central Plannning Organization. English and Arabic.

1982 edition, 360 p., contains statistical data in the following areas:

PHYSICAL ENVIRONMENT
Climatology: precipitation, temperature; *Geography*: maps.

DEMOGRAPHY
Population: census results from 1975, 1981, distribution by age and sex, distribution by geographic/administrative area, households and families, internal migration; *Vital statistics*: fertility, infant mortality, life expectancy.

ECONOMIC AFFAIRS
Agriculture and food: farming, fishing; *Commerce and business*: exports, imports, tourism; *Finance*: banking and credit, money supply; *Income and expenditure*: prices; *Industry*: construction, energy, manufacturing, transportation, water; *National accounts*: balance of payments, gross domestic product, national income; *Public finance*: government expenditure, government revenue.

SOCIAL AND CULTURAL AFFAIRS
Cultural and scientific activities: journals, cinema and performing arts, newspapers; *Education*: educational attainment, enrollments, literacy, teaching staff; *Health*: disease, hospitals, medical personnel, public health; *Housing*; *Justice*: crimes, traffic accidents; *Labor*: employment and unemployment, foreign workers, labor force, occupations; *Sports and recreation*.

Most data are for 1982 and varying numbers of earlier years. In addition to the national level, data are included for governorates.

Brief explanatory notes are provided at the beginnings of chapters and notes accompanying the tables indicate the names of the agencies furnishing the data. A description of the geographical and administrative divisions of the country is provided at the beginning of the volume.

Available from the agency, PO Box 175, Sana'a. Priced.

Available in microform: CIS: 1971; 1974/75. IDC: 1971-76.

No general statistical bulletin has been found for Yemen.

YEMEN (PEOPLE'S DEMOCRATIC REPUBLIC)

275. Statistical yearbook. 1980- Crater: Central Board of Statistics. Published jointly with the United Nations Economic Commission for Western Asia.

No general statistical bulletin has been found for the People's Democratic Republic of Yemen.

EUROPE

ALBANIA

276. *[35] Vjet Shqipëri Socialiste* [35 years of Albanian socialism]. Tirana: Drejtoria e Statistikës. Issued at irregular intervals. Albanian.

    The 1974 edition, 239 p., contains economic statistics, with some coverage of climate and geography, population, cultural affairs. education and health. Data are also given on membership in the Popullor (Assembly).

    Most data are for 1973 and the following earlier years: 1970, 1965, 1960, 1950, and 1938.

    Latest edition published: 1979. Available from the agency, Tirana. Priced.Available in microform: CIS: 1974.

277. **Vjetari statistikor i RPSH* [Statistical yearbook of the Albanian People's Republic]. 1958-73. Tirana: Drejtoria e Statistikës. Biennial for 1967-8, 1969-70 and 1971-2, otherwise annual. Albanian.

    Title varies: 1958-61 as *Anuari statistikor*. Agency varies: some years by Drejtoria e Përgjithshme e Statistikës.

    The 1971-72 edition, published in 1973, 214 p., contains statistical data in the following areas:

    PHYSICAL ENVIRONMENT
    Climatology: temperature; *Geography*: area and use of land, maps.

    DEMOGRAPHY
    Population: distribution by geographic area, households and families; *Vital statistics*: births, deaths, life expectancy, marriages.

    ECONOMIC AFFAIRS
    Agriculture: farming; *Business and commerce*: exports, imports; *Industry*: communication, construction, transportation; *Finance*: government expenditures, government revenue, national income.

    SOCIAL AND CULTURAL AFFAIRS
    Cultural and scientific activities: books, libraries, museums, newspapers, performing arts and films; *Education*: enrollments, teaching staff; *Health*: medical personnel; *Labor*: labor force.

Most data are for 1971 and these earlier years: 1970, 1965, 1960, 1950 and 1938. There is a chapter offering comparative statistics for a number of countries. Chapter 1 contains a description of administrative divisions and government organization.

The following years are available in microform: CIS: 1969-70, 1971-2.

No general statistical bulletin has been found for Albania.

ANDORRA

No general statistical yearbook or bulletin has been found for Andorra.

AUSTRIA

278. ***Statistisches Handbuch für die Republik Österreich*** [Statistical handbook of the Austrian Republic]. 1920-38, 1950- Vienna: Österreichisches Statistisches Zentralamt. German.

1950 numbered new series.

Title varies: 1935-37 as *Statistisches Handbuch für den Bundesstaat Österreich*; 1938: *Statistisches Jahrbuch für Österreich*. Agency varies: 1920 by Statistische Zentralkommission, 1921-37 by Bundesamt für Statistik, and 1938 by Statistisches Landesamt. Continues: *Österreichisches statistisches Handbuch*, 1882-1916/17, published by the Statistische Zentralkommission, 1901-16/17 and by the Statistische Central-Commission, 1882-1900.

V. 35, n.s., 1984, 664 p, contains statistical data in the following areas:

PHYSICAL ENVIRONMENT
Climatology: precipitation, sunshine, temperature; *Environmental quality*: air quality, noise pollution, protection of nature, solid waste; *Geography*: area and use of land, maps.

DEMOGRAPHY
Population: census results from 1869-1981, distribution by age and sex, distribution by geographic/administrative area, households and families, population projections, refugees; *Vital statistics*: births, including illegitimate births, causes of death, deaths, divorces, fertility, infant mortality, marriages.

ECONOMIC AFFAIRS
Agriculture and food: farming, fishing, forestry; *Commerce and business*: companies, cooperatives, domestic commerce, exports, imports, tourism; *Finance*: banking and credit, money supply, securities; *Income and expenditure*: consumption, personal income, prices; *Industry*: communication, construction, energy, manufacturing, mining, transportation; *National accounts*: balance of payments, gross domestic product, national income; *Public finance*: government expenditures and government revenue for the central, state and local level.

POLITICAL AFFAIRS
Elections.

SOCIAL AND CULTURAL AFFAIRS
Cultural and scientific activities: books and journals, cinema and performing arts, libraries, museums and galleries, newspapers, radio, television, use of time; *Education*: degrees conferred, educational attainment, enrollments, examination results, teaching staff; *Health*: disease, hospitals, medical personnel, public health; *Housing*; *Justice*: courts, traffic accidents; *Labor*: employment and unemployment, foreign workers, labor force, occupations, salaries and wages; *Religion*; *Social assistance*; *Social security*; *Sports and recreation.*

Most data are for 1983 or 1982 and varying numbers of earlier years. In addition to the national level, data are included for Länder [states], Bezirke [counties], and Gemeinden [municipalities]. There is a section with comparative statistics for selected foreign countries.

Explanatory notes are provided at the beginnings of chapters. Notes accompanying the tables indicate the names of the agencies furnishing the data. There is a detailed list of tables at the beginning of the volume and an alphabetical subject index at the end.

*Historical statistics.*Statistics for the period 1945-1965 were published by the Austrian Central Statistical Office in 1976 under the title, *Republic of Austria, 1945-1975,* 206 p. Statistics for the 19th century are found in *Statistisches Jahrbuch der österreichischen Monarchie,* 1863-81, published by the Statistische Central-Commission and the *Tafeln zur statistik der österreichischen Monarchie,* 1842-65, published by the Direktion der Administrativen Statistik.

Available from the agency, PO Box 9000, A-1033 Vienna. Price: SA570.

Available in microform: CH: 1920-38, 1950-65, and *Tafeln zur Statistik der österreichischen Monarchie,* 1842-1859; *Osterreichisches statistisches Handbuch,*1882-1916/17; *Statistisches Jahrbuch der österreichischen Monarchie,* 1863-1881. CIS: 1970-71, 1980.

279. **Statistische nachrichten** [Statistical reports]. 1923- Vienna: Osterreichisches Statistisches Zentralamt. Monthly. German.

For agency variations, see entry 278. Continues: *Mitteilungen,* 1921-23, published by the Bundesamt für Statistik.

V. 38, no. 7, 1983, n.s., 83 p., contains statistical data in the following areas:

DEMOGRAPHY
Population: microcensus results from 1981 and 1982, distribution by age and sex; *Vital statistics*: births, deaths, fertility, infant mortality.

ECONOMIC AFFAIRS
Agriculture and food: farming, forestry; *Commerce and business*: domestic commerce, exports, imports, tourism; *Finance*: banking and credit, money supply; *Income and expenditure*: consumption, prices; *Industry*: communication, construction, energy,

manufacturing, transportation; *National accounts*: gross domestic and gross national product, national income.

SOCIAL AND CULTURAL AFFAIRS
Justice: traffic accidents; *Labor*: employment and unemployment, foreign workers, labor force, salaries and wages; *Social security*.

Most data are monthly or quarterly for 12 to 18 months and annual for the latest 3 completed years; supplements offer annual statistics for 5 or more years. Latest data are for 1 or 2 months before the month of issue. Some data are given for states and there are comparative statistics for selected foreign countries. There is an alphabetical subject index at the end of the issue.

Available from the address in entry 278. Price: SA110 per issue; SA1,060 per year.

BELGIUM

280. **Annuaire statistique de la Belgique** [Statistical yearbook of Belgium]. 1870- Brussels: Institut National de Statistique. French. There is also a Dutch edition, entitled *Statistisch jaarboek van België*.

Title varies: 1912-59 as *Annuaire statistique de la Belgique et du Congo belge*. Agency varies: 1870-83 and 1907-14 by Ministère de l'Intérieur; 1884-1900 by Ministère de l'Intérieur et de l'Instruction Publique; 1901-06 and 1915-1931/32 by Ministère de l'Intérieur et de l'Hygiène; 1933-44 by Office Central de Statistique.

V. 103, 1983, 783 p., contains statistical data in the following areas:

PHYSICAL ENVIRONMENT
Climatology: precipitation, sunshine, temperature; *Environmental quality*: air pollution; *Geography*: area and use of land, maps.

DEMOGRAPHY
Population: census results from 1866-1981, distribution by age and sex, distribution by geographic/administrative area, external migration, households and families, internal migration; *Vital statistics*: births, including illegitimate births, causes of death, deaths, divorces, infant mortality, life expectancy, marriages.

ECONOMIC AFFAIRS
Agriculture and food: farming, fishing, forestry; *Commerce and business*: companies, domestic commerce, exports, imports, tourism; *Finance*: banking and credit, money supply, securities; *Income and expenditure*: consumption, personal income, prices; *Industry*: communication, construction, energy, manufacturing, mining, transportation; *National accounts*: balance of payments, gross domestic and gross national product, national income; *Public finance*: government expenditures and government revenue at the central, provincial and local levels (aggregate only for provincial and local).

POLITICAL AFFAIRS
Elections.

SOCIAL AND CULTURAL AFFAIRS
Cultural and scientific activities: books and journals, cinema and performing arts, libraries, newspapers, radio, television, science and research; *Education*: degrees conferred, educational attainment, enrollments, language of instruction, teaching staff; *Health*: disease, hospitals, medical personnel, public health; *Housing*; *Justice*: courts, crimes, traffic accidents; *Labor*: employment and unemployment, foreign workers, labor force, labor-management relations, occupations, salaries and wages; *Religion*; *Social assistance*; *Social security*; *Sports and recreation.*

Most data are for 1983 or 1982, with time series of varying lengths. In addition to the national level, data are included for regions, provinces, arrondissements [districts], and communes. There is a section of comparative statistics for selected foreign countries.

Explanatory notes, which include discussions of sources, are provided at the end of the volume. Notes accompanying the tables indicate the names of the agencies furnishing the data. There is a detailed list of tables at the beginning of the volume and an alphabetical subject index at the end. Illustrations include charts showing the organization of education.

Historical statistics. Statistics for the 19th century are found in *Statistique générale de la Belgique*: *Exposé de la situation du Royaume,* published by the Ministère de l'Intérieur, 1841-60 and by the Commission Centrale de Statistique, 1861-1900.

Available from the agency, 44 rue de Louvain, 1000 Brussels. Price FB900, domestic; FB1050, foreign.

Available in microform: CH: 1870-1945, 1947-51, 1955, 1958-62; and *Statistique générale de la Belgique*: *Exposé de la situation du Royaume,* 1841-1900, published by the Commission Centrale de Statistique, 1861-1900 and by the Ministère de l'Intérieur, 1841-60.

281. **Annuaire statistique de poche** [Statistical pocketbook]. 1965- Brussels: Institut National de Statistique. French.

An abridged edition of entry 280, offering less detailed statistics on most of the same topics. Frequently offers time series for selected years to 1950.

Latest edition published: 1983. Available from the address in entry 280. Price: FB125, domestic; FB160, foreign.

282. **Bulletin de statistique** [Statistical bulletin]. 1909- Brussels: Institut National de Statistique.

V. 69, no. 1, Jan., 1983, published Feb., 1983, 60 p., contains statistical data in the following areas:

DEMOGRAPHY
Vital statistics: births, deaths, infant mortality, marriages.

ECONOMIC AFFAIRS
Agriculture and food: farming, fishing; *Commerce and business*: domestic commerce, exports, imports, services; *Finance*: banking and credit, money supply, securities; *Income and expenditure*: prices; *Industry*: construction, energy, manufacturing, mining, transportation; *National accounts*: gross national product; *Public finance*: government expenditures, government revenue.

SOCIAL AND CULTURAL AFFAIRS
Health: disease; *Housing*; *Justice*: traffic accidents; *Labor*: employment and unemployment, labor-management relations, salaries and wages.

Most data are monthly for 12 months and annual for the 5 preceding years. Latest data is for month of publication.

Explanatory notes, which include discussions of sources, are provided at the end of the issue. There is a list of official statistical materials published by the Institute during the month.

Available from the address in entry 290. Price per issue: FB180, domestic; FB230, foreign. Price per year: FB900, domestic; FB1,200, foreign.

BULGARIA

283. *Statisticheski godishnik* [Statistical yearbook]. 1947/48- Sofia: Dŭrzhavno Upravlenie za Informatisiya. Bulgarian.

Agency name varies: 1956-68 by Tsentralno Statistichesko Upravlenie. Continues *Statisticheski godishnik na Tsarstvo Bŭlgariia/ Annuaire statistique du Royaume du Bulgarie,* 1909-42, published by Glavna Directsiia na statistikata.

1983 edition, 673 p., contains the following information:

PHYSICAL ENVIRONMENT
Climatology: precipitation, temperature; *Environmental quality*; *Geography*: area of land, maps.

DEMOGRAPHY
Population: census results from 1981, distribution by age and sex, distribution by geographic area, internal migration; *Vital statistics*: births, divorces, deaths, infant mortality, life expectancy, marriages.

ECONOMIC AFFAIRS
Agriculture: farming, forestry; *Business and commerce*: domestic commerce, exports, imports, tourism; *Finance* : savings and credit; *Income and expenditure*: consumption, personal income, prices; *Industry*: communication, construction, energy, manufacturing, mining, transportation, water; *National accounts*: social product, national income; *Public finance*: economic development.

SOCIAL AND CULTURAL AFFAIRS
Cultural and scientific activities: books and journals, cinema and performing arts, libraries, museums and galleries, radio, television, science and research; *Education*: enrollments, degrees conferred, teaching staff; *Health*: hospitals, medical personnel, public health; *Housing*; *Labor*: employment, labor force, occupations, wages; *Sports and recreation*; *Social assistance*; *Social security*.

Most data are for 1982 and the preceding 6 years, plus 1970. Time series of varying length are provided. The volume is divided into 3 parts, with Part I offering data for the whole country, Part II data for provinces, and Part III, comparative data for selected foreign countries.

Explanatory notes are provided at the beginnings of chapters and there is a detailed list of tables at the beginning of the volume.

Available from the agency, Ministerskiya Sŭvet, International Division, 2 P Volov St., Sofia. Priced.

Available in microform: CH: 1956,1959-68,1970, and *Statisticheski godishnik na Tsarstvo Bŭlgariia*,1909-42. CIS: 1970-75, 1977.

284. ***Statistical pocketbook.*** 1958- Sofia: Dŭrzhavno Upravlenie za Informatisiya.

Title varies: Some years entitled *Statistical reference book*.

Not available for examination.

This is an English version of the abridged edition of entry 283 published annually in Bulgarian from 1958 as *Statisticheski spravochnik* [Statistical manual]. Available from the Foreign Language Press, 1 Levski Street, Sofia. Priced.

No general statistical bulletin is currently published by Bulgaria.

CZECHOSLOVAKIA

285. ***Statistická ročenka*** [Statistical yearbook]. 1934- Prague: Federální Statistický Úřad. Czech. English translations of section and table headings are available separately as *Statistical yearbook of the Czechoslovak Socialist Republic: Summary sheets*.

Not published 1939-1956.

Title and agency vary: 1934-1938, *Annuaire statistique de la République Tchécoslovaque*, published by the Office de Statistique. Continues the *Manuel statistique de la République Tchécoslovaque*, 1920-1932, published by l'Office Statistique d'Etat.

1983 edition published 1983, 698 p., contains the following information:

PHYSICAL ENVIRONMENT
Climatology: precipitation, temperature; *Environmental quality*: air pollution; *Geography*: area and use of land, maps.

DEMOGRAPHY

Population: census results from 1950-1982, distribution by age and sex, distribution by geographic area, ethnic groups, households and families; *Vital statistics*: abortions, births, causes of death, deaths, divorces, infant mortality, life expectancy, marriages, reproduction rate.

ECONOMIC AFFAIRS

Agriculture and food: farming, fishing, forestry; *Commerce and business*: domestic commerce, exports, imports, tourism; *Finance*: banking and credit; *Income and expenditure*: consumption, personal income, prices; *Industry*: communication, construction, energy, manufacturing, mining, transportation, water; *National accounts*: social product, national income; *Public finance*: government expenditure, government revenue.

SOCIAL AND CULTURAL AFFAIRS

Cultural and scientific activities: books and journals, cinema and performing arts, libraries, museums and galleries, newspapers, radio, television, science and research; *Education*: enrollments, graduates of higher education institutions, teaching staff; *Health*: disease, hospitals, medical personnel, public health; *Housing*; *Justice*: traffic accidents; *Labor*: employment, foreign workers, productivity, salaries and wages; *Social assistance*; *Social security*; *Sports and recreation*.

Most data are for 1982, with time series of varying lengths, usually 5 or more years. In addition to the national level, data are included for the following: the Republics, regions, and municipalities above 10,000. There is a section devoted to comparative statistics for a number of foreign countries.

Explanatory notes are provided at the beginnings of chapters. There is an alphabetical subject index at the end of the volume and a detailed table of contents at the beginning.

Available from ARTIA, Smechsvsky 30, Prague 1. Price: kcs78.

Available in microform: CH: 1957-1970; also *Annuaire statistique de la République Tchécoslovaque*, 1934-38, and *Manuel statistique de la République Tchécoslovaque*, 1920-32. CIS: 1970-1978, with English summary sheets for 1974, 1976-78.

286. **Čísla pro Každého** [Figures for everybody]. 1958- Prague: Federální Statistický Úřad. Czech.

Brief compilation covering many of the same topics as entry 285.

Latest published: 1984, 299 p. Available from ARTIA, Smečky 30, Prague 1.

287. **Statistické Přehledy** [Statistical surveys]. 1967- Prague: Federální Statistický Úřad. Monthly. English and Russian table of contents.

Available from ARTIA, Smečky 30, Prague 1.

DENMARK

288. **Statistisk årbog/Statistical yearbook.** 1896- Copenhagen: Danmarks Statistik. Danish,

with English translations of table headings in notes at end of tables; Danish and French, 1896-1951.

Agency varies: 1896-1912 by Statistiske Bureau.

V.88, 1984, published July, 1984, 667 p., contains statistical data in the following areas:

PHYSICAL ENVIRONMENT
Climatology: precipitation, sunshine, temperature; *Environmental quality*: air and water pollution, pesticides; *Geography*: area of land, maps.

DEMOGRAPHY
Population: census results from 1976, 1979, distribution by age and sex, distribution by geographic/administrative area, external migration, households and families, internal migration, population estimates and projections; *Vital statistics*: abortions, births, causes of death, deaths, divorces, fertility, infant mortality, life expectancy, marriages.

ECONOMIC AFFAIRS
Agriculture and food: farming, fishing, forestry; *Commerce and business*: companies, domestic commerce, exports, imports, services, tourism; *Finance*: banking and credit, money supply, securities; *Income and expenditure*: consumption, personal income, prices; *Industry*: communication, construction, energy, manufacturing, mining, transportation; *National accounts*: balance of payments, gross domestic and gross national product, national income; *Public finance*: government expenditures and government revenue at all levels of government.

POLITICAL AFFAIRS
Elections and referenda.

SOCIAL AND CULTURAL AFFAIRS
Cultural and scientific activities: books and journals, cinema and performing arts, libraries, museums and galleries, newspapers, radio, television, science and research; *Education*: enrollments, teaching staff; *Health*: disease, examination of conscripts, family planning, hospitals, medical personnel, public health; *Housing*; *Justice*: correctional institutions, courts, crimes, police, traffic accidents; *Labor*: employment and unemployment, labor force, labor-management relations, salaries and wages; *Religion*; *Social assistance*; *Social security*; *Sports and recreation.*

Most data are for 1983 and/or 1982 and varying numbers of earlier years. In addition to the national level, data are included for county and muncipality. There are special sections devoted to the Faroe Islands and Greenland, and a section of comparative data for selected foreign countries.

Explanatory notes are provided at the beginnings of some chapters in Danish only. Notes accompanying the tables indicate the names of the agencies furnishing the data. Changes in tables from the previous edition are noted in the foreword, which is in Danish only. There is an alphabetical subject index in Danish at the beginning of the volume and in English at the end. A description of the main official statistical series in Danish and English and a complete list of publications of Danmarks Statistik is provided at the end of the volume.

Historical statistics. Statistics for earlier periods are found in *Sammendrag af statistiske oplysninger angaaende Kongeriget Danmark,* 1869-93, published by the Statistiske Bureau.

Available from the agency, Postboks 2550, Sejrogade 11, DK 2100, Copenhagen 0. Price: K90.00.

Available in microform: CH: 1896-1965, and *Sammendrag af statistiske oplysninger angaaende Kongeriget Danmark,* 1869-93, published by the Statistiske Bureau. CIS: 1970-75, 1977, 1980-81.

289. **Statistiske efterretninger** [Statistical news]. 1909- Copenhagen: Danmarks Statistik. Irregular. Danish.

Contents of issues vary, with each issue containing both articles and statistical tables. Articles frequently summarize inquiries published in greater detail in *Statistiske meddelelser.* Issue no. 12 of 1982, 41 p., contains data on abortions, enonomic outlook, registered vehicles, energy and prices.

Available from the address in entry 288.

FINLAND

290. **Suomen tilastollinen vuosikirja/ Statistisk årsbok för Finland/ Statistical yearbook of Finland.** 1879-1902, 1903- Helsinki: Tilastokeskus. Finnish, Swedish and English since 1953; Finnish, Swedish and French, 1933-1952; Finnish and French, 1879-1932; Swedish and French, 1879-1932; Russian, 1892-1916.

1903- numbered new series.

Title varies: 1879-1902 as *Annuaire statistique pour la Finlande*; 1903-52 as *Annuaire statistique de Finlande.* Agency varies: 1879-84 by Tilastollinen toimisto; 1885-1969 by Tilastollinen Päätoimisto.

V. 79, 1983, n.s.. published 1984, 529 p., contains statistical data in the following areas:

PHYSICAL ENVIRONMENT
Climatology: precipitation, temperature; *Geography*: area of land, maps.

DEMOGRAPHY
Population: census results from 1950-80, distribution by age and sex, distribution by geographic/administrative area, external migration, households and families, internal migration, language groups; *Vital statistics*: abortions, births, including illegitimate births, causes of death, deaths, divorces, fertility, infant mortality, life expectancy, marriages.

ECONOMIC AFFAIRS
Agriculture and food: farming, fishing, forestry; *Commerce and business*: cooperatives, enterprises, establishments, domestic commerce, exports, imports; *Finance*: banking and credit, securities; *Income and expenditure*: consumption, cost of living, personal

income, prices; *Industry*: communication, construction, energy and water, manufacturing, mining, transportation; *National accounts*: balance of payments, gross domestic product, national income; *Public finance*: government expenditures and government revenue for central government and municipalities.

POLITICAL AFFAIRS
Elections.

SOCIAL AND CULTURAL AFFAIRS
Cultural and scientific activities: books and journals, cinema and performing arts, libraries, newspapers, radio, television, science and research, including patents issued; *Education*: degrees conferred, educational attainment, enrollments, examination results, teaching staff; *Health*: disease, family planning, hospitals, medical personnel, public health; *Housing*; *Justice*: correctional institutions, courts, crimes, traffic offenses; *Labor*: employment and unemployment, labor force, labor-management relations, occupations, salaries and wages; *Religion*; *Social assistance*; *Social security*.

Most data are for 1982, with time series of varying lengths. In addition to the national level, data are included for provinces and municipalities. There is a section of comparative statistics for selected foreign countries in Swedish and Finnish only.

Notes accompanying the tables indicate the names of the agencies furnishing the data. There is a detailed list of tables at the beginning of the volume. Tables dropped, added or revised since the previous edition are listed in the foreword. Alphabetical subject indexes in English, Finnish and Swedish and a list of current official statistical publications are provided.

Latest edition published: 1984, 562 p. Available from the Government Printing Centre, PO Box 516, SF00101 Helsinki 10. Price: FM148, plus postage.

Available in microform: CH: 1879-1970. CIS: 1971-80.

291. *Tilastokatsauksia/ Statistiska översikter/ Bulletin of statistics.* 1924- Helsinki: Tilastokeskus. Quarterly and monthly since 1983; earlier, monthly only. Quarterly edition in Finnish, Swedish and English; monthly edition in Finnish, with table titles only also in Swedish and English.

Title varies: 1936-51 as *Tilastokatsauksia/ Statistiska översikter/ Recueil de statistique*; 1924-51 as *Tilastokatsauksia/ Statistiska översikter.*Agency varies: 1924-69 by Tilastollinen Päätoimisto.

V. LIX, no. 3, 1984, 108 p., of the quarterly edition, contains statistical data in the following areas:

DEMOGRAPHY
Population: distribution by age, distribution by sex, external migration; *Vital statistics*: births, deaths, marriages.

ECONOMIC AFFAIRS
Agriculture and food: farming, forestry.*Commerce and business*: domestic commerce, exports, imports, tourism; *Finance*: banking and credit, securities; *Income and expenditure*: prices; *Industry*: communication, construction, energy, manufacturing, transpor-

tation; *National accounts*: gross domestic product, national income; *Public finance*: government expenditures, government revenue.

SOCIAL AND CULTURAL AFFAIRS
Health: disease; *Justice*: crimes, traffic accidents; *Labor*: employment and unemployment, labor force, labor-management relations, salaries and wages.

Most data are monthly for 13 to 24 months and annual for 4 or 5 years. Latest data are for 3 to 4 weeks before first date covered by issue. In addition, there is a separate section of monthly or quarterly seasonally adjusted series for a year or two. A list of official statistical publications is provided at the end of the issue.

The monthly edition, subtitled *kuukausikatsaus/ månadsöversikt*, updates some of the tables in the quarterly edition, presenting monthly figures for the latest 3 months available and the last month of the previous year. Latest data are for the month before the date of issue. Since the table headings are the same as in the quarterly edition, English-speaking readers may use the quarterly edition to translate them.

Available from the address in entry 290. Price: Combined annual subscription to quarterly and monthly bulletins: FIM190, Scandinavia; FIM200, other European countries; FIM210, elsewhere. Yearly subscription to quarterly bulletin only: FIM105, 110 and 120, respectively. Individual issues of quarterly bulletin FIM25, plus postage.

FRANCE

292. **Annuaire statistique de la France** [Statistical yearbook of France]. 1878- Paris: Institut National de la Statistique et des Etudes Economiques [INSEE]. Annual, except for the following volumes: 15, 1892-94; 16, 1895-96; 34, 1914-15; 35, 1916-18; 36, 1919-20; 56, 1940-45; 58, 1948-51. French.

1952 numbered new series.

Agency name varies: 1878-1939 by the Statistique Générale de la France (also called the Bureau de la Statistique Générale), which was attached to the following: 1878-81, Ministère de l'Agriculture et du Commerce; 1882-1904, Ministère du Commerce under this name and variants; 1905-23, 1933, Ministère du Travail under this name and variants; 1924-32, 1934-36, 1938: Présidence du Conseil; 1937, 1939: Ministère de l'Economie Nationale.

V. 89 (n.s. 31), 1984, 903 p., contains statistical data in the following areas:

PHYSICAL ENVIRONMENT
Climatology: precipitation, sunshine, temperature; *Environmental quality*: air pollution, national parks, solid waste, water pollution; *Geography*: area of land, maps.

DEMOGRAPHY
Population: census results from 1968, 1975, 1982, distribution by age and sex, distribution by geographic/administrative area, households and families, internal migration; *Vital statistics*: births, including illegitimate births, causes of death, deaths, divorces, fertility, infant mortality, life expectancy, marriages.

ECONOMIC AFFAIRS

Agriculture and food: farming, fishing, forestry; *Commerce and business*: domestic commerce, enterprises, establishments, exports, imports, tourism; *Finance*: banking and credit, money supply, securities; *Income and expenditure*: consumption, personal income, prices; *Industry*: communication, construction, energy, manufacturing, mining, transportation; *National accounts*: balance of payments, gross domestic product, national income; *Public finance*: government expenditures and government revenue for the central and local governments (aggregate only).

SOCIAL AND CULTURAL AFFAIRS

Cultural and scientific activities: books, cinema and performing arts, libraries and archives, museums, radio, television; *Education*: degrees conferred, enrollments, examination results, percent of age group in school, teaching staff; *Health*: disease, hospitals, medical personnel, public health; *Housing*; *Justice*: correctional institutions, courts, crimes, traffic accidents; *Labor*: employment and unemployment, foreign workers, labor force, labor-management relations, occupations, productivity, salaries and wages; *Social assistance*; *Social security*; *Sports and recreation*.

Most data are for 1983 and the preceding 5 or more years. In addition to the national level, data are included for regions, departments, overseas departments and territories, (DOM and TOM), and cities over 50,000.

Explanatory notes, which sometimes include descriptions of governmental organization are provided at the beginnings of chapters. Agencies furnishing the data and titles of sources are listed at ends of sections. There are a detailed list of tables and an alphabetical subject index at the end of the volume. Statistical publications of INSEE and international organizations are listed and the addresses of INSEE regional offices and distribution centers are provided.

Historical statistics. Retrospective statistics are found in the following volumes: v. 57, 1946; v. 58, 1951; v.66-rétrospective, 1961; and v. 72, 1966. Both current and retrospective data are included in the volumes for 1881 to 1939.

Latest edition published: 1985, 890 p. Available from the Observatoire Economique de Paris, 195 rue de Bercy, Tour Gamma A, 75582 Paris Cedex 22. Price: F440, foreign.

Available in microform: Brookhaven: 1878-1973. CH: 1878-1965. CIS: 1970/71-77. Datamics: 1878-1946. INSEE: 1975-83. Also available in a reprint edition from Kraus, 1878-1934.

293. **Bulletin mensuel de statistique** [Monthly bulletin of statistics]. 1949- Paris: Institut National de la Statistique et des Etudes Economiques [INSEE]. French.

Continues the *Bulletin de la statistique générale de la France,* 1911-49, published by Bureau de la Statistique Générale.

[V. 35], no. 10, Oct., 1984, 102 p., contains statistical data in the following areas:

PHYSICAL ENVIRONMENT
Climatology: precipitation, sunshine, temperature.

DEMOGRAPHY
Population: monthly population; *Vital statistics*: births, causes of death, deaths, infant mortality, marriages.

ECONOMIC AFFAIRS
Agriculture and food: farming, fishing; *Commerce and business*: companies, domestic commerce, exports, imports; *Finance*: banking and credit, money supply, securities; *Income and expenditure*: prices; *Industry*: communication, construction, energy, manufacturing, mining, transportation; *National accounts*: balance of payments; *Public finance*: government expenditures, government revenue.

SOCIAL AND CULTURAL AFFAIRS
Health: disease; *Justice*: traffic accidents; *Labor*: activity of employment offices, foreign workers, labor-management relations, salaries and wages; *Social assistance*; *Social security*.

Most data are monthly for 12 to 14 months and annual for latest full year. Latest data are for month of issue or preceding month. There are also some data for weeks or 10-day periods and some for quarters. Each issue also contains retrospective statistics on one topic for a period of 9 or more years. Statistics for overseas departments and territories and for foreign countries are included.

Notes accompanying the tables indicate the names of the agencies furnishing the data. A list of INSEE publications recently released or in press is provided.

Available from the address in entry 292. Price: Annual subscriptions: paper edition: F240, domestic; F275, foreign; microform edition: F125, domestic; F155, foreign. Single copies: paper edition: F23, domestic; F28, foreign; microfiche edition: F15.

Available in microform: INSEE: 1979 to date.

GERMANY (EAST)

294. ***Statistisches Jahrbuch der Deutschen Demokratischen Republik*** [Statistical yearbook of the German Democratic Republic]. 1955- Berlin: Staatliche Zentralverwaltung für Statistik. German, with table of contents also in English, French and Russian.

V. 29, 1984, published June, 1984, 534 p., contains statistical data in the following areas:

PHYSICAL ENVIRONMENT
Climatology: precipitation, temperature; *Geography*: area of land, maps.

DEMOGRAPHY
Population: census results from 1939-1981, distribution by age and sex, distribution by geographic/administrative area, households and families, internal migration; *Vital statistics*: births, causes of death, deaths, divorces, fertility, infant mortality, life expectancy, marriages.

ECONOMIC AFFAIRS

Agriculture and food: farming, fishing, forestry; *Commerce and business*: domestic commerce, exports, handicrafts, imports, services, tourism; *Finance*: banking and credit, money supply; *Income and expenditure*: consumption, cost of living, personal income, prices; *Industry*: communication, construction, energy, manufacturing, mining. transportation, water; *National accounts*: gross domestic product, national income; *Public finance*: government expenditures, government revenue, planning and economic development.

POLITICAL AFFAIRS

Composition of assemblies and membership in organizations.

SOCIAL AND CULTURAL AFFAIRS

Cultural and scientific activities: books and journals, cinema and performing arts, libraries, museums and galleries, newspapers, radio, television, science and research, including patents registered; *Education*: educational attainment (of employed only), enrollments, graduates of higher education institutions, teaching staff; *Health*: disease, hospitals, medical personnel, public health; *Housing*; *Justice*: courts, crimes, traffic accidents; *Labor*: employment, labor force, occupations, productivity, salaries and wages; *Social security*; *Sports and recreation.*

Most data are for 1983 and varying numbers of earlier years. In addition to the national level, data are included for Bezirke [districts], Kreise [counties] and Gemeinden [municipalities]. There are two appendices containing statistics for selected foreign countries; the first includes members of Council for Mutual Economic Assistance only. A bibliography of sources for international statistics is included.

Explanatory notes are provided at the beginnings of sections. There is an alphabetical subject index in German only at the end.

Latest edition published: 1985, 536 p. Available from Staatsverlag, Otto-Grotewohl-Strasse 17, 108 Berlin. Price: DM 59.60.

Available in microform: CH: 1955-65. CIS: 1970-73.

295. ***Statistisches Taschenbuch der Deutschen Demokratiken Republik*** [Statistical pocketbook of the German Democratic Republic]. 1960- Berlin: Staatliche Zentralverwaltung für Statistik. German. Also published in English, Arabic, French, Russian, Spanish and Swedish editions.

An abridged version of entry 294. The English edition is entitled *Statistical pocketbook of the German Democratic Republic.*

No general statistical bulletin is currently published by East Germany.

GERMANY (WEST)

296. ***Statistisches Jahrbuch für die Bundesrepublik Deutschland*** [Statistical yearbook for the Federal Republic of Germany]. 1952- Wiesbaden: Statistische Bundesamt. German.

1984 edition, published Aug., 1984, 792 p., contains statistical data in the following areas:

PHYSICAL ENVIRONMENT
Climatology: precipitation, sunshine, temperature; *Environmental quality*: environmental protection investment, solid waste, water quality; *Geography*: area of land, maps.

DEMOGRAPHY
Population: census results from 1950, 1961, 1970, and 1982 microcensus, distribution by age and sex, distribution by geographic/administrative area, external migration, households and families, internal migration, population projections; *Vital statistics*: births, including illegitimate births, causes of death, deaths, divorces, fertility, infant mortality, life expectancy, marriages.

ECONOMIC AFFAIRS
Agriculture and food: farming, fishing, forestry; *Commerce and business*: companies, cooperatives, establishments, domestic commerce, exports, imports, tourism; *Finance*: banking and credit, money supply, securities; *Income and expenditure*: consumption, personal income, prices; *Industry*: communication, construction, energy, manufacturing, mining, transportation; *National accounts*: balance of payments, gross domestic product, national income; *Public finance*: government expenditures, government revenue.

POLITICAL AFFAIRS
Elections; *Foreign aid*.

SOCIAL AND CULTURAL AFFAIRS
Cultural and scientific activities: books and journals, cinema and performing arts, libraries, museums, newspapers, radio, television, science and research, including patents registered; *Education*: degrees conferred, enrollments, examination results, teaching staff; *Health*: disease, hospitals, medical personnel, public health; *Housing*; *Justice*: correctional institutions, courts, crimes, traffic accidents; *Labor*: employment and unemployment, foreign workers, labor force, labor-management relations, occupations, salaries and wages; *Religion*; *Social assistance*; *Social security*; *Sports and recreation*.

Most data are for 1983 or 1982 and varying numbers of earlier years. In addition to the national level, data are included for Länder [states], Regierungsbezirke [districts], Kreise [counties], and Gemeinden [municipalities]. There is a section devoted to East Germany and East Berlin and another with comparative statistics for selected foreign countries.

Explanatory notes are provided at the beginnings of chapters. Notes accompanying the tables indicate the names of the agencies furnishing the data. There is also a section describing sources, entitled 'Quellennachweis', which includes lists of official statistical publications of the federal government and of state statistical offices. Sources which may be consulted for further information are also listed at the end of each section of tables. There is a detailed list of tables at the beginning of the volume, as well as an alphabetical subject index at the end.

Historical statistics. Statistics for earlier periods are found in *Statistisches Jahrbuch für das Deutsche Reich*, 1880-1942, published by Statistisches Reichsamt.

Latest edition published: 1985, 776 p. Available from Kohlhammer, Mainz. Price: DM 98.

Available in microform: CH: 1952-65, and *Statistisches Jahrbuch für das Deutsche Reich*, 1880-1942, published by Statistisches Reichsamt. CIS: 1970-78.

297. **Statistical compass.** 1977- Wiesbaden: Statistische Bundesamt. English; editions are also published in French and German.

A brief summary of demographic, economic and social statistics.

Another abridged edition was published 1953-1972? in German, French, English and Spanish editions under the title, *Statistisches Taschenbuch für die Bundesrepublik Deutschland*.

Latest edition available: 1984. Available from the address in entry 296. Price: DM3.

298. **Wirtschaft und Statistik** [Economy and statistics]. 1921- Wiesbaden: Statistische Bundesamt. Monthly. German, with table of contents also in English and French for the first part.

Each issue consists of two parts; the first contains articles, many of which include statistics, while the second consists of recurring statistical tables. Tables in no. 12, Dec., 1983, 133 p., contains statistical data in the following areas:

DEMOGRAPHY
Population: external migration, households and families, internal migration; *Vital statistics*: births, including illegitimate births, deaths, divorces, marriages.

ECONOMIC AFFAIRS
Agriculture and food: farming, fishing, forestry; *Commerce and business*: domestic commerce, enterprises, exports, handicrafts, imports, tourism; *Finance*: banking and credit, money supply, securities; *Income and expenditure*: consumption, personal income, prices; *Industry*: communication, construction, manufacturing, mining, transportation; *National accounts*: gross domestic product; *Public finance*: government expenditures, government revenue.

POLITICAL AFFAIRS
Elections.

SOCIAL AND CULTURAL AFFAIRS
Cultural and scientific activities: cinema and performing arts; *Education*: enrollments, examination results; *Health*: disease, hospitals, medical personnel; *Housing*; *Justice*: traffic accidents; *Labor*: employment and unemployment, labor force, productivity, salaries and wages; *Social assistance*; *Social security*.

Most data are monthly for 12 months and annual for 5 years. Latest data are for 1 or 2 months before the date of issue. There is a cumulative table of contents for the year to date for the first part of the issue, and a list of official statistical materials released during the month.

Available from the address in entry 296. Price: DM12.70 per issue.

GIBRALTAR

299. ***Abstract of statistics.*** 1972- Gibraltar: Economic Planning and Statistics Office.

1983 edition, 74 p., contains statistical data in the following areas:

PHYSICAL ENVIRONMENT
Climatology: precipitation, sunshine, temperature.

DEMOGRAPHY
Population: census results from 1961-1981, distribution by age and sex, households and families, population estimates; *Vital statistics*: births, deaths, life expectancy, marriages.

ECONOMIC AFFAIRS
Commerce and business: exports, imports, tourism; *Finance*: banking and credit; *Income and expenditure*: consumption, prices; *Industry*: communication, energy, transportation, water; *National accounts*: gross domestic and gross national product, national income; *Public finance*: government expenditures, government revenue.

SOCIAL AND CULTURAL AFFAIRS
Education: enrollments, teaching staff; *Health*: disease, hospitals, public health; *Housing*; *Justice*: correctional institutions, crimes, traffic accidents; *Labor*: employment and unemployment, foreign workers, labor force, occupations, salaries and wages; *Religion*.

Most data are for 1983 and varying numbers of earlier years. Explanatory notes and an indication of the names of the agencies furnishing the data accompany the tables. There is a detailed list of tables at the beginning of the volume.

Available from the Stationery Office, Government Secretariat, Gibraltar. Price: £2.00.

GREECE

300. ***Statistical yearbook of Greece/ Statistikē epetēris tēs Hellados.*** 1930- Athens: Ethnikē Statistikē Hyperēsia. Greek and English; 1930-39 in Greek and French.

New series begun 1954; publication suspended 1940-53.

Title varies slightly. Agency varies: 1930-39 by Genikē Statistikē Hyperēsia.

1982 edition, published 1983, 484 p., contains statistical data in the following areas:

PHYSICAL ENVIRONMENT
Climatology: precipitation, temperature; *Environmental quality*: radioactivity in Athens area; *Geography*: area of land, maps.

DEMOGRAPHY
Population: arrivals and departures, census results from 1821-1981, distribution by age and sex, distribution by geographic/administrative area, external migration, households and families, population estimates; *Vital statistics*: births, including illegitimate births, causes of death, deaths, infant mortality, life expectancy, marriages.

ECONOMIC AFFAIRS
Agriculture and food: farming, fishing, forestry; *Commerce and business*: domestic commerce, establishments, exports, imports, tourism; *Finance*: banking and credit, money supply, securities; *Income and expenditure*: consumption, personal income, prices; *Industry*: communication, construction, energy, manufacturing, mining, transportation; *National accounts*: balance of payments, gross domestic product, national income; *Public finance*: government expenditures and government revenue for central government and municipalities.

SOCIAL AND CULTURAL AFFAIRS
Cultural and scientific activities: journals, cinema and performing arts, museums and galleries, newspapers; *Education*: educational attainment, enrollments, graduates of higher education institutions, teaching staff; *Health*: disease, hospitals, medical personnel, public health; *Housing*; *Justice*: correctional institutions, courts, crimes, traffic accidents; *Labor*: employment and unemployment, foreign workers, labor force, occupations, salaries and wages; *Social assistance*; *Social security*.

Most data are for 1981 or 1980 and varying numbers of earlier years. In addition to the national level, data are included for region, department, cities over 10,000 and inhabited islands. There is a section of comparative statistics for selected foreign countries.

Commentaries are provided at the beginnings of chapters. Notes accompanying the tables indicate the names of the agencies furnishing the data. If no other source is indicated, the National Statistical Office is responsible for collecting the data. There is a detailed list of tables at the beginning of the volume.

Available from the agency, 14 Lycourgou St., Athens. Priced.

Available in microform: CH: 1930-64. CIS: 1970-76, 1978.

301. *Synoptikē statistikē epetēris/Concise statistical yearbook.* 1962- Athens: National Statistical Office/Ethnikē Statistikē Hyperēsia. English and Greek.

This is a condensed version of entry 299.

Available from the address given in entry 299. Priced.

302. *Mēniaion statistikon deltion/ Monthly statistical bulletin.* 1956- Athens: National Statistical Office / Ethnikē Statistikē Hyperēsia.

V. 28, no. 5, May, 1983, 90 p., contains statistical data in the following areas:

PHYSICAL ENVIRONMENT
Climatology: precipitation, sunshine, temperature; *Environmental quality*: radioactivity in Athens area.

DEMOGRAPHY
Population: arrivals and departures, distribution by age and sex, population estimates; *Vital statistics*: births, causes of death, deaths, infant mortality, marriages.

ECONOMIC AFFAIRS
Agriculture and food: farming, fishing, forestry; *Commerce and business*: domestic commerce, exports, imports, tourism; *Finance*: banking and credit, securities; *Income and expenditure*: prices; *Industry*: communication, construction, energy, transportation; *Public finance*: government expenditures, government revenue.

SOCIAL AND CULTURAL AFFAIRS
Cultural and scientific activities: Health: disease, hospitals; *Justice*: traffic accidents; *Labor*: employment and unemployment, foreign workers, salaries and wages.

Most data are monthly for 12 months and annual for the preceding 3 to 6 years. Latest data are for 2 months prior to the date of the issue. Notes accompanying a few of the tables indicate the names of the agencies furnishing the data.

Available from the address in entry 299. Priced.

GREENLAND

See DENMARK.

GREAT BRITAIN

See UNITED KINGDOM.

HUNGARY

303. ***Statisztikai évkönyv*** [Statistical yearbook]. 1871- Budapest: Központi Statisztikai Hivatal. Hungarian, with supplement containing English translation available for some years under the title, *Statistical yearbook: English translation of the text*. English and Russian editions also published some years.

Title and languages vary: 1871-1890 as *Magyar statisztikai évkönyv/ Statistisches Jahrbuch für Ungarn* in Hungarian and German; 1893-1900 as *Magyar statisztikai évkönyv: Uj folyam*, in Hungarian and German; 1901-41 as *Annuaire statistique hongrois*, in French, German and Hungarian.

1942-1948 not published.

1983 edition, published 1984, 408 p., contains statistical data in the following areas:

PHYSICAL ENVIRONMENT
Climatology: precipitation, sunshine, temperature; *Environmental quality*: protection of nature, solid waste; *Geography*: area and use of land, maps.

DEMOGRAPHY
Population: distribution by age and sex, distribution by geographic/administrative area, households and families, internal migration; *Vital statistics*: abortions, births, including illegitimate births, causes of death, deaths, divorces, infant mortality, life expectancy, marriages.

ECONOMIC AFFAIRS
Agriculture and food: farming, fishing, forestry; *Commerce and business*: companies, domestic commerce, exports, imports, services, tourism; *Income and expenditure*: consumption, prices; *Industry*: communication, construction, energy, manufacturing, mining, transportation, water; *National accounts*: gross domestic and net national product, national income; *Public finance*: government expenditures, government revenue, planning and economic development.

SOCIAL AND CULTURAL AFFAIRS
Cultural and scientific activities: books and journals, cinema and performing arts, computers, libraries, museums and galleries, newspapers, radio, television, science and research; *Education*: degrees conferred, educational attainment, enrollments, examination results, teaching staff; *Health*: disease, family planning, hospitals, medical personnel, public health; *Housing*; *Justice*: correctional institutions, courts, crimes, traffic accidents; *Labor*: employment, labor force, occupations, productivity, salaries and wages. *Social assistance*; *Social security*; *Sports and recreation*.

Most data are for 1983 and selected earlier years, most frequently 1980-1982, 1975 and 1970. In addition to the national level, there are separate sections offering data for megyek [counties] and selected foreign countries. There are also some data for towns.

There is a detailed list of tables at the beginning of the volume and an alphabetical subject index at the end.

Available from the agency, Keleti Káoly u. 5-7, 1024 Budapest. Priced.

Available in microform: CH: 1949/55-1965 and *Magyar statisztikai évkönyv*, 1872-1941. CIS: 1970, 1972, 1979 of Hungarian ed., 1971, 1973-74 of English ed. and 1979 of *Statistical yearbook*: English translation of the text.

304. *Magyar statisztikai zsebkönyv* 1931- [Statistical pocketbook of Hungary]. 1931- Budapest: Központi Statisztikai Hivatal. English, German, Hungarian, and Russian editions.

An abridged version of entry 302.

Latest edition published: 1982. Available from the address given in entry 303. Priced.

305. *Statisztikai havi közlemények* [Monthly bulletin of statistics]. 1897- Budapest: Központi Statisztikai Hivatal. Hungarian, with translations of English, German and Russian table headings in a supplement.

Title varies: 1937-56 as *Statisztikai negyedévi közlemények*.

No. 10, 1983, 102 p., contains statistical data in the following areas:

PHYSICAL ENVIRONMENT
Climatology: temperature.

DEMOGRAPHY
Population; *Vital statistics*: causes of death.

ECONOMIC AFFAIRS
Agriculture and food: farming; *Commerce and business*: domestic commerce, exports, imports, tourism; *Finance*: money in circulation; *Income and expenditure*: prices; *Industry*: construction, transportation.

SOCIAL AND CULTURAL AFFAIRS
Cultural and scientific activities: books; *Education*: enrollments; *Health*: disease, hospitals, medical personnel; *Justice*: traffic accidents; *Labor*: employment.

Each issue consists of 2 parts; the first offers monthly statistics for 18 to 24 months and annual for the 5 preceding years. The second part offers quarterly, semi-annual or annual statistics. In addition to the national level, there is a section of comparative data for selected foreign countries. A list of official statistical materials in print and a subject index are provided.

Available from the address in entry 303. Priced.

ICELAND

306. *Tölfraedihandbók/Statistical abstract of Iceland.* 1967- Reykjavik: Hagstofa Islands/ Statistical Bureau. (Statistics of Iceland II, 82.) Irregular; previous editions published 1967, 1974. Icelandic and English.

1984 edition, 268 p., contains statistical data in the following areas:

PHYSICAL ENVIRONMENT
Climatology: precipitation, sunshine, temperature; *Geography*: area and use of land.

DEMOGRAPHY
Population: census results from 1703-1960, distribution by age and sex, distribution by geographic/administrative area, external migration, households and families, internal migration, population projections; *Vital statistics*: abortions, births, including illegitimate births, causes of death, deaths, divorces, fertility, infant mortality, life expectancy, marriages.

ECONOMIC AFFAIRS
Agriculture and food: farming, fishing; *Commerce and business*: cooperatives, domestic commerce, establishments, exports, imports, tourism; *Finance*: banking and credit, money supply; *Income and expenditure*: consumption, cost of living, personal income, prices; *Industry*: communication, construction, energy, manufacturing, transportation; *National accounts*: balance of payments, gross national product, national income; *Public finance*: government expenditures and government revenue for the central and communal governments.

POLITICAL AFFAIRS
Elections.

SOCIAL AND CULTURAL AFFAIRS
Cultural and scientific activities: books and journals, cinema and performing arts, libraries, museums and galleries, newspapers, radio, television; *Education*: degrees conferred, enrollments, examination results, teaching staff; *Health*: disease, family

planning (sterilizations only), hospitals, medical personnel; *Housing*; *Justice*: courts, crimes, traffic accidents; *Labor*: unemployment, labor force, labor-management relations, salaries and wages; *Religion*; *Social assistance*; *Social security*; *Sports and recreation* .

Most data are for 1983 or 1982 with many long time series. There are some monthly figures. In addition to the national level, data are included for regions, counties and towns.

Explanatory notes are provided at the beginnings of some sections and at the foot of some tables. Sources for tables are listed at the end of the volume. There is a detailed list of tables at the beginning of the volume and an alphabetical subject index at the end.

Historical statistics. Statistics for earlier periods may be found in *Arbók Hagstofu Islands*, 1930, and *Sammendrasg af statistiske oplysninger om Island...*, 1907, published by the Statens Statistiske Bureau.

Available from the agency, Hverfisgata 8-10, Reykjavik. Priced.

No general statistical bulletin for Iceland is currently published.

IRELAND

307. **Statistical abstract of Ireland.** 1931- Dublin: Central Statistics Office.

1980 edition, published 1983, 386 p., contains statistical data in the following areas:

PHYSICAL ENVIRONMENT
Climatology: precipitation, sunshine, temperature; *Geography*: area of land, maps.

DEMOGRAPHY
Population: arrivals and departures, census results from 1841-1979, distribution by age and sex, distribution by geographic/administrative area, external migration, households and families, internal migration; *Vital statistics*: births, including illegitimate births, causes of death, deaths, fertility, infant mortality, life expectancy, marriages.

ECONOMIC AFFAIRS
Agriculture and food: farming, fishing, forestry; *Commerce and business*: companies, cooperatives, domestic commerce, exports, imports, tourism; *Finance*: banking and credit, money in circulation, securities; *Income and expenditure*: consumption, personal income, prices; *Industry*: communication, construction, energy, manufacturing, transportation; *National accounts*: balance of payments, gross national product, national income; *Public finance*: government expenditures and government revenue for the central and local governments (aggregate only).

POLITICAL AFFAIRS
Defense; *Elections*.

SOCIAL AND CULTURAL AFFAIRS
Cultural and scientific activities: Irish language, libraries, patents issued, radio, television; *Education*: educational attainment, enrollments, examination results, graduates of higher education institutions, teaching staff; *Housing*; *Justice*: correctional institutions, courts, crimes, traffic accidents; *Labor*: employment, labor force, labor-management relations, occupations, salaries and wages; *Religion*; *Social assistance*; *Social security*.

Most data are for 1980, with varying numbers of earlier years. In addition to the national level, data are included for provinces, counties and county boroughs. There is an appendix with data for Northern Ireland which contains cross references to tables in the *Abstract* with similar data for Ireland.

Commentaries are provided at the beginnings of sections. Sources of tables are listed after the table of contents. An alphabetical subject index and a detailed list of tables are provided.

Historical statistics. Population statistics for earlier periods may be found in *Irish historical statistics: population 1821-1971,* edited by W.E. Vaughan and A. J. Fitzpatrick (A new history of Ireland II), Dublin, Royal Irish Academy, 1978, 372 p.

Available from the Government Publications Sales Office, Sun Alliance House, Molesworth St., Dublin 2. Price: £10.70.

Available in microform: CIS: 1970/71, 1972/73-1974/75.

308. **Irish statistical bulletin.** 1965- Dublin: Central Statistics Office. Quarterly.

Continues: *Irish trade journal,* 1925-37 and *Irish trade journal and statistical bulletin,* 1937-63, both issued by the Dept. of Industry and Commerce.

Available from the Government Publications Sales Office, Sun Alliance House, Molesworth St., Dublin 2. Priced.

ITALY

309. **Annuario statistico italiano** [Italian statistical abstract]. 1878- Rome: Istituto Centrale di Statistica (ISTAT). Italian.

Agency varies: 1878-1922 by Direzione Generale della Statistica.

1984 edition, 423 p., contains statistical data in the following areas:

PHYSICAL ENVIRONMENT
Climatology: precipitation, temperature; *Geography*: area of land, maps.

DEMOGRAPHY
Population: census results from 1861-1981, distribution by age and sex, distribution by geographic/administrative area, external migration, households and families, internal migration, population projections; *Vital statistics*: abortions, births, including illegitimate births, causes of death, deaths, divorces, fertility, infant mortality, life expectancy, marriages.

ECONOMIC AFFAIRS
Agriculture and food: farming, fishing, forestry; *Commerce and business*: domestic commerce, enterprises, exports, imports, tourism; *Finance*: banking and credit, money supply, securities; *Income and expenditure*: consumption, prices; *Industry*: communication, construction, energy, manufacturing, mining, transportation; *National accounts*: balance of payments, gross domestic product, national income; *Public finance*: government expenditures and government revenue for the central and local governments (aggregate only).

POLITICAL AFFAIRS
Elections.

SOCIAL AND CULTURAL AFFAIRS
Cultural and scientific activities: books and journals, cinema and performing arts, libraries, museums and galleries, newspapers, radio, television, science and research; *Education*: degrees conferred, enrollments, teaching staff; *Health*: disease, hospitals, public health; *Housing*; *Justice*: correctional institutions, courts, crimes, traffic accidents; *Labor*: employment and unemployment, labor force, labor-management relations, salaries and wages; *Social assistance*; *Social security*; *Sports and recreation*.

Most data are for 1983 or 1982 and the preceding 1 to 4 years. In addition to the national level, data are included for regions and provinces. There are comparative statistics for selected foreign countries.

Explanatory notes are provided at the beginnings of chapters. Sources of tables are given in the methodological note at the end of the volume. There is a detailed list of tables at the beginning of the volume. A bibliography of ISTAT publications is provided.

Historical statistics. Sommario di statistiche storiche dell'Italia 1861-1975, ISTAT, 197 187 p. Offers annual, quinquennial and decennial series.

Available from the agency, Via Cesare Balbo 16, 00100 Rome. Price: L11,000.

Available in microform: CH: 1878-1965. CIS: 1970-80.

310. **Compendio statistico italiano** [Italian statistical compendium]. 1927- Rome: Istituto Centrale di Statistica (ISTAT). Italian.

An abridged version of the preceding entry.

Available from the address in entry 309. Priced.

311. **Bolletin mensile de statistica** [Monthly bulletin of statistics]. 1926- Rome: Istituto Centrale di Statistica (ISTAT). Italian.

V. 58, no. 8-9, Aug.-Sept., 1983, 166 p., contains statistical data in the following areas:

PHYSICAL ENVIRONMENT
Climatology: precipitation, temperature.

DEMOGRAPHY
Population: population estimates; *Vital statistics*: births, causes of death, deaths, infant mortality.

ECONOMIC AFFAIRS
Agriculture and food: farming, fishing, forestry; *Commerce and business*: domestic commerce, exports, imports, tourism; *Finance*: banking and credit, money supply; *Income and expenditure*: cost of living, prices; *Industry*: construction, energy, manufacturing, transportation; *Public finance*: situation of Treasury.

SOCIAL AND CULTURAL AFFAIRS
Education: enrollments; *Health*: disease, hospitals, medical personnel; *Justice*: correctional institutions, courts, crimes; *Labor*: employment, labor force, labor management relations, occupations, salaries and wages.

Most data are monthly for 24 months. Latest data are for 2 months prior to the date of the issue. In addition to the national level, data are included for provinces and municipalities.

Available from the address given in entry 309. Priced.

LIECHTENSTEIN

312. **Statistisches Jahrbuch** [Statistical yearbook]. 1960- Vaduz: Amt für Volkswirtschaft. German.

Title varies: Earlier, *Statistisches Tabellenwerk*.

1983 edition, published Dec., 1983, 362 p., contains statistical data in the following areas:

PHYSICAL ENVIRONMENT
Climatology: precipitation, sunshine, temperature; *Environmental quality*: garbage removal; *Geography*: area of land, maps.

DEMOGRAPHY
Population: census results from 1930, distribution by age and sex, distribution by geographic/administrative area, external migration, households and families; *Vital statistics*: births, causes of death, deaths, infant mortality, marriages.

ECONOMIC AFFAIRS
Agriculture and food: farming, forestry; *Commerce and business*: domestic commerce, exports, imports, tourism; *Finance*: banking and credit; *Income and expenditure*: prices; *Industry*: communication, construction, energy, manufacturing, transportation; *National accounts*: gross domestic product, national income; *Public finance*: government expenditures, government revenue.

POLITICAL AFFAIRS
Elections.

SOCIAL AND CULTURAL AFFAIRS
Cultural and scientific activities: libraries, museums, native language of population, radio; *Education*: enrollments, teaching staff; *Health*: disease, medical personnel; *Housing*; *Justice*: courts, traffic accidents; *Labor*: employment and unemployment, foreign workers, labor force, salaries and wages; *Religion*; *Social security*; *Sports and recreation*.

Most data are for 1982 and varying numbers of earlier years. In addition to the national level, data are included for Gemeinden [municipalities]. Notes accompanying the tables indicate the names of the agencies furnishing the data. There is a detailed list of tables at the beginning of the volume.

Latest edition published: 1984, 376 p. Available from the agency, FL-9490 Vaduz.

Available in microform: CIS: 1971-72.

No general statistical bulletin has been found for Liechtenstein.

LUXEMBOURG

313. **Annuaire statistique** [Statistical yearbook]. 1955- Luxembourg: Service Central de la Statistique et des Etudes (STATEC). French.

1983/84 edition, published Jan., 1984, 460 p., contains statistical data in the following areas:

PHYSICAL ENVIRONMENT
Climatology: precipitation, sunshine, temperature; *Environmental quality*; air and water pollution; *Geography*: area of land, maps.

DEMOGRAPHY
Population: census results from 1871-1981, distribution by age and sex, distribution by geographic/administrative area, external migration, households and families; *Vital statistics*: births, including illegitimate births, causes of death, deaths, divorces, fertility, infant mortality, life expectancy, marriages.

ECONOMIC AFFAIRS
Agriculture and food: farming, fishing, forestry; *Commerce and business*: domestic commerce, enterprises, exports, imports, handicrafts, services, tourism; *Finance*: banking and credit, money supply, securities; *Income and expenditure*: consumption, cost of living, personal income, prices; *Industry*: communication, construction, energy, manufacturing, mining, transportation, water; *National accounts*: balance of payments, gross domestic product, national income; *Public finance*: government expenditures, government revenue.

POLITICAL AFFAIRS
Elections.

SOCIAL AND CULTURAL AFFAIRS

Cultural and scientific activities: books and journals, cinema and performing arts, frequency of family names and given names, newspapers, patents, science and research; *Education*: enrollments, examination results, teaching staff; *Health*: body measurements, disease, family planning. hospitals, medical personnel, public health; *Housing*; *Justice*: correctional institutions, traffic accidents; *Labor*: employment and unemployment, foreign workers, labor force, labor-management relations, occupations, salaries and wages; *Religion*; *Social assistance*; *Social security*; *Sports and recreation*.

Most data are for 1983 or 1982 and the preceding 4 years, plus selected earlier years to 1938. In addition to the national level, data are included for localities. There are comparative statistics for selected foreign countries.

Explanatory notes, which include bibliographies, are provided at the beginnings of chapters. Sources for each table are listed in the section entitled 'Centralisation statistique', near the end of the volume. There is a detailed list of tables at the beginning of the volume and an alphabetical subject index at the end. A bibliography of official statistical materials is included.

Historical statistics. Statistics for earlier periods may be found in the 1973 edition, entitled *Annuaire statistique rétrospectif,* 536 p., and the addendum to it published in 1974, 66 p.

Available from the agency, PO Box 304, L-2013, Luxembourg. Priced.

Available in microform: CIS: 1970-73, 1975, 1977-80.

314. ***Bulletin du STATEC*** [Bulletin of STATEC]. 1963- 8 issues a year. French.

Each issue contains articles on statistical topics and reports on the activities of STATEC. Topics covered in 1984 included the results of the agricultural census of 1983, buildings finished in 1982, recent demographic developments, legislative elections 1945-1984, principal enterprises, retail prices 1983, traffic accidents.

Available from the address in entry 313. Priced.

MALTA

315. ***Annual abstract of statistics.*** 1947- Valletta: Central Office of Statistics.

No. 37, 1983, published 1984, 259 p., contains statistical data in the following areas:

PHYSICAL ENVIRONMENT
Climatology: precipitation, sunshine, temperature; *Geography*: area of land.

DEMOGRAPHY
Population: arrivals and departures, census results from 1957 and 1967, distribution (projected) by age and sex, distribution by geographic/administrative area, external migration, population estimates and projections; *Vital statistics*: births, including illegitimate births, causes of death, deaths, infant mortality, life expectancy, marriages.

ECONOMIC AFFAIRS
Agriculture and food: farming, fishing, land tenure; *Commerce and business*: companies, cooperatives, exports, imports, tourism; *Finance*: banking and credit, money supply; *Income and expenditure*: consumption, prices; *Industry*: communication, construction, energy, manufacturing, quarrying, transportation, water; *National accounts*: balance of payments, gross domestic and gross national product, national income; *Public finance*: government expenditures and government revenue, including lottery.

POLITICAL AFFAIRS
Elections.

SOCIAL AND CULTURAL AFFAIRS
Cultural and scientific activities: cinema and performing arts, libraries, museums and galleries, radio, television; *Education*: degrees conferred, enrollments, teaching staff; *Health*: disease; *Justice*: correctional institutions, courts, crimes, traffic accidents; *Labor*: employment and unemployment, labor-management relations, occupations, salaries and wages; *Social security*.

Most data are for 1983 and varying numbers of earlier years, usually 7. In addition to the national level, data are included for selected localities.

Explanatory notes which include discussions of sources are provided at the beginnings of chapters. Notes accompanying some of the tables indicate the names of the agencies furnishing the data. There is a detailed list of tables at the beginning of the volume.

Available from the Information Division, Auberge de Castille, Castille Place, Valletta. Price: £-M1.

Available in microform: CIS: 1970/71-77.

316. ***Quarterly digest of statistics.*** 1960- Valletta: Central Office of Statistics.

No. 98, June, 1984, 70 p., contains statistical data in the following areas:

PHYSICAL ENVIRONMENT
Climatology: precipitation, sunshine, temperature.

DEMOGRAPHY
Population: arrivals and departures, external migration, internal migration, population estimates; *Vital statistics*: births, deaths.

ECONOMIC AFFAIRS
Agriculture and food: farming, fishing; *Commerce and business*: exports, imports, tourism; *Finance*: banking and credit, money supply; *Income and expenditure*: prices; *Industry*: transportation; *Public finance*: government expenditures, government revenue.

SOCIAL AND CULTURAL AFFAIRS
Health: disease; *Justice*: traffic accidents; *Labor*: employment and unemployment.

Most data are monthly for 12 months, quarterly for 2 years, and annual for 6 years. The latest data are for the date of the issue.

Available from the address in entry 315. Price: 40c.

MONACO

No current general statistical yearbook or bulletin is published by Monaco.

NETHERLANDS

317. ***Statistical yearbook of the Netherlands.*** 1850/81- The Hague: Centraal Bureau voor de Statistiek (CBS). English only since 1969/70. Previously published in the following languages: 1850/81, 1850/83: French; 1883-1939: Dutch and French; 1940-42: Dutch and German; 1943/46-1967/68: Dutch and English.

1887-1921 published in 2 parts : [1] Binnenland; [2] Koloniën.

Title varies: 1850/81, 1850/83: *Annuaire statistique pour le Royaume des Pays-Bas*; 1883-1897: *Jaarcijfers/ Annuaire statistique des Pays-Bas*; 1898-1922: *Jaarcijfers voor het Koninkrijk der Nederlanden/ Annuaire statistique [pour le Royaume] des Pays-Bas*; 1923-38: *Jaarcijfers voor Nederland/ Annuaire statistique pour les Pays-Bas*; 1940-42: *Jaarcijfers voor Nederland*; 1943-67/68: *Jaarcijfers voor Nederland/ Statistical yearbook of the Netherlands.* Agency varies: 1850-83 by Société de Statistique des Pays-Bas; 1883-84: Vereeniging voor de Statistiek in Nederland; 1885-92: Statistisch Instituut voor de Vereeniging voor de Statistiek in Nederland/ Institut Statistique fondé par la Société de Statistique des Pays-Bas; 1893-97: Centrale Commissie voor de Statistiek/ Commission Centrale de Statistique; 1898-1966: Centraal Bureau voor de Statistiek/ Central Bureau of Statistics [Bureau Centrale de Statistique before 1940].

1983 edition, published Feb., 1984, 428 p., contains statistical data in the following areas:

PHYSICAL ENVIRONMENT
Climatology: precipitation, sunshine, temperature; *Environmental quality*: air pollution, solid waste, recycling, use of pesticides, waste water treatment; *Geography*: area and use of land, maps.

DEMOGRAPHY
Population: distribution by age and sex, distribution by geographic/administrative area, external migration, households and families, internal migration, population projections; *Vital statistics*: births, including illegitimate births, causes of death, deaths, divorces, fertility, infant mortality, life expectancy, marriages.

ECONOMIC AFFAIRS
Agriculture and food: farming, fishing; *Commerce and business*: domestic commerce, enterprises, establishments, exports, imports, tourism; *Finance*: banking and credit, money supply, securities; *Income and expenditure*: consumption, personal income, prices; *Industry*: communication, construction, energy, manufacturing, mining, transportation; *National accounts*: balance of payments, gross domestic product, national income; *Public finance*: government expenditures and government revenue for central government, provinces and municipalities (aggregate only for latter two).

POLITICAL AFFAIRS
Elections.

SOCIAL AND CULTURAL AFFAIRS
Cultural and scientific activities: books, cinema and performing arts, libraries, museum and galleries, radio, television, science and research; *Education*: degrees conferre enrollments, examination results, teaching staff; *Health*: disease, hospitals, medic personnel, public health; *Housing*; *Justice*: correctional institutions, courts, crime police, traffic accidents; *Labor*: employment and unemployment, foreign workers, lab force, labor-management relations, occupations, salaries and wages; *Religion*; *Soci assistance*; *Social security*; *Sports and recreation.*

Most data are for 1982 or 1981 and the preceding 2 years, plus 1970 and 1975. I addition to the national level, data are included for regions/ provinces and municipal ties.

Explanatory notes are provided at the beginnings of chapters. There is a key to source used for each table, followed by a a bibliography of publications of the CBS, near th end of the volume. If an agency other than the CBS has furnished the informatio the name of the agency furnishing the data accompanies the table. There is a detaile list of tables at the beginning of the volume and an alphabetical subject index at th end. Among the illustrations is a chart showing the educational system.

Historical statistics. Compilations of statistics from 1899 to the date of publication hav been published in Dutch by the CSB at irregular intervals since 1959 under the tit *[80] Jaar statistiek in tijdreeksen.* Tables of contents in English are included. Statisti for the mid-nineteenth century are found in *Statistisch jaarboek voor het koningrijk d Nederlanden...,* 1851-68, published by the Departement van Binnenlandsche.

Available from the government printer, Staatsuitgeverij, Christoffel Plantijnstraat, Th Hague. Priced.

Available in microform: CH: 1850/51-1965/66 and *Statistisch Jaarboek,* 1851-81. CI: 1971-74, 1976-80.

318. **Statistisch zakboek** [Statistical pocketbook]. 1924- The Hague: Centraal Bureau vo de Statistiek (CBS). Dutch.

The 1981 ed., published Oct., 1981, 388 p., covers most of the same topics as th preceding entry in less detail.

Available from the government printer, Staatsuitgeverij, Christoffel Plantijnstraat, Th Hague. Priced.

Available in microform: CIS: 1970, 1975.

319. **Statistisch magazine.** [Statistical magazine]. 1981- The Hague: Centraal Bureau vo de Statistiek (CBS).

Each issue contains articles on various statistical topics. Subjects in v. 3, no. 1, 198 73 p., include the Dutch population in 1980, and price indexes.

Historical statistics. Monthly and quarterly demographic, economic and social data for earlier periods are found in *Maandschrift van het CBS* [Monthly bulletin of the CBS], 1944-1980, published in Dutch, with tables of contents and an annual appendix containing explanatory notes in English.

Available from the government printer, Staatsuitgeverij, Christoffel Plantijnstraat, The Hague. Priced.

NORTHERN IRELAND

See UNITED KINGDOM.

NORWAY

320. **Statistisk årbok** [Statistical yearbook]. 1879- Oslo: Statistisk Sentralbyrå. Norwegian and English.

V. 103, 1984, published Aug., 1984, 518 p., contains statistical data in the following areas:

PHYSICAL ENVIRONMENT
Climatology: precipitation, temperature; *Environmental quality*: recycling, waste treatment; *Geography*: area of land, maps.

DEMOGRAPHY
Population: census results from 1769-1980, distribution by age and sex, distribution by geographic/administrative area, external migration, households and families, internal migration, population projections; *Vital statistics*: abortions, births, including illegitimate births, causes of death, deaths, divorces, fertility, infant mortality, life expectancy, marriages.

ECONOMIC AFFAIRS
Agriculture and food: farming, fishing, forestry; *Commerce and business*: domestic commerce, establishments, exports, imports, services, tourism; *Finance*: banking and credit, money supply, securities; *Income and expenditure*: consumption, personal income, prices; *Industry*: communication, construction, energy, manufacturing, mining, transportation; *National accounts*: balance of payments, gross domestic product, national income; *Public finance*: government expenditure and government revenue for the central and local governments.

POLITICAL AFFAIRS
Elections; *Foreign aid*.

SOCIAL AND CULTURAL AFFAIRS
Cultural and scientific activities: books and journals, cinema and performing arts, libraries, newspapers, radio, television, science and research, use of Norwegian language in schools and government service, use of time; *Education*: degrees conferred, enrollments, teaching staff; *Health*: disease, family planning, height of conscripts, hospitals, medical personnel, public health; *Housing*; *Justice*: correctional institutions,

courts, crimes, traffic accidents; *Labor*: employment and unemployment, foreign workers, labor force, labor-management relations, occupations, salaries and wages; *Religion*; *Social assistance*; *Social security*; *Sports and recreation*.

Most data are for 1983 or 1982 and varying numbers of earlier years. In addition to the national level, data are included for counties and municipalities. Also included are separate tables for Svalbard and a section of comparative data from selected foreign countries. This last section has no English translations of table headings.

Notes accompanying the tables indicate the names of the agencies furnishing the data. There is a detailed list of tables at the beginning of the volume and there are alphabetical subject indexes in Norwegian and English at the end. Recent publications of the Statistisk Sentralbyrå are listed at the end of the volume.

Historical statistics. Statistics for earlier periods are found in the Statistisk Sentralbyrå's *Historisk statistikk/ Historical statistics*, 1978, 650 p., which offers time series of varying lengths through 1975. Earlier editions of this title were published in 1914, 1926, 1948, 1958 (supplement to 1948), and 1968.

Latest edition published: 1985, 528 p. Available from Universitetsforlaget, Postboks 8134, 0033, Oslo 1. Price: NKr 40.00.

Available in microform: CH: 1879-1965 and 1968 of *Historisk statistikk*. CIS: 1970-79.

321. **Statistisk månedshefte/ Monthly bulletin of statistics.** Oslo: Statistisk Sentralbyrå Norwegian and English.

No. 10 of 1983, 111 p., contains statistical data in the following areas:

DEMOGRAPHY
Population: external migration, internal migration; *Vital statistics*: births, deaths, divorces, marriages.

ECONOMIC AFFAIRS
Agriculture and food: fishing; *Commerce and business*: domestic commerce, exports imports; *Finance*: banking and credit, securities; *Income and expenditure*: prices *Industry*: communication, construction, manufacturing, transportation; *National accounts*: balance of payments, gross domestic product; *Public finance*: government expenditures, government revenue.

SOCIAL AND CULTURAL AFFAIRS
Justice: crimes, traffic accidents; *Labor*: employment and unemployment, labor force salaries and wages.

Most data are monthly or quarterly for 1 to 3 years and annual for 5 to 8 years. Late data are for the month before month of issue. There is a section of comparative da from selected foreign countries. A detailed list of tables at the beginning of the volum indicates whether tables are published monthly, quarterly or semi-annually.

Available from the address given in entry 320. Price: NKr15.00 per issue ar NKr150.00 per year.

POLAND

322. ***Rocznik statystyczny*** [Statistical yearbook]. Warsaw: Główny Urząd Statystyczny. 1930-39, 1947- Polish, with table of contents available in English for some issues; 1920/21-1938 in Polish and French.

No volumes published between no. 14, 1950 and no. 15, 1955.

Continues: *Rocznik statystyki Rzeczypospolitej Polskiej/ Annuaire statistique de la République Polonaise*, 1920/21-29.

1983 edition, 574 p., contains statistical data in the following areas:

PHYSICAL ENVIRONMENT
Climatology: precipitation, sunshine, temperature; *Environmental quality*: level and cleanliness of principal rivers, air and water pollution, investment outlays on water management and protection, selected animals protected, national parks, utilization of wastes; *Geography*: area and use of land, maps.

DEMOGRAPHY
Population: results from 1946-1978, distribution by age and sex, distribution by geographic area, external migration, households and families, internal migration, population estimates; *Vital statistics*: births, divorces, deaths, causes of death, fertility, infant mortality, life expectancy, marriages.

ECONOMIC AFFAIRS
Agriculture and food: agriculture in non-socialized and socialized economies, forestry; *Commerce and business*: domestic commerce, exports, imports, services; *Finance*: banking and credit, currency in circulation; *Income and expenditure*: consumption, household budgets, household income, prices; *Industry*: communication, construction, energy, handicrafts, manufacturing, mining, transportation; *National accounts*: gross national product, national income, inter-industry flows; *Public finance*: government expenditure and government revenue for the central and provincial governments (aggregate only).

POLITICAL AFFAIRS
Membership of Parliament and People's Councils, trade unions.

SOCIAL AND CULTURAL AFFAIRS
Cultural and scientific activities: books and journals, libraries, museums and galleries, newspapers, performing arts, radio, television, science and research; *Education*: enrollments, educational attainment, graduates of higher education institutions, teaching staff; *Health*: disease, hospitals, medical personnel, public health; *Housing*; *Justice*: correctional institutions, courts, crimes; *Labor*: employment, labor force, labor productivity, salaries and wages; *Religion*; *Social assistance*; *Social security*; *Sports and recreation*.

Most data are for 1982 and the preceding year, plus 1975, 1970 and 1960. In addition to the national level, data are included for counties (voivods) and towns. There is a section devoted to statistics from selected foreign countries. Notes accompanying the tables indicate the names of the agencies furnishing the data and sources for the foreign section are listed.

Explanatory notes are provided at the beginnings of chapters. There is an alphabetical subject index at the end of the volume and a detailed table of contents at the beginning of the volume.

For sale abroad by Ars Polona-Ruch ul. Krakowskie Przedmieście 7, PO Box 1001, 00-068 Warsaw. Priced.

The following years are available in microform: CH: 1920/21-1930; 1947-1950; 1955-1965. CIS: 1970-73, 1975-80, and English table of contents available for 1978-80.

323. *Mały rocznik statystyczny* [Concise statistical yearbook]. 1958- Warsaw: Główny Urząd Statystyczny. Polish, English, French, German and Russian editions.

An abridged version of entry 322. Latest English edition, 1984, 398 p. A briefer version of the yearbook, *Informator statystyczny* (English title: *Poland: statistical data*), has also been published annually since 1977. Both versions available from the address given in entry 322. Priced.

324. *Biuletyn statystyczny* [Statistical bulletin]. 1957- Warsaw: Główny Urząd Statystyczny. Polish, with table of contents in both Polish, English and Russian.

Each issue is divided into three parts: Part I contains tables published regularly on a monthly, quarterly or annual basis; Part II contains occasional tables; and Part III, comparative statistics for a number of countries. The quarterly issues published in February, May, August and November, are organized somewhat differently from the others, with Part II containing periodic (quarterly) tables and occasional tables, and Part III devoted to provinces rather than foreign countries.

V. XXVII, no. 321, Sept.,1983, 55 p., contains the following data in Part I: Population, births, marriages, deaths and natural increase, farming, free market prices of agricultural products, logging, transportation of timber, domestic commerce, exports, imports, retail prices of selected foods, industry, construction, flats completed, transportation, investment outlays, employment, hours of work, salaries and wages, social security. Part II includes tables on retail prices of selected seasonal vegetables and fruits; average consumption of basic foodstuffs per capita in households by socio-economic group; average income and expenditure per capita in households by socio-economic group.

The latest data are for the month before the date of the issue. Monthly figures are included for a 6 to 13 month period and annual data for the latest 2 full years, plus 1978 and 1975.

Available from the address given in entry 322. Priced.

PORTUGAL

325. *Anuário estatístico; continente, Açores e Madeira / Annuaire statistique; continent,*

Açores et Madère. 1875- Lisbon: Instituto Nacional de Estatística (INE). Portuguese and French.

Not published 1876-83, 1887-91, 1893-99. Volumes for 1962-73 issued in 2 vols.: V. 1, Metrópole; v. 2, Provincias ultramarinos (Vol. 2 issued separately as *Anuário estatístico do ultramar [do império colonial]*, 1943-61).

Title varies slightly: 1875 as *Anuário estatístico do Reino de Portugal.* Agency varies: 1875, 1884 by Repartição de Estatística do Ministerio das Obras Publicas, Comércio e Indústria; 1885-86 by Direcção Geral do Comércio e Indústria of the same ministry; 1892-1904/05 by Direcção Geral da Estatística e dos Propios Nacionaes of the Ministerio da Fazenda; 1906/07-36 by Direcção Geral da Estatística of the Ministerio das Finanças.

1982 edition, 292 p., contains statistical data in the following areas:

PHYSICAL ENVIRONMENT
Climatology: precipitation, sunshine, temperature; *Geography*: area of land, maps.

DEMOGRAPHY
Population: arrivals and departures, census results from 1864-1981, distribution by age and sex, distribution by geographic/administrative area, external migration, households and families; *Vital statistics*: births, causes of death, deaths, divorces, infant mortality, marriages.

ECONOMIC AFFAIRS
Agriculture and food: farming, fishing, forestry; *Commerce and business*: companies, domestic commerce, establishments, exports, imports, tourism; *Finance*: banking and credit, securities; *Income and expenditure*: consumption, family income, prices; *Industry*: communication, construction, energy, manufacturing, mining, transportation, water; *National accounts*: balance of payments, gross domestic product, national income; *Public finance*: government expenditures, government revenue.

SOCIAL AND CULTURAL AFFAIRS
Cultural and scientific activities: books, cinema and performing arts, libraries, museums and galleries, newspapers, radio, television; *Education*: enrollments, students finishing courses, teaching staff; *Health*: disease, hospitals, medical personnel, public health; *Housing*; *Justice*: correctional institutions, courts, crimes, traffic acccidents; *Labor*: employment and unemployment, emigrant workers, labor force, occupations, salaries and wages; *Sports and recreation*; *Social security*.

Most data are for 1982 and 2 preceding years. In addition to the national level, data are included for regions, including the autonomous regions of the Azores and Madeira, districts, and urban centers. There is a section of comparative data for selected foreign countries.

Explanatory notes, which include discussions of sources, are provided at the beginnings of chapters and notes accompanying some of the tables indicate the names of the agencies furnishing the data. There is a detailed list of tables at the beginning of the volume. Tables added or deleted since the previous edition are listed after the introductory note. A list of publications of the INE is provided at the end of the volume.

Latest edition published: 1984/1985, 275 p. Available from the agency, Avenida António Joséde Almeida, 1078 Lisbon. Price: esc1100.

Available in microform: CH: 1875, 1884-86, 1892, 1900, 1903-25, 1928-29, 1933, 1937-70. CIS: 1971-73, 1975-76.

326. ***Boletim mensal de estatística*** [Monthly bulletin of statistics]. 1929- Lisbon: Instituto Nacional de Estatística (INE). Portuguese and French.

For agency name changes, see entry 325.

V. LV, no. 1, 1983, 88 p., contains statistical data in the following areas:

ECONOMIC AFFAIRS
Agriculture and food: farming, fishing; *Commerce and business*: domestic commerce, exports, imports, tourism; *Finance*: banking and credit; *Income and expenditure*: consumption, prices; *Industry*: communication, construction, energy, transportation.

SOCIAL AND CULTURAL AFFAIRS
Cultural and scientific activities: cinema and performing arts; *Housing*; *Justice*: traffic accidents; *Labor*: labor force, salaries and wages.

Data are for the latest month available and the same month of the preceding year or two years. Notes accompanying the tables indicate the names of the agencies furnishing the data. There is a list of publications of the INE inside back cover.

Available from the address given in entry 325. Price: esc250 per issue; esc 2,500 per year.

ROMANIA

327. ***Anuarul statistic al Republicii Socialiste România.*** [Statistical yearbook of the Romanian Socialist Republic]. 1904- Bucharest: Direcţia Centrală de Statistică. Romanian. An English translation of table headings is available for some years as *Statistical yearbook of the Socialist Republic of Romania: translation of texts.*

Title varies: 1957-65, *Anuarul statistic al R.P.R.*; *Anuarul statistic al României*, 1904-40.

The 1982 edition, 365 p., contains statistical data in the following areas:

PHYSICAL ENVIRONMENT
Climatology: precipitation, temperature; *Geography*: area and use of land, maps.

DEMOGRAPHY
Population: census results from 1930-1977, distribution by age and sex, distribution by geographic/administrative area, population estimates.*Vital statistics*: births, deaths, divorces, fertility, infant mortality, life expectancy, marriages.

ECONOMIC AFFAIRS

Agriculture and food: farming, forestry; *Commerce and business*: cooperatives, domestic commerce, exports, handicrafts, imports, services, tourism; *Income and expenditure*: consumption; *Industry*: communication, construction, energy, manufacturing, mining, transportation; *National accounts*: social product, national income; *Public finance*: government expenditures and government revenue for the central and local governments (aggregate only).

SOCIAL AND CULTURAL AFFAIRS

Cultural and scientific activities: books and journals, cinema and performing arts, libraries, museums and galleries, newspapers, radio, television; *Education*: enrollments, graduates of all levels of education; *Health*: hospitals, medical personnel, public health; *Housing*; *Labor*: employment, labor force, labor productivity, salaries and wages; *Social assistance*; *Social security*.

Most data are for 1981 and the following earlier years: 1975, 1965, 1950 and 1938. In addition to the national level, data are included for judeţe [counties] and municipalities. There is a section of comparative statistics for selected foreign countries.

Explanatory notes are provided at the beginnings of chapters. There is a detailed list of tables at the beginning of the volume. A chapter on the administrative and territorial organization of Romania is included.

Available from the agency, Str. Stavropoleos Nr. 6, Bucharest. Priced.

Available in microform: CH: 1904, 1909, 1912-29, 1931-40 of *Anuarul statistic al României*. CIS: 1971, 1973, 1975-77 and English supplement for 1975-77.

An abridged version of the yearbook, entitled *Breviarul statistic al R.P.R.* in Romanian and *Statistical pocket book of the Socialist Republic of Romania*, in English, was published from 1957 to 1971 (English title 1961-65 was *Rumanian statistical pocket book*).

328. ***Buletinul statistic trimestrial*** [Quarterly statistical bulletin]. 1957-71. Bucharest: Direcţia Centrală de Statistică. Romanian.

This bulletin, which was mainly devoted to economic data, included some demographic information.

SAN MARINO

329. **Annuario statistico** [Statistical yearbook]. 1972/80?- San Marino: Ufficio Statale di Statistica. Irregular. Italian.

Continues: *Sintesi statistica socio-economica*, 1962-71?

1972/80 edition, 3 v., contains statistical data in the following areas:

PHYSICAL ENVIRONMENT
Climatology: precipitation, temperature; *Geography*: area of land, maps.

DEMOGRAPHY
Population: census results from 1864-1976, distribution by age and sex, distribution by geographic/administrative area, external migration, households and families; *Vital statistics*: births, including illegitimate births, causes of death, deaths, divorces, fertility, infant mortality, marriages.

ECONOMIC AFFAIRS
Agriculture and food: farming; *Commerce and business*: domestic commerce; *Industry*: communication, construction, manufacturing, transportation; *National accounts*: gross domestic product.

POLITICAL AFFAIRS
Elections.

SOCIAL AND CULTURAL AFFAIRS
Cultural and scientific activities: cinema and performing arts, libraries, newspapers, radio, television; *Education*: degrees conferred, educational attainment, enrollments, literacy, teaching staff; *Health*: disease, hospitals, medical personnel, public health; *Housing*; *Justice*: courts, traffic accidents; *Labor*: employment, labor force; *Social assistance*; *Social security*.

Most data are for 1972-1980. In addition to the whole country, data are included for castelli [districts]. There are detailed lists of tables at the beginnings of volumes.

Available from the agency, via Carducci 145, San Marino. Priced.

330. ***Bollettino di statistico*** [Statistical bulletin]. 1972- San Marino: Ufficio Statale di Statistica. Monthly. Italian.

V. 13, no.6/7, June-July, 1984, 35 p., contains statistical data in the following areas:

PHYSICAL ENVIRONMENT
Climatology: precipitation, temperature; *Geography*: maps.

DEMOGRAPHY
Population: external migration; *Vital statistics*: births, causes of death, deaths, infant mortality, marriages.

ECONOMIC AFFAIRS
Commerce and business: tourism; *Income and expenditure*: consumption, prices; *Industry*: construction, transportation.

SOCIAL AND CULTURAL AFFAIRS
Education: educational attainment; *Health*: disease; *Justice*: courts; *Labor*: employment, unemployment and underemployment, labor force, labor-management relations; *Religion*.

Most data are monthly for 3 months and annual for 5 years. Latest data are for months of issue. There are a few tables with comparative statistics for foreign countries.

Available from the agency, via Carducci 145, San Marino. Priced.

SCOTLAND

See UNITED KINGDOM.

SOVIET UNION

331. *Narodnoe Khoziaistvo SSSR: Statisticheskii ezhegodnik* [National economy of the USSR: Statistical yearbook]. 1956- Moscow: Tsentral'noe Statisticheskoe Upravlenie. Russian. Jubilee editions published 1957, 1966, 1971, 1976 and 1981.

1982 edition published 1982, 624 p., contains the following information:

PHYSICAL ENVIRONMENT
Geography: area of land.

DEMOGRAPHY
Population: census results from 1979, distribution by sex, distribution by geographic/administrative area, ethnic groups, households and families, population estimates and projections; *Vital statistics*: births, deaths.

ECONOMIC AFFAIRS
Agriculture and food: farming, forestry; *Commerce and business*: cooperatives, domestic commerce, exports, imports, services; *Income and expenditure*: personal income; *Industry*: communication, construction, energy, manufacturing, mining, transportation; *National accounts*: national income; *Public finance*: government expenditures, government revenue, planning and economic development.

SOCIAL AND CULTURAL AFFAIRS
Cultural and scientific activities: books and journals, cinema and performing arts, libraries, museums and galleries, newspapers, science and research; *Education*: educational attainment, enrollments, teaching staff; *Health*: disease, hospitals, medical personnel, public health; *Housing*; *Labor*: employment, labor force, labor productivity, occupations, salaries and wages; *Social security*; *Sports and recreation*.

Most data are for 1982 and the preceding 2 years, plus 1975, 1970, 1965, and 1940. In addition to the national level, data are included for individual republics, krays and oblasts. Explanatory notes are provided at the beginnings of chapters. There is a detailed list of tables at the end of the volume.

Latest edition published: 1983, 607 p. Available from Finansy i Statistika Publishers, Moscow. Price: 2R, 50k.

Available in microform: CH: 1956-65. CIS: 1970, 1972-75, and 1922/72.

332. *The USSR in figures for [year]: brief statistical handbook*. 1957- Moscow: Tsentral'noe Statisticheskoe Upravlenie. English. There are also editions in French, German, Russian and Spanish.

This is an abridged edition of entry 331. The 1983 edition, 239 p., also includes data on environmental protection, class composition, consumption, radio, television and graduates of higher education institutions.

Most data are for 1983 and the preceding 3 years, plus selected earlier years, usually 1975, 1970, 1940. In addition to the national level, some data are included for constituent republics, cities over 500,000, capitals of republics, and foreign countries.

Sources are not given. There is a detailed table of contents at the end of the volume.

Available from: Finansy i Statistika Publishers, Moscow. Price: 50k.

Available in microform: CIS: 1971-78 (1971 and 1972 in Russian edition).

333. ***Vestnik statistiki*** [Statistical herald]. 1919-29, 1949- Moscow: Tsentral'noe Statisticheskoe Upravlenie. Frequency varies; monthly from 1958. Russian.

In addition to articles, bibliographical information and statistical news, each issue contains a statistical appendix, 'Statisticheskie materialy', whose content varies from issue to issue. Subjects covered in recent issues include census results, industrial production, national income, economic planning, and women.

Available from the address in entry 331. Priced.

SPAIN

334. ***Anuario estadístico de España: Edición extensa*** [Statistical yearbook of Spain: Comprehensive edition]. 1912- Madrid: Instituto Nacional de Estadística (INE). Spanish.

Not published 1935-42.

Agency varies: 1912, 1915-20: Dirección General de Geográfico y Estadística; 1921/22-1922/23, 1943: Dirección General de Estadística; 1923/24-24/25: Jefatura Superior de Estadística; 1925/26-28: Servicio General de Estadística; 1929-34: Dirección General del Instituto Geográfico, Cadastral y de Estadística. Continues same title for 1859-67, published by Comisión de Estadística General del Reino, 1860, Junta General de Estadística, 1862-63, 1866-67, and Dirección General de Estadística, 1870.

V. LVII, 1983, 800 p., contains statistical data in the following areas:

PHYSICAL ENVIRONMENT
Climatology: precipitation, sunshine, temperature; *Geography*: area of land, maps.

DEMOGRAPHY
Population: census results from 1857-1981 and non-official censuses 1594-1797, distribution by age and sex, distribution by geographic/administrative area, external migration, internal migration, population estimates; *Vital statistics*: births, including illegitimate births, causes of death, deaths, annulments and separations, infant mortality, life expectancy, marriages.

ECONOMIC AFFAIRS
Agriculture and food: farming, fishing, forestry; *Commerce and business*: exports, imports, tourism; *Finance*: banking and credit, money in circulation, securities; *Income and expenditure*: consumption, prices; *Industry*: communication, construction, energy, manufacturing, transportation; *National accounts*: balance of payments, gross domestic product, national income; *Public finance*: government expenditures and government

revenue for the central, provincial and municipal levels (aggregates by province for municipal governments).

POLITICAL AFFAIRS
Elections.

SOCIAL AND CULTURAL AFFAIRS
Cultural and scientific activities: books and journals, cinema and performing arts, libraries, newspapers, radio, television; *Education*: enrollments, examination results, literacy, students of higher education institutions finishing their studies, teaching staff; *Health*: body measurements of males, disease, hospitals, medical personnel, public health; *Housing*; *Justice*: correctional institutions, courts, crimes, traffic accidents; *Labor*: employment and unemployment, foreign workers, labor force, labor-management relations, salaries and wages; *Religion*; *Social assistance*; *Social security*; *Sports and recreation.*

Part I offers data for the national level, as well as a section of comparative data for selected foreign countries, while Part II contains data for provinces, including the external territories in North Africa (Ceuta, Melilla, etc.) Most data in Part I are for 1983 or 1982 and the preceding 9 years; figures in Part II are for the latest available year only.

Explanatory notes, which include sources for additional information, are provided at the beginnings of chapters. Notes accompanying the tables indicate the names of the agencies furnishing the data. A detailed list of tables at the beginning of the volume lists tables included for the first time. There is an alphabetical subject index following the table of contents. A bibliography of official statistical materials is provided.

Historical statistics. Time series for the period 1900-1970 may be found in *Estadísticas basicas de España, 1900-1970,* 610 p., published by the Confederación Española de Caja de Ahorros in Madrid in 1975. Some data by province are provided and sources are indicated at the end of tables.

Available from the agency, Paseo de la Castellana, 183, Madrid 16. Price: Paper edition: ptas 3,897, including postage. Microfiche edition: ptas 793.

Available in microform: CH: 1858-67, 1912-34, 193-70. CIS: 1972, 1977-79. INE: 1858-1983.

335. **Anuario estadística de España: Edición manual** [Statistical yearbook of Spain: pocket edition]. 1912- Madrid: Instituto Nacional de Estadística. Spanish.

For agency variations, see entry 334.

The 1983 edition of this abridged version of entry 334 covers most of the same topics, but offers shorter time series, usually 5 years at most.

Available from the agency, Paseo de la Castellana, 183, Madrid 16. Price: ptas 1,614, including postage.

Available in microform: CIS: 1970-71, 1973-76.

336. *Boletín de estadística* [Bulletin of statistics]. 1918- Madrid: Instituto Nacional de Estadística. Spanish.

For agency variations, see entry 334.

V. XLI, no. 442, July-Aug., 1983, 166 p., contains statistical data in the following areas:

DEMOGRAPHY
Population: census results from 1900-1981, external migration, internal migration; *Vital statistics*: births, causes of death, deaths, marriages.

ECONOMIC AFFAIRS
Commerce and business: exports, imports, services, tourism; *Finance*: banking and credit, securities; *Income and expenditure*: consumption, prices; *Industry*: communication, construction, manufacturing, transportation; *National accounts*: balance of payments; *Public finance*: government expenditures, government revenue.

SOCIAL AND CULTURAL AFFAIRS
Cultural and scientific activities: radio, television; *Health*: disease; *Justice*: correctional institutions; *Labor*: labor force, salaries and wages.

Most data are monthly for 12 months and annual for 5 years. Latest data are for the month before the date of the issue. Data are included for both the national and provincial levels and there is a section of comparative data for selected foreign countries. A list of the most recent publications of the INE is included on the inside of the front cover.

Available from the address given in entry 334. Price: ptas 668 per issue; ptas 3,897 per year.

SWEDEN

337. *Statistisk årsbok för Sverige/ Statistical abstract of Sweden.* 1914- Stockholm: Statistiska Centralbyrån (SCB). English and Swedish; Swedish and French, 1914-51.

Title varies: 1914-1951: *Statistisk årsbok för Sverige/ Annuaire statistique de la Suède.* Agency name varies: 1914-26: Kungl.[Kungliga] Statistiska Centralbyrån. Continues: *Sveriges officiella statistik i sammandrag*, published annually, 1870-1913, by the Statistiska Centralbyrån as no. 1 in its *Statistisk tidskrift*, 1860-1913.

V. 70, 1984, published Nov., 1983, 569 p., contains statistical data in the following areas:

PHYSICAL ENVIRONMENT
Climatology: precipitation, temperature; *Environmental quality*: air pollution, nature reserves, pesticide use, water pollution; *Geography*: area and use of land, maps.

DEMOGRAPHY
Population: census results from 1750-1980, distribution by age and sex, distribution by geographic/administrative area, external migration, households and families, internal migration, population projections; *Vital statistics*: abortions, births, including illegit-

imate births, causes of death, deaths, divorces, fertility, infant mortality, life expectancy, marriages.

ECONOMIC AFFAIRS
Agriculture and food: farming, fishing, forestry; *Commerce and business*: companies, domestic commerce, enterprises, exports, imports, services, tourism; *Finance*: banking and credit, securities; *Income and expenditure*: consumption, cost of living, personal income, prices; *Industry*: communication, construction, energy, manufacturing, mining, transportation, water; *National accounts*: balance of payments, gross domestic product, national income; *Public finance*: government expenditures and government revenue for the central government, counties, municipalities and ecclesiastical districts.

POLITICAL AFFAIRS
Elections and referenda; *Foreign aid*.

SOCIAL AND CULTURAL AFFAIRS
Cultural and scientific activities: books and journals, cinema and performing arts, libraries, museums and galleries, newspapers, radio, television, science and research; *Education*: degrees conferred, enrollments, teaching staff; *Health*: disease, hospitals, medical personnel, public health; *Housing*; *Justice*: correctional institutions, courts, crimes, traffic accidents; *Labor*: employment and unemployment, labor costs in mining and manufacturing, labor force, labor-management relations, occupations, salaries and wages; *Religion*; *Social assistance*; *Social security*; *Sports and recreation*.

Most data are for 1982 and varying numbers of earlier years, usually 3 to 10. In addition to the national level, data are included for provinces, counties and municipalities. There is a section of comparative statistics for selected foreign countries; no English translations are provided for this section.

Explanatory notes are provided in a special section. Notes accompanying the tables indicate the names of the agencies furnishing the data. There are detailed lists of tables at the beginnings of chapters and alphabetical subject indexes in Swedish and English at the end. Changes in tables from the previous edition are listed in front of the indexes.

Historical statistics. Statistics from the middle of the 18th century or earlier may be found in *Historisk statistik för Sverige/ Historical statistics of Sweden,* published by the Statistiska Centralbyrån. V. I, 2nd ed., 1969, covers population; v. II, 1959, covers climate, land tenure, agriculture, forestry and fishing; and v. III, 1972, covers foreign trade.

Latest edition published: 1986, 580 p. Available from SCB-Distribution, S-70189 Orebro. Price: SKr215.

Available in microform: CH: 1914-65 and *Statistisk tidskrift,* 1860-1913. CIS: 1970-79.

338. ***Allmän månadsstatistik*** [Monthly digest of Swedish statistics]. 1963- Stockholm: Statistiska Centralbyrån. English and Swedish.

V. 21, no. 11 of 1983, published Nov., 1983, 96 p., contains statistical data in the following areas:

DEMOGRAPHY
Population: external migration; *Vital statistics*: births, deaths, divorces, marriages.

ECONOMIC AFFAIRS
Agriculture and food: farming, fishing; *Commerce and business*: domestic commerce, exports, imports; *Finance*: banking and credit, securities; *Income and expenditure*: prices; *Industry*: communication, construction, energy, manufacturing, mining, transportation; *National accounts*: balance of payments; *Public finance*: government expenditures, government revenue.

SOCIAL AND CULTURAL AFFAIRS
Justice: crimes, traffic accidents; *Labor*: employment and unemployment, labor force, labor-management relations, salaries and wages.

Most data are monthly for 24 months and annual for 1 to 5 years. The latest data are for 2 months before the date of issue. There is a section of comparative data for selected foreign countries. There is a detailed list of tables at the beginning of the issue. The annual supplement published in January contains a list of sources for each table, a bibliography of materials published by the SCB and an annual subject index.

Available from the address in entry 337. Price: SKr25 per issue; SKr220 per year.

SWITZERLAND

339. ***Statistisches Jahrbuch der Schweiz/ Annuaire statistique de la Suisse.*** 1891- Bern: Bundesamt für Statistik/ Office Fédéral de la Statistique. German and French.

Agency varies: 1891-1913 by Statistisches Bureau des Eidgenössischen Departements des Innern/ Bureau de Statistique du Département Fédérale de l'Intérieur; 1914-16 by Statistisches Bureau des Finanzdepartements/ Bureau de Statistique du Département des Finances; 1917-78 by Eidgenössisches Statistisches Amt/Bureau Fédéral de Statistique.

92nd year, 1984, published Nov., 1984, 658 p., contains statistical data in the following areas:

PHYSICAL ENVIRONMENT
Climatology: precipitation, sunshine, temperature; *Environmental quality*: solid waste disposal; *Geography*: area and use of land.

DEMOGRAPHY
Population: census results from 1850-1980, distribution by age and sex, distribution by geographic/administrative area, external migration, households and families, internal migration; *Vital statistics*: births, including illegitimate births, causes of death, deaths, divorces, infant mortality, life expectancy, marriages.

ECONOMIC AFFAIRS
Agriculture and food: farming, fishing, forestry; *Commerce and business*: companies, domestic commerce, enterprises, exports, imports, services, tourism; *Finance*: banking and credit, money supply, securities; *Income and expenditure*: consumption, cost of living, personal income, prices; *Industry*: communication, construction, energy,

manufacturing, mining, transportation; *National accounts*: balance of payments, gross domestic product, national income; *Public finance*: government expenditures and government revenue for the central government, cantons and communes (aggregate by cantons for communes).

POLITICAL AFFAIRS
Elections; *Foreign aid given*.

SOCIAL AND CULTURAL AFFAIRS
Cultural and scientific activities: books and journals, cinema and performing arts, libraries, native language spoken, newspapers, radio, television, science and research; *Education*: degrees conferred, enrollments, examination results, teaching staff; *Health*: disease, medical personnel, public health; *Housing*; *Justice*: courts, crimes, traffic accidents; *Labor*: employment and unemployment, foreign workers, labor force, labor-management relations, salaries and wages; *Religion*; *Social assistance*; *Social security*; *Sports and recreation*.

Most data are for 1983 or 1982 and varying numbers of preceding years. In addition to the national level, data are included for cantons and selected cities. There is also a section of comparative statistics for selected foreign countries.

Table sources and a list of the latest publications of the agency are listed at the end of the volume. There are lists of tables at the beginning of the volume and alphabetical subject indexes in German and French at the end. Tables included in the previous edition that have been omitted from the present one are listed in the index.

Available from the agency, Hallwylstrasse 15, CH-3003, Bern. Price: FrS 74.00.

Available in microform: CH: 1891-1965.

340. *La Vie économique: Rapports économiques et de statistique sociale* [Economic life: Economic reports and social statistics]. 1928- Bern: Département Fédéral de l'Economie Publique. Monthly, with quarterly supplements. French. There is also a German edition, entitled *Die Volkswirtschaft, wirtschaftliche, sozialstatistische und arbeitsrechtliche Mitteilungen*.

Issued as supplement to the *Schweizerischen Handelsamtsblatt* 1929-41.

Each issue contains regularly published tables in addition to articles including statistical data on a variety of topics. V. 57, no. 8, August, 1984, 83 p., included the following tables: general economic indicators, labor market, results of a survey of consumer attitudes, retail and wholesale prices, and vital statistics (births, deaths, marriages, internal migration). Topics covered in articles included: economically active population according to the 1980 population census, health costs, employment, wages and hours, activities of labor-management tribunals, tourism, government revenue and expenditures for all levels of government, subsidies for professional education, production of slaughterhouses, and results of the April, 1984 census of livestock. In addition to monthly issues, there are quarterly supplements presenting reports of the Commission pour les Questions Conjoncturelles [Commission for Economic Research] and special issues, each devoted to a single topic. A cumulative list of the latter published from 1928 onwards is found on the last page of the issue.

Most data in the regular tables are for the month before the date of the issue and some earlier months. General economic indicators are monthly for latest 4 months, quarterly for 6 quarters, and annual for 3 years. Notes accompanying the tables indicate the source of the information.

Available from: La Feuille Officielle Suisse du Commerce, CP 2170, 3001, Bern.Price: SF88 per year.

UNITED KINGDOM

341. ***Annual abstract of statistics.*** 1840/53- London, Central Statistical Office.

Publication suspended 1939-45; resumed with v. 84, 1935-46.

Title varies: 1840/53-1924/38 as *Statistical abstract for the United Kingdom*. Agency varies: 1840/53-1924/38 by Board of Trade.

No. 121, 1985, published January, 1985, 343 p., contains statistical data in the following areas:

PHYSICAL ENVIRONMENT
Climatology: precipitation, sunshine, temperature; *Environmental quality*: expenditure on pollution control; *Geography*: area of land.

DEMOGRAPHY
Population: arrivals and departures, census results from 1801, 1851, 1901-1981, distribution by age and sex, distribution by geographic/administrative area, external migration, households and families, internal migration, population estimates and projections; *Vital statistics*: births, including illegitimate births, causes of death, deaths, divorces, fertility, infant mortality, life expectancy, marriages.

ECONOMIC AFFAIRS
Agriculture and food: farming, fishing, forestry; *Commerce and business*: companies, domestic commerce, exports, imports, services, tourism; *Finance*: banking and credit, money supply, securities; *Income and expenditure*: consumption, personal income, prices; *Industry*: communication, construction, energy, manufacturing, mining, transportation, water; *National accounts*: balance of payments, gross domestic and gross national product, national income; *Public finance*: government expenditures and government revenue for the central government and local authorities (aggregates for the U.K., England and Wales, Northern Ireland, and Scotland for local authorities).

POLITICAL AFFAIRS
Defense; *Elections*; *Foreign aid*.

SOCIAL AND CULTURAL AFFAIRS
Cultural and scientific activities: cinema, books and journals, newspapers, radio, television, science and research; *Education*: degrees conferred, enrollments, examination results, percent of age group in school, teaching staff; *Health*: disease, hospitals, medical personnel, public health; *Housing*; *Justice*: correctional institutions, courts, crimes,

police, traffic accidents; *Labor*: employment and unemployment, labor force, labor-management relations, salaries and wages; *Social assistance*; *Social security*.

Most data are for 1983 or 1982 and the preceding 10 years for the entire U.K.; there are some tables offering figures for Great Britain, England and Wales, Northern Ireland, and Scotland.

Explanatory notes are provided at the beginnings of chapters. Notes accompanying the tables indicate the names of the agencies furnishing the data and the 'Index of sources', at the end of the volume lists both author and title of sources used by table number. There is a detailed list of tables at the beginning of the volume and an alphabetical subject index at the end. New or revised tables are starred in the table of contents; changes in tables are also noted in the introduction.

Historical statistics. Statistics for earlier periods may be found in *Abstract of British historical statistics* by Brian Mitchell, 1962, 513 p., and *Second abstract of British historical statistics* by Mitchell and H. G. Jones, 1971, 227 p., both published by the Cambridge University Press.

Latest published: 1986, 340 p. Available from Her Majesty's Stationery Office, PO Box 276, London, SW8 5DT or from HMSO agents overseas (U. S. agent is Bernan Associates, Inc., 9730-E George Palmer Highway, Lanham, Md., 20706). Price: £17.50.

Available in microform: CH: 1928-77. CIS: 1970-. Microform Ltd.: 1860 to date.

342. **Monthly digest of statistics.** 1946- London: Central Statistical Office.

No. 466, Oct., 1984, 126 p., contains statistical data in the following areas:

PHYSICAL ENVIRONMENT
Climatology: precipitation, sunshine, temperature.

DEMOGRAPHY
Population: distribution by age and sex, *Vital statistics*: births, deaths, marriages.

ECONOMIC AFFAIRS
Commerce and business: domestic commerce, exports, imports; *Finance*: banking and credit, money supply, securities; *Income and expenditure*: consumption, personal income, prices; *Industry*: communication, construction, energy, manufacturing, mining, transportation; *National accounts*: balance of payments, gross domestic and gross national product; *Public finance*: government expenditures, government revenue.

SOCIAL AND CULTURAL AFFAIRS
Cultural and scientific activities: cinema, television; *Health*: public health; *Justice*: crimes, traffic accidents; *Labor*: employment and unemployment, labor force, labor-management relations, salaries and wages; *Social assistance*; *Social security*.

Most data are monthly or quarterly for 11 months and annual for 5 or 6 years. Latest data are for 1 or 2 months before the date of the issue. In addition to the U. K., some data are offered for Great Britain, England and Wales, Northern Ireland, and Scotland.

Explanatory notes are contained in supplements published with January issue. Notes accompanying the tables indicate the names of the agencies furnishing the data. There is a detailed list of tables at the beginning of the issue and an alphabetical subject index at the end.

Available from the addresses in the preceding entry. Price: £7.95 per issue; £100 per year.

NORTHERN IRELAND

343. ***Northern Ireland annual abstract of statistics.*** 1982- Belfast: Department of Finance and Personnel. Annual.

Continues: *Digest of statistics for Northern Ireland*, 1954-1981, published by the Economic Section of the Cabinet Office.

No. 2, 1983, 176 p., contains statistical data in the following areas:

PHYSICAL ENVIRONMENT
Climatology: precipitation, sunshine, temperature; *Environmental quality*: air and water pollution.

DEMOGRAPHY
Population: census results from 1961, 1966, 1971, distribution by age and sex, distribution by geographic/administrative area, external migration, households and families, population estimates and projections; *Vital statistics*: births, deaths, infant mortality, life expectancy, marriages.

ECONOMIC AFFAIRS
Agriculture and food: farming, fishing, forestry; *Commerce and business*: companies, tourism; *Finance*: banking and credit, securities; *Income and expenditure*: consumption, personal income, prices; *Industry*: communication, energy, manufacturing, transportation, water; *National accounts*: gross domestic product, national income; *Public finance*: government expenditures and government revenue for Northern Ireland.

SOCIAL AND CULTURAL AFFAIRS
Cultural and scientific activities: television (licenses only); *Education*: degrees conferred, enrollments, examination results, teaching staff; *Health*: hospitals, public health; *Housing*; *Justice*: correctional institutions, courts, crimes, deaths and injuries connected with the civil disturbances, police and Ulster Defence Regiment, terrorist activities, traffic accidents; *Labor*: employment and unemployment, labor force, labor-management relations, salaries and wages; *Social assistance*; *Social security*.

Most data are for 1982 and varying numbers of earlier years, usually 7 to 9. There are some quarterly figures. In addition to the national level, some data are included for district council areas.

Explanatory notes are provided at the beginnings of chapters. Notes accompanying the tables indicate the names of the agencies furnishing the data. There is a detailed list of tables at the beginning of the volume. A list of official statistical materials published by Northern Ireland and the U.K. is provided inside the back cover.

Latest edition published: No. 3, 1984, 184 p. Available from Her Majesty's Stationery

Office, PO Box 276, London, SW8 5DT or from HMSO agents overseas (U. S. agent is Bernan Associates, Inc., 9730-E George Palmer Highway, Lanham, Md., 20706). Price: £11.50.

344. ***Ulster year book: the official handbook of Northern Ireland.*** 1926- Belfast: Northern Ireland Information Office. Annual; triennial until 1969.

Agency name varies: 1957-1960/62 by General Register Office [Office of the Registrar General].

The 1985 edition, 300 p., contains statistical tables intermixed with narrative. Data in the following areas are included:

PHYSICAL ENVIRONMENT
Climatology: precipitation, sunshine, temperature; *Environmental quality*: parks and reserves, pollution; *Geography*: land use, maps.

DEMOGRAPHY
Population: census results from 1821, 1841, 1871-1981, distribution by age and sex, distribution by geographic/administrative area, external migration; *Vital statistics*: births, including illegitimate births, causes of death, deaths, divorces, fertility, infant mortality, life expectancy, marriages.

ECONOMIC AFFAIRS
Agriculture and food: farming, fishing, forestry; *Commerce and business*: tourism; *Finance*: banking and credit; *Industry*: communication, construction, energy, manufacturing, mining, transportation, water; *Public finance*: government expenditures and government revenue.

POLITICAL AFFAIRS
Elections.

SOCIAL AND CULTURAL AFFAIRS
Cultural and scientific activities: libraries, newspapers, radio, television; *Education*: enrollments, teaching staff; *Health*: hospitals, public health; *Housing*; *Justice*: correctional institutions, courts, crimes, police, security, traffic accidents; *Labor*: employment and unemployment, labor union membership, salaries and wages; *Religion*; *Social assistance*; *Social security*; *Sports and recreation.*

Most data are for 1983 and varying numbers of earlier years. In addition to Northern Ireland as a whole, data are included for counties/ county boroughs and cities.

There is an alphabetical subject index at the end and a bibliography of materials about Northern Ireland which includes official statistical publications.

Available from the Government Bookshop, 80 Chichester St., Belfast, BT1 4JY, and from Bernan Associates, Inc., 9730-E George Palmer Highway, Lanham, Md., 20706. Price: £10.00.

SCOTLAND

345. ***Scottish abstract of statistics.*** 1971- Edinburgh: Scottish Office.

Continues in part: *Digest of Scottish statistics*, 1953-71.

No. 13, 1984, 162 p., contains statistical data in the following areas:

PHYSICAL ENVIRONMENT
Climatology: precipitation, sunshine, temperature; *Environmental quality*: air pollution; *Geography*: maps.

DEMOGRAPHY
Population: census results from 1801-1981, distribution by age and sex, distribution by geographic/administrative area, external migration, households and families, population estimates and projections; *Vital statistics*: abortions, births, including illegitimate births, causes of death, deaths, divorces (court actions only), infant mortality, marriages.

ECONOMIC AFFAIRS
Agriculture and food: farming, fishing, forestry; *Commerce and business*: exports, imports; *Finance*: banking and credit; *Income and expenditure*: consumption, personal income; *Industry*: communication, construction, energy, manufacturing, mining, transportation, water; *National accounts*: gross domestic product; *Public finance*: government expenditures and government revenue for Scotland and local authorities (aggregate only), planning and economic development.

SOCIAL AND CULTURAL AFFAIRS
Cultural and scientific activities: cinema and performing arts, television (licenses only); *Education*: enrollments, qualifications of school leavers, teaching staff; *Health*: dental services, disease, family planning, hospitals, medical personnel, public health; *Housing*; *Justice*: correctional institutions, courts, crimes, police, traffic accidents; *Labor*: employment and unemployment, labor force, labor-management relations, labor productivity in coal mines, occupations, salaries and wages; *Recreation*; *Social assistance*; *Social security*.

Most data are for 1982 or 1981 and the preceding 8 years. In addition to the national level, data are included for regions and districts.

Explanatory notes are provided at the beginnings of chapters. Notes accompanying the tables indicate the names of the agencies furnishing the data. There is a detailed list of tables at the beginning of the volume which lists changes in tables from the previous edition. A list of official statistical publications and an alphabetical subject index are provided.

Available from Her Majesty's Stationery Office, PO Box 276, London, SW8 5DT or from HMSO agents overseas (U. S. agent is Bernan Associates, Inc., 9730-E George Palmer Highway, Lanham, Md., 20706). Price: £24.50.

WALES

346. ***Digest of Welsh statistics.*** 1954- Cardiff: Welsh Office. Annual.

No. 30, 1984, published Nov., 1984, 200 p., contains statistical data in the following areas:

PHYSICAL ENVIRONMENT
Climatology: precipitation, sunshine, temperature; *Environmental quality*: air pollution, land reclamation, national and county parks, water pollution; *Geography*: area and use of land, maps.

DEMOGRAPHY
Population: census results from 1871-1981, distribution by age and sex, distribution by geographic/administrative area, households and families, population estimates and projections; *Vital statistics*: abortions, births, including illegitimate births, causes of death, deaths, divorces, marriages.

ECONOMIC AFFAIRS
Agriculture and food: farming, fishing, forestry; *Commerce and business*: domestic commerce, tourism; *Income and expenditure*: consumption, personal income, prices; *Industry*: communication, construction, energy, manufacturing, mining, transportation; *National accounts*: gross domestic product, national income; *Public finance*: government expenditures, government revenue.

POLITICAL AFFAIRS
Elections.

SOCIAL AND CULTURAL AFFAIRS
Cultural and scientific activities: cinema and performing arts, libraries and archives, museums and galleries, radio, television, Welsh language; *Education*: degrees conferred, enrollments, examination results, teaching staff; *Health*: disease, public health; *Housing*; *Justice*: courts, crimes, traffic accidents; *Labor*: employment and unemployment, labor force, labor-management relations, occupations, salaries and wages; *Religion*; *Social assistance*; *Social security*.

Latest data are for 1984; most figures are for 1983 or 1982 and the preceding 4 to 9 years, plus 1970/71. There are some monthly and quarterly figures. In addition to Wales as a whole, data are included for counties. There are also some figures for the United Kingdom and for cities.

Notes accompanying the tables indicate the names of the agencies furnishing the data. There is a detailed list of tables at the beginning of the volume and an alphabetical subject index at the end. Appendices contain county profiles; maps and definitions of various types of districts; and references for further information. Official statistical publications are listed inside the back cover.

Available from Publications Unit, Economic and Statistical Services Division, Welsh Office, New Crown Building, Cathays Park, Cardiff CF1 3NQ. Price: £4.00.

YUGOSLAVIA

347. *Statistički godišnjak Jugoslavije* [Statistical yearbook of Yugoslavia]. 1954- Belgrade: Savezni Zavod za Statistiku. Serbo-Croatian, with translations of the detailed table of contents for the whole volume and table headings and methodological explanations for Part I available in English, French and Russian.

Spine title: *Statistički godišnjak SFRJ*. Title varies slightly: 1954-62, *Statistički godišnjak FNRJ*; 1963-67, *Statistički godišnjak SFRJ*. Continues: *Statistički godišnjak/ Annuaire statistique*, 1929-40, published by Opsta Drzavna statistika.

1984 edition, 788 p., contains statistical data in the following areas:

PHYSICAL ENVIRONMENT
Climatology: precipitation, temperature; *Environmental quality*: national parks; *Geography*: area and use of land, maps.

DEMOGRAPHY
Population: census results from 1921-1981, distribution by age and sex, distribution by geographic/administrative area, ethnic groups, households and families; *Vital statistics*: births, including illegitimate births, causes of death, deaths, divorces, fertility, infant mortality, life expectancy, marriages.

ECONOMIC AFFAIRS
Agriculture and food: farming, fishing, forestry; *Commerce and business*: domestic commerce, exports, handicrafts, imports, tourism; *Finance*: banking and credit, money in circulation; *Income and expenditure*: consumption, personal income, prices; *Industry*: communication, construction, energy, manufacturing, mining, transportation, water; *National accounts*: balance of payments, gross domestic product, national income; *Public finance*: government expenditures and government revenue for all levels of government.

POLITICAL AFFAIRS
Members of assemblies and other organizations.

SOCIAL AND CULTURAL AFFAIRS
Cultural and scientific activities: books and journals, cinema and performing arts, libraries, museums and galleries, newspapers, radio, television, science and research; *Education*: degrees conferred, educational attainment of persons employed, enrollments, teaching staff; *Health*: disease, hospitals, medical personnel, public health; *Housing*; *Justice*: courts, crimes; *Labor*: employment and unemployment, labor force, salaries and wages; *Social assistance*; *Social security*; *Sports and recreation*.

Most data are for 1983 or 1982 and 4 or more preceding years. The volume contains 5 parts with the following territorial coverage: 1. Yugoslavia as a whole; 2. individual republics and autonomous regions; 3. communes; 4. towns; and 5. selected foreign countries. Each part offers less detailed coverage than the preceding part.

Explanatory notes which include discussions of sources are provided at the beginning of the volume. Notes accompanying some of the tables indicate the names of the agencies furnishing the data. There is a detailed list of tables at the beginning of the volume and an alphabetical subject index at the end.

Available from the agency, PO Box 203, 11000 Belgrade. Priced.

Available in microform: CH: 1954-65 and 1929-40 of *Statistički godišnjak/ Annuaire statistique,* published by Opsta Drzavna statistika. CIS: 1970-77 and English translations of table headings and explanatory notes, 1975-77.

348. **Statistički kalendar Jugoslavije** [Statistical calendar]. 1955- Belgrade: Savezni Zavod za Statistiku.

An abridged version of the preceding entry available in Serbo-Croat, Slovene, Macedonian, English, French, German and Russian. English title: *Statistical pocketbook of Yugoslavia.*

Available from the agency, PO Box 203, 11000 Belgrade. Priced.

349. **Statistički bilten** [Statistical bulletins]. 1953- Belgrade: Savezni Zavod za Statistiku. Irregular. Serbo-Croat, with English and French translations of the text.

Each issue is devoted to a different topic. Regularly published statistical tables contained in issue No. 1202, June, 1982, 68 p., includes data in the following areas:

ECONOMIC AFFAIRS
Commerce and business: domestic commerce, exports, imports, tourism; *Finance*: banking and credit, money in circulation; *Income and expenditure*: cost of living, personal income, prices; *Industry*: construction, manufacturing.

SOCIAL AND CULTURAL AFFAIRS
Labor: employment, salaries and wages.

Most data are monthly for 24 months and annual for 6 years. Latest data are for 2 months before the date of the issue. There is a cumulative index inside the back cover.

Available from the agency, PO Box 203, 11000 Belgrade. Priced.

OCEANIA

AUSTRALIA

350. **Year book Australia.** 1908- Canberra: Australian Bureau of Statistics. Annual, except for the following volumes which cover 2 years: no. 35, 1942/43; no. 36, 1943/44; no. 37, 1946/47; no. 61, 1975/76; and no. 62, 1977/78.

Title varies: 1973-75/76 as *Official yearbook of Australia*; 1908-72 as *Official yearbook of the Commonwealth of Australia.* Agency varies: 1906-72 by Commonwealth Bureau of Census and Statistics.

Consists of statistical data intermixed with narrative. No. 68, 1984, 757 p., contains statistical data in the following areas:

PHYSICAL ENVIRONMENT
Climatology: precipitation, sunshine, temperature; *Geography*: area and use of land, maps.

DEMOGRAPHY
Population: arrivals and departures, census results from 1947-1981, distribution by age and sex, distribution by geographic/administrative area, ethnic groups, external migration, households and families, internal migration, population estimates and projections; *Vital statistics*: births, including illegitimate births, causes of death, deaths, divorces, fertility, infant mortality, life expectancy, marriages.

ECONOMIC AFFAIRS
Agriculture and food: farming, fishing, forestry; *Commerce and business*: domestic commerce, establishments, exports, imports, services, tourism; *Finance*: banking and credit, money supply, securities; *Income and expenditure*: consumption, personal income, prices; *Industry*: communication, construction, energy, manufacturing, mining, transportation, water; *National accounts*: balance of payments, gross domestic product, national income; *Public finance*: government expenditures and government revenue for all levels of government (aggregate only for local).

POLITICAL AFFAIRS
Defense; *Elections*; *Foreign aid.*

SOCIAL AND CULTURAL AFFAIRS
Cultural and scientific activities: radio, television, science and research; *Education*: degrees conferred, enrollments, teaching staff; *Health*: disease, public health; *Housing*; *Justice*: crimes, police, traffic accidents; *Labor*: employment and unemployment, foreign workers, labor force, labor-management relations, salaries and wages; *Social assistance*; *Social security*.

Most data are for 1983 or 1982 and the preceding 5 years. In addition to the national level, data are included for states and territories, including the external territories of Australian Antarctic Territory, Christmas Island, Cocos Island, Coral Sea Islands, Heard Island and McDonald Islands, and Norfolk Island, and for major cities.

New material and changes introduced in this edition are described in the introduction. There is an alphabetical subject index which includes references to other volumes of the *Yearbook*. Bibliographies are included at the end of some chapters. Special features include explanations of the governmental system, the text of the Constitution, and lists of the following: members of the Federal cabinet, governors and prime ministers of the states, leaders of the opposition on both federal and state levels, and a list of prime ministers from 1901 to 1983.

Historical statistics. Statistics to the beginning of the 20th century or earlier are included in nos. 13 and 14, 1920 and 1921. For more information on historical statistics, see Jennifer Ann Finlayson, *Historical statistics of Australia; a select list of official sources,* Canberra: Department of Economic History, Research School of Social Sciences, Australian National University, 1970, 55 p.

Latest edition published: 1985, 705 p. Available from the Australian Government Publishing Service, PO Box 84, Canberra, ACT 2601. Price: $A37.80, including postage.

Available in microform: CIS: 1970-73.

351. **Pocket year book Australia.** 1909- Canberra: Australian Bureau of Statistics.

No. 69, 1984 edition, 112 p., contains statistical data in the following areas:

PHYSICAL ENVIRONMENT
Climatology: precipitation, temperature; *Geography*: area of land, maps.

DEMOGRAPHY
Population: arrivals and departures, census results from 1971-1981, distribution by age and sex, distribution by geographic/administrative area, ethnic groups, external migration, population estimates and projections; *Vital statistics*: births, causes of death, deaths, divorces, infant mortality, marriages.

ECONOMIC AFFAIRS
Agriculture and food: farming, fishing, forestry, land tenure; *Commerce and business*: domestic commerce, exports, imports, tourism; *Finance*: banking and credit, money supply, securities; *Income and expenditure*: consumption, prices; *Industry*: construction, energy, manufacturing, mining, transportation; *National accounts*: balance of payments, gross domestic product; *Public finance*: government expenditures and government revenue for all levels of government (aggregate only).

POLITICAL AFFAIRS
Defense; Membership of parliaments.

SOCIAL AND CULTURAL AFFAIRS
Education: enrollments, teaching staff; *Justice*: traffic accidents; *Labor*: employment and unemployment, labor force, labor-management relations, salaries and wages; *Social assistance*; *Social security*.

Most data are for 1983 and the preceding 2 years. In addition to the national level, data are included for states and major cities. There is one table with comparative statistics for foreign countries. Commentaries are provided at the beginnings of a few chapters. There is a list of tables at the beginning of the volume and an alphabetical subject index at the end.

Available from the Australian Government Publishing Service, PO Box 84, Canberra, ACT 2601. Price: $A4.35, including postage.

352. ***Monthly summary of statistics.*** 1912- Canberra: Australian Bureau of Statistics. Quarterly until June, 1976.

Title varies: 1912-1976 as *Quarterly summary of Australian statistics*; 1976-78 as *Monthly review of business statistics*.

Oct., 1984, 47 p., contains statistical data in the following areas:

DEMOGRAPHY
Population: arrivals and departures, external migration, population estimates; *Vital statistics*: births, deaths, infant mortality, marriages.

ECONOMIC AFFAIRS
Commerce and business: domestic commerce, exports, imports; *Finance*: banking and credit, securities; *Income and expenditure*: prices; *Industry*: communication, construction, energy, manufacturing, mining, transportation; *National accounts*: balance of payments, gross domestic product.

SOCIAL AND CULTURAL AFFAIRS
Justice: traffic accidents; *Labor*: employment and unemployment, labor force, labor-management relations, salaries and wages.

Most data are monthly or quarterly for two years and annual for the preceding 3 years. A list of official statistical publications is found inside the cover.

Available from the address in entry 350. Price: $A42.00 per year.

FIJI

353. ****Annual statistical abstract.*** 1969-1970/71. Suva: Bureau of Statistics.

1970/71 edition, 325 p., contains statistical data in the following areas:

PHYSICAL ENVIRONMENT
Climatology: precipitation, temperature.

DEMOGRAPHY

Population: arrivals and departures, census results from 1881-1966, distribution by age and sex, distribution by geographic/administrative area, external migration, households and families, population estimates, racial groups.*Vital statistics*: births, causes of death in hospitals, deaths, fertility, infant mortality, life expectancy, marriages.

ECONOMIC AFFAIRS

Agriculture and food: farming, forestry, land tenure; *Commerce and business*: companies, establishments, exports, imports, tourism; *Finance*: banking and credit, money supply; *Income and expenditure*: consumption, personal income, prices; *Industry*: communication, construction, energy, manufacturing, mining, transportation, water; *National accounts*: balance of payments, gross domestic product, input-output tables, national income; *Public finance*: government expenditures, government revenue.

SOCIAL AND CULTURAL AFFAIRS

Cultural and scientific activities: radio; *Education*: educational attainment, enrollments, examination results, teaching staff; *Health*: disease, family planning, hospitals, public health; *Justice*: correctional institutions, courts, crimes, police, traffic accidents; *Labor*: employment, and unemployment, labor force, labor-management relations, occupations, salaries and wages; *Religion*.

Most data are for 1970 and 1971 and varying numbers of preceding years, usually 10. In addition to the national level, data are included for provinces. Commentaries which include discussions of sources are provided at the beginnings of chapters. There is a detailed list of tables at the beginning of the volume.

Available in microform: CIS: 1970/71; IDC: 1969, 1970/71.

354. *Current economic statistics.* 1969- Suva: Bureau of Statistics.

The July, 1983 issue, 116 p., contains demographic and economic statistics, including population distribution by sex and by towns and urban areas, ethnic origin, households and population estimates, banking and credit, companies, construction, exports, imports, industry, prices, public finance, tourism, and transport. Figures are quarterly for 3 quarters. Latest data are for quarter ending in month before date of issue.

Available from the Government Printing and Stationery Department, PO Box 98, Suva. Priced.

FRENCH POLYNESIA

355. *Bilan statistique de l'année* [Statistical account for the year]. Papeete: Institut Territorial de la Statistique. 1981?- French.

1983 edition (Dossier de l'ITSTAT no. 8), published Dec., 1984, 82 p., contains statistical data in the following areas:

DEMOGRAPHY

Population: census results from 1977, 1983, distribution by age, distribution by sex,

OCEANIA : FRENCH POLYNESIA

distribution by geographic/administrative area, ethnic groups; *Vital statistics*: births, deaths, infant mortality, life expectancy.

ECONOMIC AFFAIRS
Agriculture and food: farming, fishing; *Commerce and business*: exports, imports, tourism; *Finance*: banking and credit, money supply; *Income and expenditure*: prices; *Industry*: construction, energy, transportation; *Public finance*: government expenditures, government revenue.

SOCIAL AND CULTURAL AFFAIRS
Education: diplomas conferred, enrollments, examination results; *Labor*: employment and unemployment, labor force, occupations, salaries and wages.

Most data are for 1983 and varying numbers of earlier years. In addition to the national level, data are included for subdivisions and communes.

Commentaries are provided at the beginnings of chapters and sections and a chronology of the main economic and social events of the year is provided. Notes accompanying the tables indicate the names of the agencies furnishing the data.

A new yearbook, entitled *Tableaux de l'économie Polynésienne* [Tables of the Polynesian economy], is scheduled to begin publication in 1985.

Historical statistics. Statistics for earlier years may be found in the 1972 edition of the *Annuaire statistique* [Statistical yearbook], 154 p., published by the Institut Territorial de la Statistique.

Available from the agency, BP 395, Papeete. Price: CFP500, domestic; CFP700, foreign.

356. **Te avei'a; bulletin d'information statistique** [Te avei'a; bulletin of statistical information]. Papeete: Institut Territorial de la Statistique. Quarterly; monthly before 1982.

The January, 1981 issue contains data on banking and credit, employment, farming, fishing, prices, government expenditure and revenue, salaries and wages, tourism and transportation. Demographic and social statistics are covered in other issues.

Available from the address in entry 355. Price: CFP350 per issue, foreign; CFP1,200 per year, foreign.

See also entries under FRANCE.

GUAM

357. **Annual economic review.** Agana: Economic Research Center of the Department of Commerce.

A statistical abstract has been published as an appendix to the *Review* since 1979. The 1980 edition, 143 p., contains statistical data in the following areas:

DEMOGRAPHY
Population: census results from 1980 (prelim.), distribution by age and sex, distribution by geographic/administrative area, ethnic groups, households and families, population projections; *Vital statistics*: births, including illegitimate births, causes of death, deaths, divorces, infant mortality, life expectancy, marriages.

ECONOMIC AFFAIRS
Agriculture and food: farming; *Commerce and business*: exports, imports, tourism; *Finance*: banking and credit; *Income and expenditure*: consumption, personal income, prices; *Industry*: communication, construction, energy, transportation, water; *Public finance*: government expenditures, government revenue.

POLITICAL AFFAIRS
Elections.

SOCIAL AND CULTURAL AFFAIRS
Education: enrollments, teaching staff; *Housing*; *Justice*: traffic accidents; *Labor*: employment and unemployment, foreign workers, labor force; *Social assistance*.

Most data are for 1979 and varying numbers of earlier years. In addition to the national level, some data are included for election districts. Notes accompanying the tables indicate the names of the agencies furnishing the data.

Historical statistics. Statistics for earlier periods may be found in U. S., Department of the Interior, *Guam: Annual report to the Secretary of the Interior,* 1950/51-1970, Washington: GPO, [I35.15/1].

Available from Economic Research Center, Department of Commerce, Agana, 96910.

No general statistical bulletin is published for Guam.

See also entries under the UNITED STATES.

KIRIBATI

The first statistical abstract is scheduled for publication in 1986.

358. ***National development plan, 1983-1986.*** Bairiki: Statistics Office, 1984. 167 p.

Data on the following topics are included:

PHYSICAL ENVIRONMENT
Geography: area of land, maps.

DEMOGRAPHY
Population: census results from 1978, population estimates and projections.

ECONOMIC AFFAIRS
Agriculture and food: farming, fishing; *Commerce and business*: exports, imports, tourism; *Finance*: credit; *Industry*: communication, energy, manufacturing, mining, transportation; *National accounts*: government expenditures, government revenue, planning and economic development.

POLITICAL AFFAIRS
Foreign aid.

SOCIAL AND CULTURAL AFFAIRS
Cultural and scientific activities: libraries; *Education*: degrees and diplomas received, enrollments, examination results, teaching staff; *Health*: family planning, public health; *Justice*: correctional institutions, police; *Labor*: employment, unemployment, overseas employment, labor force.

Available from the Statistics Office, Ministry of Finance, PO Box 67, Bairiki, Tarawa. Price $10.00.

No general statistical bulletin is published for Kiribati.

NAURU

No general statistical yearbook or bulletin has been found for Nauru.

NEW CALEDONIA

359. ***Tableaux de l'Economie Calédonienne*** [Tables of the Caledonian economy]. 1982- Noumea: Direction Territoriale de la Statistique et des Etudes Economiques. French.

Replaces: *Annuaire statistique de la Nouvelle Calédonie,* 1973-83, published by the Service de la Statistique.

Available from the agency, BP 823, Noumea. Price: CFP1,000, foreign.

Available in microform: IDC: 1973-79 of the *Annuaire statistique.*

No general statistical bulletin has been found for New Caledonia.

See also entries under FRANCE.

NEW ZEALAND

360. ***New Zealand official yearbook.*** 1892- Wellington, Statistics Department.

Agency varies: 1893-1914 by Registrar General's Office; 1915-55 by Census and Statistics Department [Office].

[No.] 89, 1984, published Dec., 1984, 1054 p., contains statistics intermixed with narrative descriptions and a statistical summary near the end of the volume. Topics covered included the following:

PHYSICAL ENVIRONMENT
Climatology: precipitation, sunshine, temperature; *Environmental quality*: environmental protection, land reserved for recreation; *Geography*: area and use of land, maps.

DEMOGRAPHY

Population: census results from 1961 and 1981, distribution by age and sex, distribution by geographic/administrative area, ethnic groups, external migration, households and families, population estimates and projections; *Vital statistics*: births, including ex-nuptial births, causes of death, deaths, divorces, infant mortality, life expectancy, marriages, reproductive index.

ECONOMIC AFFAIRS

Agriculture and food: farming, fishing, forestry; *Commerce and business*: companies, domestic commerce, exports, imports, services, tourism; *Finance*: banking and credit, money supply; *Income and expenditure*: consumption, personal income, prices; *Industry*: communication, construction, energy, manufacturing, mining, transportation; *National accounts*: balance of payments, gross domestic product, national income; *Public finance*: government expenditures and government revenue for the central government and local authorities (aggregate only).

POLITICAL AFFAIRS

Defense; *Elections*; *Foreign Aid*.

SOCIAL AND CULTURAL AFFAIRS

Cultural and scientific activities: books, cinema and performing arts, libraries, newspapers, radio, television, science and research, including patents issued; *Education*: educational attainment, enrollments, examination results, graduates of higher education institutions, teaching staff; *Health*: disease, hospitals, medical personnel, public health; *Housing*; *Justice*: correctional institutions, courts, crimes, traffic accidents; *Labor*: employment and unemployment, foreign workers, labor force, labor-management relations, occupations, salaries and wages; *Religion*; *Social Assistance*; *Social Security*; *Sports and Recreation*.

The section on the latest statistical information at the end of the volume usually provides data for the year ended March or June, 1984. Otherwise, latest data are usually for the year ended March, 1983 and the preceding 2 to 4 years. Longer time series appear in the statistical summary. In addition to the national level, data are included for North and South Islands, counties, districts, cities and boroughs. Information is also provided for the Ross Dependency, and Tokelau.

There is a subject index at the end of the volume. Sources for further information are listed at the end of each section and a bibliography of Department of Statistics publications is provided at the end of the volume, along with a list of books about New Zealand. Other features include: a brief history of the country and a chronology of events from 1642 to 1983; a description of the governmental system; lists of cabinet level officials, past and present governors and prime ministers, and members of the House of Representatives. Each year a special article is included; in 1984, it described INFOS, a computerized information system.

Historical statistics. A compilation of statistics from the mid-nineteenth century to 1975, entitled *New Zealand: A handbook of historical statistics*, by Gerald T. Bloomfield, 429 p., was published by G.K. Hall, Boston, in its series, *International historical statistics* in 1984. In addition to New Zealand, data are included for the Cook Islands, Niue, Tokelau Islands and Western Samoa for the period 1901-1976. Statistics for earlier periods may also be found in *Statistics of the Dominion of New Zealand, 1853-1920*, published by the Census and Statistics Department.

Latest edition published: 1985, 1074 p. Available from the Government Bookshop, Mulgrave St. (Private Bag), Wellington. Price: $NZ19.50.

Available in microform: CIS: 1970-80.

361. **New Zealand pocket digest of statistics.** 1936- Wellington, Statistics Department.

1984, 242 p., contains statistical data in the following areas:

PHYSICAL ENVIRONMENT
Climatology: precipitation, sunshine, temperature; *Geography*: area of land, maps.

DEMOGRAPHY
Population: census results from 1971-1981, distribution by age and sex, distribution by geographic/administrative area, ethnic groups, external migration, households, internal migration, population estimates and projections; *Vital statistics*: births, including illegitimate births, causes of death, deaths, divorce decrees, fertility, infant mortality, life expectancy, marriages.

ECONOMIC AFFAIRS
Agriculture and food: farming, fishing, forestry; *Commerce and business*: domestic commerce, establishments, exports, imports, tourism; *Finance*: banking and credit, money supply; *Income and expenditure*: consumption, personal income, prices; *Industry*: communication, construction, energy, manufacturing, mining, transportation; *National accounts*: balance of payments, gross domestic product, national income; *Public finance*: government expenditures and government revenue for the central government and local authorities (aggregate only).

POLITICAL AFFAIRS
Elections; *Foreign Aid*.

SOCIAL AND CULTURAL AFFAIRS
Cultural and scientific activities: newspapers, patents issued, radio, television; *Education*: educational attainment, enrollments; *Health*: cigarette smoking, disease, hospitals, public health; *Housing*; *Justice*: correctional institutions, courts, traffic accidents; *Labor*: employment and unemployment, labor force, labor-management relations, occupations, salaries and wages; *Religion*; *Social assistance*; *Social security*.

Latest data are for 1984 and varying numbers of earlier years, usually 5 or 10. There are some monthly and quarterly data. In addition to the national level, data are included for statistical divisions, cities and boroughs, and the external territories other than the Ross Dependency. There are a few tables offering international comparisons.

The introduction includes a list of statistical terms used and there are explanatory notes at the beginning of some tables. Notes accompanying most of the tables indicate the names of any external agencies furnishing the data. There is an alphabetical subject index at the end. Special features include a list of publications of the Department of Statistics, a chronology of historical events, and a list of members of the cabinet, diplomatic corps, and the House of Representatives.

Available from the Government Bookshop, Mulgrave St. (Private Bag), Wellington. Price: $NZ3.95

362. ***Monthly abstract of statistics.*** 1914- Wellington, Statistics Department.

Oct., 1984 issue, 137 p., contains statistical data in the following areas:

DEMOGRAPHY
Population: distribution by age and sex, distribution by geographic/administrative area, external migration, population projections; *Vital statistics*: births, including ex-nuptial births, deaths, marriages.

ECONOMIC AFFAIRS
Agriculture and food: farming; *Commerce and business*: domestic commerce, exports, imports; *Finance*: banking and credit, money supply; *Income and expenditure*: prices; *Industry*: construction, energy, manufacturing, transportation; *National accounts*: balance of payments, gross domestic product.

SOCIAL AND CULTURAL AFFAIRS
Health: disease; *Labor*: employment and unemployment, labor force, labor-management relations, salaries and wages; *Social security*.

Most data are monthly for 12 months, quarterly for 2 years and/or annual for 1 to 7 years. Latest data are for the month before the month of issue. Unless otherwise indicated in notes accompanying the tables, the Department of Statistics is the source of data. There is a detailed list of tables at the beginning of the issue and a list of publications of the Statistics Department.

Available from the Government Bookshop, Mulgrave St. (Private Bag), Wellington. Price: $NZ5.00 per issue; $NZ50.00 per annum.

NIUE

363. ***Abstract of statistics.*** 1974- Niue Island: Statistics Unit of the Department of Economic Development.

Latest edition published: 1983, published March, 1985, 60p. For agency address, see next entry.

364. ***Quarterly abstract of statistics.*** Niue Island: Statistics Unit of the Department of Economic Development.

March, 1985, 17 p., contains statistical data in the following areas:

PHYSICAL ENVIRONMENT
Climatology: precipitation, temperature.

DEMOGRAPHY
Population: arrivals and departures, census results from 1981 and mini-census, 1984, population estimates; *Vital statistics*: births, deaths, infant mortality, marriages.

ECONOMIC AFFAIRS
Agriculture and food: farming; *Commerce and business*: exports, handicrafts; *Income and expenditure*: prices; *Industry*: energy, manufacturing, transportation.

Most data are quarterly for 4 quarters and annual for 1 year. The latest data are for the quarter before the date of the issue.

Notes accompanying some of the tables give the names of agencies furnishing the data. There is a detailed list of tables at the beginning of the issue.

Available from the agency, PO Box 42, Niue Island, South Pacific.

PACIFIC ISLANDS (TRUST TERRITORY)

365. **Annual report to the United Nations on the administration of the Trust Territory of the Pacific Islands.** 1947/48- Washington, D.C.: U. S. Department of State.

Agency varies: 1948-51 by the Department of the Navy; 1952-53 by the Department of the Interior.

1983 edition covering Oct. 1, 1982-Sept. 30, 1983, 380 p. [S1.70: 162] (Department of State Publication 9379; International organization and conference series 162). In addition to data presented in the text, it contains tables on the following topics in the section entitled 'Statistical organization':

DEMOGRAPHY
Population: census results from 1980, population estimates and projections; *Vital statistics*: births, causes of death, deaths, infant mortality.

ECONOMIC AFFAIRS
Agriculture and food: farming, fishing; *Commerce and business*: establishments, exports, imports, tourism; *Income and expenditure*: prices; *Industry*: energy, water; *Public finance*: government expenditures and government revenue for the Northern Marianas, the Federated States of Micronesia and individual states of the latter.

POLITICAL AFFAIRS
Results of plebescite on future political status of Federated States of Micronesia.

SOCIAL AND CULTURAL AFFAIRS
Education: enrollments, teaching staff; *Health*: disease, hospitals, medical personnel, public health; *Justice*: correctional institutions, crimes, police, traffic accidents; *Labor*: employment, foreign workers, occupations, salaries and wages.

Most data are for 1983 or 1982 and varying numbers of earlier years. There are some monthly figures. In addition to the the Trust Territory, data are included for the Republic of the Marshall Islands, the Republic of Palau, the Federated States of Micronesia and the Commonwealth of the Northern Mariana Islands. Subject coverage for the different areas varies considerably.

Notes accompanying some of the tables indicate the names of agencies furnishing the data. A list of tables in the statistical organization section appears at the beginning of that section; there is also a list of tables included in the text following the table of contents.

Available from the State Dept., Washington, D.C. 20402.

366. **Bulletin of statistics.** 1978?- Saipan, Mariana Islands: Office of Planning and Statistics of the Office of the High Commissioner. Quarterly.

Population and vital statistics data are included in some issues.

Available from the agency, Office of the High Commissioner, Saipan, Mariana Islands 96950.

See also entries under UNITED STATES.

PAPUA NEW GUINEA

367. **Summary of statistics.** 1970/71- Port Moresby: National Statistical Office.

Agency name varies: 1970/71-1976/77 by Bureau of Statistics.

1979 edition, published Aug., 1982, 127 p., contains statistical data in the following areas:

PHYSICAL ENVIRONMENT
Climatology: precipitation, temperature; *Geography*: area of land, maps.

DEMOGRAPHY
Population: arrivals and departures, census results from 1966-1971, distribution by age and sex, distribution by geographic/administrative area, external migration, internal migration, population estimates and projections, racial groups; *Vital statistics*: births, deaths.

ECONOMIC AFFAIRS
Agriculture and food: farming, fishing, forestry; *Commerce and business*: companies, domestic commerce, exports, imports; *Income and expenditure*: prices; *Industry*: communication, construction, energy, manufacturing, mining, transportation; *National accounts*: gross domestic product, national income; *Public finance*: government expenditures, government revenue.

POLITICAL AFFAIRS
Members of Parliament and local councils.

SOCIAL AND CULTURAL AFFAIRS
Cultural and scientific activities: languages spoken; *Education*: educational attainment, enrollments, graduates of higher education institutions, literacy, teaching staff; *Health*: disease, family planning, hospitals, medical personnel, public health; *Housing*; *Justice*: courts, crimes, police; *Labor*: employment and unemployment, non-citizen workers, labor force, labor-management relations, occupations.

Most data are for 1979 and the preceding 2 to 4 years. In addition to the national level, data are included for regions, provinces and major urban areas.

Commentaries which include discussions of sources are provided at the beginnings of sections. Unless otherwise indicated in notes accompanying the tables, the National Statistical Office has compiled the data. There is a detailed list of tables at the beginning of the volume. A list of official statistical materials and a description of political and economic institutions and the educational system are included.

Available from the agency, PO Wards Strip.

Available in microform: CIS: 1976/77, 1977. IDC: 1970/71-1976/77.

368. *Abstract of statistics.* 1972- Port Moresby: National Statistical Office. Quarterly.

Statistics are mainly economic, although some population data are included.

Available from the address in the preceding entry.

SOLOMON ISLANDS

369. *Statistical yearbook.* 1970- Honiara: Statistics Office.

Not published 1974-78.

Title varies: 1970-73 as *Annual abstract of statistics.* Agency varies: 1970-73 by Statistical Office.

1980 edition, 202 p., contains statistical data in the following areas:

PHYSICAL ENVIRONMENT
Climatology: precipitation; *Geography*: area of land, maps.

DEMOGRAPHY
Population: census results from 1970, 1976, distribution by age and sex, distribution by geographic/administrative area, ethnic groups, population estimates and projections.

ECONOMIC AFFAIRS
Agriculture and food: farming, fishing, forestry, land tenure; *Commerce and business*: companies, cooperatives, exports, imports, tourism; *Finance*: banking and credit, money supply; *Income and expenditure*: prices; *Industry*: communication, construction, energy, transportation; *National accounts*: balance of payments, gross domestic product; *Public finance*: government expenditures and government revenue for central government and provinces.

SOCIAL AND CULTURAL AFFAIRS
Education: enrollments, teaching staff; *Health*: disease, hospitals, medical personnel, public health; *Justice*: traffic accidents; *Labor*: employment, salaries and wages; *Religion*.

Most data are for 1979 and the preceding 8 years. In addition to the national level, data are included for provinces. Commentaries are provided at the beginnings of sections. Sources are discussed in the foreword and notes accompanying a few of the tables indicate the names of the agencies furnishing the data.

Available from the agency, PO Box G6, Honiara.

Available in microform: CIS: 1970-73, 1979. IDC: 1971-73, 1979-80.

370. **Quarterly digest of statistics.** 1971- Honiara: Statistics Office.

TONGA

371. **Statistical abstract.** 1971- Nuku'alofa: Statistics Department. Irregular.

1983 edition, published Dec., 1983, 217 p., contains data on the following topics:

PHYSICAL ENVIRONMENT
Climatology: precipitation, temperature; *Geography*: area and use of land, maps.

DEMOGRAPHY
Population: census results from 1956-1976, distribution by age and sex, distribution by geographic/administrative area, households and families; *Vital statistics*: births, causes of death, deaths, infant mortality.

ECONOMIC AFFAIRS
Agriculture and food: farming; *Commerce and business*: exports, imports, tourism; *Finance*: banking and credit, money supply; *Income and expenditure*: consumption, prices; *Industry*: communication, energy, manufacturing, transportation, water; *National accounts*: balance of payments, gross domestic product, national income; *Public finance*: government expenditures, government revenue, planning and economic development.

SOCIAL AND CULTURAL AFFAIRS
Education: educational attainment, enrollments, teaching staff; *Health*: disease, family planning, hospitals, medical personnel, public health; *Housing*; *Justice*: courts, crimes, traffic accidents; *Labor*: employment and unemployment, labor force, occupations; *Religion*.

Most data are for 1980 and 5 or more preceding years. In addition to the national level, some data are included for census district. There is a detailed list of tables at the beginning of the volume.

Available from the agency, PO Box 149, Nuku'alofa. Priced.

No statistical bulletin has been found for Tonga.

TUVALU

372. **Statistical yearbook.** 1976- Suva, Fiji: U.N. Economic and Social Commission for Asia and the Pacific, U.N. Development Advisory Team for the Pacific.

1978 edition, published 1979, 31 p., contains statistical data in the following areas:

PHYSICAL ENVIRONMENT
Climatology: precipitation, temperature.

DEMOGRAPHY
Population: census results from 1979 (prelim.) and the 1973 census of the Gilbert and Ellice Islands, distribution by age and sex, distribution by geographic/administrative area, ethnic groups, population estimates.

ECONOMIC AFFAIRS
Commerce and business: exports, imports; *Finance*: banking and credit; *Income and expenditure*: consumption, prices; *Industry*: energy; *Public finance*: government expenditures, government revenue.

SOCIAL AND CULTURAL AFFAIRS
Labor: labor force.

Most data are for 1978 and the preceding year. In addition to the national level, data are included for islands.

Available from the U.N. Economic and Social Commission for Asia and the Pacific, Sala Santitham, Rajadamnern Ave., Bangkok, Thailand.

No statistical bulletin has been found for Tuvalu.

VANUATU

373. **Statistical indicators.** 1980?- Port-Vila: National Planning and Statistics Office. Quarterly.

3rd qtr, 1984, 40 p., contains statistical data in the following areas:

PHYSICAL ENVIRONMENT
Geography: area of land.

DEMOGRAPHY
Population: arrivals and departures, census results from 1979, distribution by age and sex, distribution by geographic/administrative area, ethnic groups, external migration, households and families, population estimates.

ECONOMIC AFFAIRS
Commerce and business: exports, imports, tourism; *Finance*: banking and credit, money supply; *Income and expenditure*: prices; *Industry*: construction, energy, transportation.

Most data are monthly or annual for 5 years. Latest data are for the quarter of the issue. In addition to the national level, data are included for districts and local government regions.

Available from the agency, PO Box 741, Lolam House, Port-Vila.

WESTERN SAMOA

374. **Annual statistical abstract.** 1966- Apia: Department of Statistics.

[No.] 17, 1982 edition, 93 p., contains statistical data in the following areas:

PHYSICAL ENVIRONMENT
Climatology: precipitation, sunshine, temperature; *Geography*: maps.

DEMOGRAPHY
Population: arrivals and departures, census results from 1956-1981, distribution by age and sex, external migration, population estimates; *Vital statistics*: births, causes of death, deaths, divorces, infant mortality, marriages.

ECONOMIC AFFAIRS
Agriculture and food: farming; *Commerce and business*: companies, exports, imports; *Finance*: banking and credit, money supply; *Income and expenditure*: consumption, prices; *Industry*: communication, construction, energy, transportation; *Public finance*: government expenditures, government revenue.

SOCIAL AND CULTURAL AFFAIRS
Cultural and scientific activities: cinema, newspapers; *Education*: enrollments, examination results, teaching staff; *Health*: disease, hospitals, public health; *Justice*: correctional institutions, courts, crimes, traffic accidents; *Labor*: employment and salaries (in government sector only).

Most data are for 1982 and varying numbers of earlier years, usually 2 to 7. In addition to the national level, data are included for districts. Notes accompanying the tables indicate the names of the agencies furnishing the data. There is a detailed list of tables at the beginning of the volume.

Latest edition published: 1983, 99 p. Available from the agency, PO Box 1151, Apia. Price: $WS1.00, plus postage.

Available in microform: CIS: 1970-74, 1976. IDC: 1966-80.

No statistical bulletin has been found for Western Samoa.

Z 7551 .W47 1986
Westfall, Gloria.
Bibliography of official
 statistical yearbooks and

FEB 1 7 1989